BREATHE

INHALE TRUTH - EXHALE LIFE

CHARLOTTE GAMBILL

Published in Great Britain in 2018 by Charlotte Gambill
charlottegambill.com

Copyright © Charlotte Gambill 2018

The moral right of the author has been asserted
A CIP record of this book is available from the British Library
ISBN 978-0-9568564-5-6

BREATHE ━━━━━━━━━━━━━

Then He said to me, "Prophesy to the breath; prophesy, son of man, and say to it, 'This is what the Sovereign Lord says: Come, breath, from the four winds and breathe into these slain, that they may live.'" So I prophesied as He commanded me, and breath entered them; they came to life and stood up on their feet - a vast army.
Ezekiel 37:9-10 (NIV)

Go ahead, take a minute and catch your breath, just breathe. How often are we unaware of the very action that keeps us alive, how many times do we waste our breath or become short of breath? We need to breathe and we need His breath, the breath of life. Ezekiel, when viewing the valley of dry bones, was asked by God, 'can they live?' God's answer was to tell Ezekiel to prophesy to the breath.

What miracle is within your very breath? What life is held within your lungs? Where do you need to prophesy to your problems, speak to you storms? Where do you need to inhale truth so you can exhale life? This devotional invites you to go on a 365 day journey, taking alternate days to meditate on His word and then prophesy to your world. So why not join me as we learn to breathe again.

But be doers of the word, and not hearers only, deceiving yourselves.
James 1:22 (NKJV)

When I put this devotional together, my original aim was to give you, the reader, 365 different thoughts. I set off down that road and was full steam ahead when I felt God edit my thinking. Our lives are already filled with reading, information assimilation, learning and I know we can begin to add God's word into the pile of all the other words. That's when God gave me the title of breathe. This isn't about stuffing your mind with more information, it's about imparting and even more about application. The Bible tells us in James we are not to just be hearers of the word but doers, as one without the other is lifeless. This devotional is therefore deliberately 365 days but with a day to read and a day to do. I want you to be able to find that rhythm for your life that is His rhythm of grace. So let's maximise the journey ahead by breaking down a little more how those days could look.

Inhale
On the inhale days, take a deep breath in of God's word, read the scripture and go and read the things that happen around the scripture. And read the lesson that is attached to that verse, allow it to go into your heart and not just be something you glance over. It is not a skim reading exercise, it's your inhale deep day. Breathe it in, it's new air for your lungs to circulate. On these inhale days you may visit the same theme more than once, that's because some things need you to breathe them in several times before you actually can fully speak them out. So on your inhale day, you will need to create space to focus, be still, pray and seek how this air needs to circulate in your life. End each of your inhale days with a place you know God is highlighting for you to invite Him into. Close that day with prayer and get ready to then take the next day to make some decisions or changes to bring that breath to life.

Exhale
The following day, you will find a mainly blank page. That's because it's now your time to make some choices, even address some changes. This is the work out the word day; what sank in yesterday is to be built on today. On the exhale page are some recurring words: think it; speak it; be it. These are your nudge points to ask you, how are you now going to practically exhale what you inhaled? We can't just live a life that only breathes in, we would blow up. We need to breathe out too. These days are to challenge you, to check in with yourself, asses how you are doing. These days, if you use them to do the work that the word has prompted, will help you look at how you can grow and apply

what God is speaking to your spirit. How can you change your thinking to align to His word? What confession needs changing to add life to your lungs and the lungs of those around you? How can you be kindness, be light, be strong?

My prayer is this alternate day of breathing in then breathing out will add new energy and rhythm to your life. We can all wait for circumstances or people to challenge us to change but surely the best change is the one we volunteer ourselves, the one that comes not out of guilt but out of willingness and eagerness to become all He says we can become.

So now you have your work set out it's time to get to it:
time to inhale truth and exhale life.

Father, Thank You for my friend who is about to take this one-year journey with You. Thank You for what You are already doing in their life. Lord, I pray as everyday they sit and devote time to be with You that they would discover more of who You are and whose they are. Open their eyes and guide each step, strengthen and refresh them, spirit and soul. I pray You would take what's within these pages and make it personal to them and all that concerns them. Thank You God, for Your words that are life and light to our path. Teach us to not just take a breath but to breathe you in so we can prophesy your life to the relationships and communities we are placed within. Teach us to breathe again. Amen.

Charlotte Gambill

BREATHE

INHALE TRUTH - EXHALE LIFE

"Prophesy to the breath; prophesy, son of man, and say to it, 'This is what the Sovereign Lord says: Come, breath, from the four winds and breathe into these slain, that they may live.'" So I prophesied as He commanded me, and breath entered them; they came to life and stood up on their feet - a vast army. Ezekiel 37:9-10 (NIV)

Ezekiel was shown a field full of dry bones and God asked him, 'can these bones live?' Maybe Ezekiel thought God would perform a miracle but God's miracle was within Ezekiel's own mouth as he was instructed to speak to the breath. We are the carriers of the breath of God. It's His breath in our lungs, His breath that gives life. He is the air we breathe and we are the breath the world needs to receive. Where do you need to breathe? Where has your breath become intoxicated with worry or fear? What bad breath is affecting your relationships, limiting your future. Where are you short of breath? Where do you face dry bones and are asking God, can this live, will it ever change? God's reply back to you and I is, it's time to breathe.

Inhale deeply and exhale slowly. Be more aware of the breath we are taking in and the air we are letting out. Breathing is something we can do without thinking but when our breathing is not right it changes everything and suddenly it becomes all we notice. Breathing facilitates our being, everything we do and everything we are requires us to keep breathing.

Today, take some time to breathe in and look at where it may be time for you to prophesy to your dry bones, to learn how to breathe life into what needs to be revived. Inhale and become aware of your breathing rhythm, think about the breath of God within you and how well it flows through you. Then tomorrow exhale, take time to identify and write down the changes you are seeking to make, the places where this needs to be applied. Become more of who God says you are so you can breathe clearer in the weeks and months ahead.

Over the next 365 days, retrain your breathing and allow your lungs to be refilled, allow your breath to find its rhythm again. This devotional will lead you not to just read but also respond: one day inhale and read the truth and the next day take time to exhale that breath in thoughts, words and deeds. This is designed to make you more aware of what you are taking into your life, your heart, your soul so you can become more effective in how you breathe out. So come with me on a journey, make a time everyday to catch your breath and, by so doing, change your life. So if you're ready, let's go.

THINK IT ━━━━━━━━━━━━━━━━

SPEAK IT ━━━━━━━━━━━━━━━━

BE IT ━━━━━━━━━━━━━━━━━━

EXHALE

He got up, rebuked the wind and said to the waves, "Quiet! Be still!" Then the wind died down and it was completely calm. Mark 4:39 (NIV)

We all face storms in life, maybe you are in one right now or maybe you are just coming out of one. By their nature, storms are noisy, they make the wind howl and the waves crash. Storms can bring thunder and lightning, torrential rain and even hurricanes. Nature's storms are not quiet and neither are the spiritual and circumstantial storms that descend on our lives and render us speechless, making them even more powerful. So how do you find your voice in the storm, what should you say to it? We have to learn that in Christ we have the authority to overwhelm the noise with the clarity of the word of God, to shout to the fear 'be still', to say to the dark 'let there be light'.

Speak loud: many people panic and scream for help in the storm but what about standing your ground and answering the storm with the promises of God that were there before the storm hit and will be there after it has died out. The word of God in your mouth is far more powerful than the waves and wind that are trying to cause you to doubt so speak the word, find the shout and let the storm know you are not backing down.

Speak faith: speak to the storm from a place of faith not fear. Your confidence is not in what you see but in what is unseen so trust in the unfailing love of God, rest in His capacity not in your own ability. Don't allow fear to take the microphone, instead let faith chose the vocabulary; faith for the future, faith in your good Father. Faith knows how to fight so let faith reply to the waves that are trying to ruin your day.

Speak now: don't save your words until the wind dies down. Declare truth over your life, speak truth over lies: pray, praise, thank, now. Sometimes the storm can make us breathless but today, catch your breath and speak your truth.

When Jesus was asleep in the storm and the fearful disciples woke Him up, He spoke to the storm to be still and it was so. He didn't scream or panic. He spoke loud and clear and immediately the storm was put in its place. It had to obey the boundaries that His word placed it within. We can loose and bind things with our words, release and resist with our own confession, so if you're in the storm, maybe it's time it heard your voice. Inhale this truth today and then take time to write down the areas where you are facing storms, so you can begin to plan how you can think, speak and become more stable in the storm.

THINK IT ━━━━━━━━━━━ **04**

SPEAK IT ━━━━━━━━━━━━━━━━

BE IT ━━━━━━━━━━━━━━━

EXHALE

And I am convinced and sure of this very thing, that He who began a good work in you will continue until the day of Jesus Christ, developing and perfecting and bringing it to full completion in you. Philippians 1:6 (AMP)

Have you ever started reading a book and then due to either lack of time, distraction, boredom or a lack of commitment, stopped reading? You put the book down, leaving the page you last read folded so when you return you will know where to pick the story back up. Yet too often we don't return. We never complete the story, leaving unfinished plots and half developed characters inside those unread pages. That story can remain stuck for years or never get finished. The same is true in our journey through life.

Your life is like that book. It is a story that is developing and evolving. Each year a new chapter is written, milestones are reached and the adventure unfolds just a little more. With your growth, diligence and commitment to keep turning the pages, more of the story is revealed. Therefore when we get distracted or weary, we have to resist the temptation of exiting our own story. Everyday is an opportunity to turn the page, to write the next line. Each day presents new hope, strength, the potential of new relationships and discovering new scenery. It is our constant commitment to stay engaged in the story that opens up more possibilities.

Both of my children love to read, I mean love to read; they go through at least a book every two weeks. Yet I have discovered that they also have become selective about what books they will read. If the author fails to develop a character, or the plot seems to meander for too long, they lose interest and start to read a different book instead. I explain they may just have to give this story a little more time to unfold, to appreciate not every book has to start and finish the same way. But they abandon what they have deemed as boring to pick up something with a little more action.

Immaturity will have you compare your story with others. It's not hard to find a plot you may prefer or a character you would like to swap places with. But maturity knows that not all stories unfold at the same pace but we do all have the same author. God is the one who holds the plot for your life and He doesn't want you to quit your story because it doesn't look like someone else's. Every one of our journeys will venture from valley to mountaintop; we all have a story to write and a page to turn so commit to writing yours well. Don't be overwhelmed by all the things you can't predict in the plot, instead commit to the next page you can turn today. Some things you are seeking are awaiting you further in this unfolding story, so read on.

SPEAK IT ━━━━━━━━━━━━━━━

BE IT ━━━━━━━━━━━━━━━

Therefore, since we are surrounded by such a great cloud of witnesses, let us throw off everything that hinders and the sin that so easily entangles. And let us run with perseverance the race marked out for us. Hebrews 12:1 (NIV)

Every week we have rubbish collectors come to our home. However they will only take from us what we remember to put out on the street for collection. If we fail to put the rubbish outside then they won't come inside our home and collect it for us. Nor will they wait for us to remember it's collection time, they don't knock on the door to alert us of the moment we are about to miss. They simply come and take what you have bagged up and left. Uncollected rubbish can become a real problem. Its contents now rot in your home and the smell becomes toxic and unsanitary.

We must remember that we too have to empty the rubbish out of our lives. Spiritually you need to be active in placing the things that are no longer purposeful for your future, nor healthy for your consumption, into the bin. Then you must also place the trash in a place where it can be removed and not leave it where it can rot. Put the offense out and let grace take it, take the bad attitude out and allow forgiveness to collect it. Remove the rotting relationship and the negative thinking, put it out of your life where it can be removed from your neighbourhood. When the rubbish of yesterday remains in your today, it will contaminate what is fresh with the stale. Don't be negligent with your rubbish disposal. Today, take the trash out, leave it where it belongs, don't keep searching through it, it's rubbish and it needs to be removed so you can move on. Your heart is not built to hold waste so don't be wasteful.

Here's one last thing to note, rubbish collection happens on a regular basis on my street, every week they show up. So don't wait for a huge clear out once a year, it will be too much, too heavy and overwhelming. If we don't stay vigilant on our trash removal we will begin to suffer from hoarder syndrome. Our accumulation of toxic thinking, past relationships, overflowing piles of offences, will all begin to take over our homes! It will make our space smaller, restricting our movement, entry and access points. It will make our lives hard to visit and less welcoming to any of the new thoughts, opportunities and people God wants to send to our address. You are not called to keep the trash nor hoard the hurt! So today, be diligent in the daily disciplines of removing rot, letting go of waste and start embracing the new space your diligence will extend to you.

THINK IT ━━━━━━━━━━━━━━━━━━

SPEAK IT ━━━━━━━━━━━━━━━━━━━━━

BE IT ━━━━━━━━━━━━━━━━━━━━━

EXHALE

Fixing our eyes on Jesus, the pioneer and perfecter of faith. For the joy set before Him He endured the cross, scorning its shame, and sat down at the right hand of the throne of God. Hebrews 12:2 (NIV)

Have you heard the expression 'what you focus on develops'? It is so true for all our lives. The more attention we give something and the more we feed it, the greater its chances are of growing but what is equally true is the more we starve something, the less it gains strength. Where we place our focus, concentration and meditation is crucial! This can be difficult to manage particularly in times of pain. The power of pain is that it has an ability to demand attention. Pain shouts to each part of your life 'look at me, tend to me, adjust around me!' Yet though pain needs to be handled it does not always need or deserve centre stage.

Pain is often an integral part of the progress we seek. You can't grow without stretching, you can't get stronger without building more stamina, you can't birth something without enduring labour. Pain can either be seen as your enemy or you can make it your training partner, even your friend. Pain has within it the ability to hurt but also the capacity to help. The difference in the outcome of pain is in the focus we give it; before we allow pain to speak we must determine the number of lines it will be given in our script. For example, when you may have had the awkward, even uncomfortable, encounter of listening to a woman's labour story, it will no doubt involve some pages of pain and yet they will be told from a perspective of joy as that pain was what helped bring forth the baby. The storyteller sits lovingly holding the baby; pain had a part but the joy of the newborn has the centre stage and the bundle of joy has everyone's attention in the room.

Jesus and His journey to the cross beautifully illustrates this once again. The cross was the most agonising death imaginable, the pain was unbearable but it was not given Jesus' full attention, it was "the joy set before Him". It was you and I that became the central scene! Jesus taught us in His most painful hours that though pain has a voice, it does not get all the lines.

Though no one enjoys pain, I am learning more and more to listen to it and allow what it is saying to help me in my understanding. So instead of feeling defeated or deflated by an area that is aggravating you, decide to be a student of the symptoms. Develop a cure instead of a complaint, see the future alongside the current frustration and let the cure have the leading lines.

Today, what are you magnifying? The pain or the prize? The hurt or the healing? The labour or the reward? It's your choice so choose wisely.

INHALE

THINK IT ━━━━━━━━━━━━━━

SPEAK IT ━━━━━━━━━━━━━━━━━━━

BE IT ━━━━━━━━━━━━━━━━━━

EXHALE

When his master heard the story his wife told him, saying, "This is how your slave treated me," he burned with anger. Joseph's master took him and put him in prison, the place where the king's prisoners were confined. But while Joseph was there in the prison, the Lord was with him. Genesis 39:19-21 (NIV)

Have you ever felt misunderstood? Your words were taken out of context or your actions misinterpreted, maybe what you meant to be helpful someone has read as hurtful? Misunderstandings are frequent occurrences on this journey through life and therefore we need to know how to neutralise the power they hold or we will waste years trying to prove what doesn't need proving. Misunderstanding creates a minefield of dangers; it is a breeding ground for wrong assumptions and a holding pattern for hurts. It separates friends, tears people from communities; it replaces truth with lies and divides what God wants to unite. The phantom menace of misunderstanding is more sinister than we often realise and therefore it is a perpetrator we need to get better in recognising and in responding to. Misunderstanding can become a set of unspoken feelings that create an ocean of confusion and eventually strand people on an island called isolation. So today, what misunderstanding do you need to stop feeding? We all have questions unanswered, and offenses that want to fester. Don't allow the misunderstanding to change the places you should be and the life you are called to fulfill.

When Joseph was thrown in prison for something he did not even do, he had to deal not only with the false accusations but the misunderstanding surrounding his own integrity and actions. Where he had been entrusted, he was now being judged for being untrustworthy, where he had been seen as safe hands, he was accused of being one whose hands had caused harm. Joseph went to prison convicted for a crime he didn't commit and misunderstood by people who he had only ever tried to help. Yet Joseph did not sit in prison trying to tell everyone how misunderstood he was, instead he closed the gap and let his life tell its own story. He silenced the misunderstanding with his upstanding character; he chose not to let the misjudgement create a gap between him and Pharaoh. These choices ensured when the time was right, Joseph could re-enter the world he was destined to help lead.

Often we allow the space misunderstanding creates to be so wide it prevents us ever getting back to the places God had planned for us to play our part in. Don't uproot because of misunderstanding, it's not worth it, rather dig deeper. We are all imperfect people trying to figure out how to get along, so let's close the gap. Don't allow the menace called misunderstanding to cause you to miss out on any places or people where your future may be calling.

THINK IT ━━━━━━━━━━━━━━ **12**

SPEAK IT ━━━━━━━━━━━━━━━

BE IT ━━━━━━━━━━━━━━━

He says, "Be still, and know that I am God; I will be exalted among the nations, I will be exalted in the earth." Psalm 46:10 (NIV)

Have you ever seen a hyperactive child or had a thrill seeking adrenaline junkie friend? Someone who is constantly moving, searching for the next activity, not prepared to slow down for the fear that it will somehow make life less amazing or appealing? In a world that constantly bombards our senses and demands our responses, stillness can be a hidden and under-appreciated skill. Being still can almost sound like an old fashioned way of life and a sign you are becoming dull or unexciting. Yet without stillness we invite illness, sickness of soul and burn out of body. We allow doing to replace being and our own health, relationships and families suffer when we cannot be still for long enough to sustain what is being entrusted to us.

Discerning the difference between busy and productive is often something we can struggle with. Activity does not necessarily mean productivity. If we make opportunities, demands and prominence our goals we will only strive and stress. We will replace real progress with manufacturing our own sense of success. True growth is found when you are as at home in the quiet as you are in the busy. When your sense of identity is not in what you do but in whose you are and when you are content in the still, as well as the crazy.

Often a life that is all go lacks the 'know'. What we discover in the stillness sustains us in the busyness. It is the knowledge of His greatness that quiets our neediness. When we are still, we can be refilled. When we are still we can see wonder over works and spirit over self. We need to increase our knowing, so we need to still our being. In all the many things you have to do, make room for this very important thing. Make time everyday to just be still, to say thank you to your Creator, to enjoy the things around you and to breathe in the possibilities and the future. It is in the stillness you will find the ability to be witness to all of God's greatness.

If we want to know more of Him today, we simply need to hear and see less of us. Decreasing our noise allows more room for His voice. Pray today for more of Him and commit to a greater knowledge that will demand a deeper stillness. Make a note of places you find it hard to be still and then make some choices about how you will reclaim that place of peace and things you can put into action to help you get back the space to breathe.

THINK IT ━━━━━━━━━━━━━━━ **14**

SPEAK IT ━━━━━━━━━━━━━━━━━

BE IT ━━━━━━━━━━━━━━━━━

EXHALE

You prepare a table before me in the presence of my enemies. You anoint my head with oil; my cup overflows. Psalm 23:5 (NIV)

It's always good to remember that while attributes like consistency, discipline, hard work, commitment, loyalty, truth and persistence may not appear exciting, these are the very qualities that make the exciting possible. Think of the most fabulous day, a wedding that was breathtaking, a party that was so elegant, a house beautifully furnished, art magnificently painted, those things we appreciate and admire did not just happen - they were the result of the many things that we admire less. They are the result of disciplines that aren't exciting or elegant but just plain hard work.

No great adventure happens without greater preparation. God is into preparation, He has prepared a table for you and I am pretty sure that table will be a beautiful sight to see. John the Baptist was even given the title, 'Preparer of the Way', that's how important preparation was for Jesus to accomplish what He was sent for. No graduation day arrives without much revision and examination. No miraculous breakthroughs happen on the back of apathy. So when you're in the stages of preparation, don't hold off the celebration. Get excited about the work that is helping you reach the place where you want to be. Be excited about the power of the preparation and be expectant, as you stay disciplined. When we delay our excitement we can resent our journey. But when you have an understanding that what you do now will lead to where you want to be later, you see something to celebrate everyday.

So let's break that down into the day before you. If you are working on a project for your job, think ahead to all the things this can achieve, the strength it is building, the people you are meeting. If today it looks like taking care of your family, raising kids, think of the seeds you are sowing that will enable their future to flourish. Every part of the preparation is a shift to our progress. See the areas we look past and celebrate now.

Today find joy in the simple things, because they are what make possible the spectacular days! He has predestined good things for your future, He has gone before you in preparation of all the things He has purposed you to do. Preparation speaks of value and priority towards the place or person it is lavished and directed. Spontaneity is good and can be a lot of fun but preparation is wise and often an unsung hero of the day. Let's start a preparation revolution. Encourage those who are willing to be prepared, the ones who prepare the ground now for the harvest that comes later. What do you need to stop avoiding and start preparing for? Today is as good a day as any to be prepared.

SPEAK IT ━━━━━━━━━━━━━━━

BE IT ━━━━━━━━━━━━━━━

EXHALE

Trust God from the bottom of your heart; don't try to figure out everything on your own. Listen for God's voice in everything you do, everywhere you go; He's the one who will keep you on track. Don't assume that you know it all. Run to God! But don't, dear friend, resent God's discipline; don't sulk under His loving correction. It's the child He loves that God corrects. Proverbs 3:6-12 (MSG)

Trust shows itself in many different ways; we can trust someone with our property, show trust by giving someone a new opportunity or it can look like stepping into a new relationship. Trust, just like our faith, has many different levels. Trust is a journey we have to choose to embrace. When we first said yes to God's Lordship of our life, we accepted we had a need for a Heavenly Father and the journey of His Fathering in our lives began. Trust is the travelling companion we all need to move this journey from the starting point into new adventures. God wants you to invite Him in, not just to provide and guide but to discover a depth of trust that lets Him correct and at times discipline you.

God is a good Father and each aspect of His Fathering of our lives requires our trust. Often God's correction in our lives seems costly, having to work against our own sense of what we feel is just or even what feels good. One of the areas where this shows up is in the way we communicate, particularly to people who may have been unkind, misjudged and mistreated us. In these moments of vulnerability we must learn to trust His way of handling what often our own unchecked emotions would mishandle. Magnifying God's voice first in these situations means submitting to our own voice being changed as He shapes us.

When we talk to God first it often changes to whom and how we talk next. Conversations are good, sharing can be healthy and voicing concerns or questions is part of the journey. If we want to be more healthy than hurtful, more hopeful than doubtful, then we have to take it to God first. He is always available, He's a great listener, He doesn't get upset when you're upset. He will never add fuel to a fire that needs putting out. He may not even reply to your question or your concern, but time just talking with Him will always alter your tone and often diffuse your dilemma. Talk to Him everyday and let Him direct you what to say next.

Today, can you trust God with the most difficult of situations, the things that right now you are upset or anxious over? This verse asks you to trust in Him and let your concern cause you to run to Him. Inhale this truth today and then tomorrow make some choices that will make your breath carry more of this.

THINK IT ━━━━━━━━━━━━━━

18

SPEAK IT ━━━━━━━━━━━━━━━━━━━━━

BE IT ━━━━━━━━━━━━━━━━━━━

EXHALE

"Suppose one of you wants to build a tower. Won't you first sit down and estimate the cost to see if you have enough money to complete it?" Luke 14:28 (NIV)

I remember trying to book seats online for a show my kids really wanted to go and see. I was shown a picture of the inside of the arena and asked to click where we would want to sit. Of course I clicked the nearest seats to the front that were still available, but that led me to the price page for those tickets and well, let's just say I soon went back to look for seats on the back row. The best seats don't come at a cheap price.

Spiritually we need to appreciate the same principle. Many may want to lead, but the real question is, can you afford the ticket right now? Some may ask to be given greater opportunity and yet we must first ask, are we willing for the greater responsibility? Others seek promotion, but are less committed to its increased demand for deeper discipline and devotion. The Bible is very clear in this matter and says we should count the cost. When James and John were arguing over who would get the best seat, Jesus told them to stop arguing about something they had no understanding of. The cost of the seats was beyond their reach, and yet often we allow our zeal to override our knowledge. Maybe the season that we want of expansion first needs a season of investment.

When I was a student I used to walk around the grocery store with a calculator, as I knew I only had a certain limit for my food spend. Maybe we need to calculate the things we put in our trolley spiritually so we don't keep finding ourselves under resourced and over extended. Count the cost of service and then sign up. Count the cost of leading and then take your place. Know the price of the dream before you start to demand. We need to ensure we can afford the emotional withdrawals that may follow the seat you are spiritually seeking. I believe God extends to all grace, favour and opportunity. His heart is not to withhold from you, but to protect and grow what is within you first. He does not want you or I to have to be removed from a seat we prematurely occupied. When we understand the price, we find more grace. Let's not complain about our view and instead work on our perspective.

Let's aim for the best view but not then ask for a budget deal. Jesus paid the highest price for you and I. It's the willingness to pay that often leads you far more effectively into doing things God's way. What seat are you wanting to select today? Make notes of what you may need to accrue to take care of what that seat may cost.

THINK IT ━━━━━━━━━━━━━ 20

SPEAK IT ━━━━━━━━━━━━━━━

BE IT ━━━━━━━━━━━━━━━

Then Joseph said to his brothers, "Come close to me." When they had done so, he said, "I am your brother Joseph, the one you sold into Egypt! And now, do not be distressed and do not be angry with yourselves for selling me here, because it was to save lives that God sent me ahead of you." Genesis 45:4-5 (NIV)

When we face situations that are uncomfortable, when we feel tested, offended or overwhelmed, we have to make a choice as to what we will do next. Will we ignore the issue, respond or run? Most times the latter of these choices seems the most attractive. I mean, who wants to stay around the mess and clean it up? I have known of individuals and families that just decided they couldn't face what was in front of them so they relocated to a place they hoped would keep them far from ever seeing or hearing about a problem again. There are some occasions where relocation is the right thing to do, but we can't keep moving when things get messy, we can't walk out on every situation that turns sour. We can't live our life on the run when actually God wants us to dig into His love and grace and find a way to maybe stay in the place that we want to escape. We all need to learn in some of those hard times and places how to begin again.

It takes boldness, humility and trust in God to begin again. Beginning again means while facing the hurt, you are also willing to find the healing, it means being bigger than the offense or the pain and committing to find a way forward. Many marriages that ended maybe needed to begin again, many friendships that were abandoned could have looked different if they had chosen to begin again. Jonah wanted to run from Nineveh, he wanted to escape God's plan, but after a little help from a passing whale, God had him begin again in his call to Nineveh. Jacob and Esau separated on bad terms, hating each other and resenting one another but God's plan was to create a moment of reuniting, so they could begin again. Joseph had every reason to never return to his family and yet when they were reunited, he chose that moment as his opportunity to restrict what evil and jealousy had tried to stop.

It's not easy but it is possible. Like Joseph, maybe it will demand more from you than running ever will, as it will ask you to forgive further, love deeper and do better than was done to you. Yet in beginning again, we salvage so much that the enemy intends for us to waste. Today, are you running from something you need to run back towards? Where could you put your energy into beginning again and by so doing secure something that is not worth losing? Where do you need to love again, believe again, heal again and begin again?

THINK IT ━━━━━━━━━━━━━ **22**

SPEAK IT ━━━━━━━━━━━━━━━━━━

BE IT ━━━━━━━━━━━━━━━━━━

EXHALE

To the weak I became weak, to win the weak. I have become all things to all people so that by all possible means I might save some. 1 Corinthians 9:19-23 (NIV)

Sometimes certain days don't remind you of the good but the bad. Father's Day, Mother's Day, an anniversary, Christmas; for some these evoke happy memories but for others they are a painful reminder of loss, hurt, betrayal. While the world tries to legislate days for us all to celebrate, life just isn't that way. We all have different journeys and what may be happy times for one, can be the darkest of times for others. That is why we must always be able to step out of our shoes and into one another's. Paul wrote in the book of 1 Corinthians that he had become all things to all men, that he had chosen to embrace not just his own journey but take the time to appreciate the journey that others were on too. Paul's compassion quota was high and he was appealing to the religious to become less religious and more real. In doing so he risked being wrongly judged by those observing his life, that somehow his entering into others worlds would lead to a compromising in his own. Yet Paul demonstrated that in order to reach more people, we need to be able to see more, feel more and hear more than just the noise of our own lives.

Where can you be more compassionate? Who do you need to take a little longer to get to know or pray a little more to try and understand? When Jesus met Zacchaeus He didn't expose him, He covered him; He knew he was embarrassed so He went to his home, He knew he was excluded and so He included him. Jesus touched lepers because He knew no one would go near them, that what would mean more than just words was that he would actually reach out and make contact. Jesus knew how to hold a child's attention and also engage with every person He met from rich young rulers to the widows and orphans. We all have those we find easier to get along with than others, however we need to be mindful that our group should never become exclusive or dismissive of others who may look or act different. Let's make room for the conversations that increase our compassion and expand our circle of love.

Compassion is an action, it is more than words, it's a shift in our hearts that changes our approach from simply helping someone to being able to hear what is unspoken and see what is hidden. Today, let's all make some time to grow in our compassion and in so doing expand our reach into one another's lives with more grace and understanding. With Christ as our example, we all have more we can do to be those who are not just passionate but also compassionate.

THINK IT ━━━━━━━━━━ 24

SPEAK IT ━━━━━━━━━━━━━━

BE IT ━━━━━━━━━━━━━━

EXHALE

Be very careful, then, how you live - not as unwise but as wise, making the most of every opportunity, because the days are evil. Therefore do not be foolish, but understand what the Lord's will is. Ephesians 5:15-17 (NIV)

When a pilot wants to ensure a good landing, they must commit to a thought through approach. The approach needs calculation and expertise. The pilot ascertains distance, speed, the weight of the vessel and cargo on board. The investment into the approach will determine the safety of the landing. This same principle can be applied in our lives. Too often we are more hasty than careful to land in our next desired location. We want to land the job, relationship, ministry, now. So we give impatience the control panel, making our landings unpredictable and our crew nervous. A landing that is too fast or a descent that's too steep is dangerous; everything we are carrying can be lost through carelessness. If we want to reduce casualties, then we must take the time to approach our next destination well.

There is much to consider, so let's take the next few days to think about how we simplify the landings our life will require. Here are the first two things to bear in mind as we seek not just to fly high but also learn how to land well.

1. Adjust your speed - every pilot knows you cannot hit the ground at the same speed you were travelling when you were thousands of miles above the earth. To avoid crash landing casualties, the speed has to be altered. The same is true in our lives. The speed in which we try and approach a landing is crucial. We have to become sensitive to the setting and find the appropriate speed so that our landing is a blessing and not a disaster. Not everything has to be said now, not each idea must be launched now, adjust the speed and steady the carrier. Let's land intact.

2. Remember the weight of what's on board - the cargo we carry, especially the older we get and the more we lead others through life, should always bear an impact on the way we fly. When I was younger I had a convertible. It was fun to drive. Then I had children and found out babies don't like the wind blowing through their gappy teeth or few strands of hair, car seats don't fit under convertible roofs and two doors are fun when only two people are in the car. The passengers changed the purpose of the vehicle and so now your life may need to do the same. You land differently when you see who is strapped in the plane with you.

Today, where do you need to adjust your speed or remember the cargo you carry? Where can you become more approach aware? Be patient, if something is worth landing, it is worth landing well.

THINK IT ▬▬▬▬▬▬▬▬▬▬▬▬▬ 26

SPEAK IT ▬▬▬▬▬▬▬▬▬▬▬▬▬▬▬▬▬

BE IT ▬▬▬▬▬▬▬▬▬▬▬▬▬▬▬▬▬

EXHALE

Be very careful, then, how you live - not as unwise but as wise, making the most of every opportunity, because the days are evil. Therefore do not be foolish, but understand what the Lord's will is. Ephesians 5:15-17 (NIV)

Previously we considered how we can learn to better land the plane of our lives. Today let's pick that thought up once more. Too often our approach to bringing things to a close is done with little finesse and a lot of unnecessary drama. How many more bad breakups do we need to see? How many times have church splits been an avoidable train crash? How many people have you come across who had wounds that are as a result of someone's kamikaze flying? There are many things beyond our control when we fly, however, there are things we should and could get better at. So what about landing the situations we are in, how do we continue to get more skilled in this responsibility? If we have already learnt to change our speed and assess our cargo, let's add a few more things to the checklist.

3. Remember other planes are landing too - we can get so caught up in our destination that we forget others are on a journey too. Have you ever been on a plane in the blue skies high above all the noise of the world and then out of the plane window seen other airplanes? At first it can be a little disconcerting, why are they up in the sky at the same time as you? The truth is, at any given time thousands of aircrafts are criss-crossing the skies and as long as the pilot is tuned into the air traffic-controller, no collisions need to happen. Be aware of His voice so that your landing doesn't collide with others.

4. Your approach requires coordinates to be set to land - we often set off into new adventures so excited about what's next without giving too much thought to the landing stage of our journey. However, before an aircraft can take off it has to programme in where it will land, otherwise it may run out of fuel mid-journey. Don't allow your approach to be governed by changing emotions. Set the dial up front on your attitude, speech and actions to ensure you have what you need on board to complete the journey ahead.

5. Don't forget people who may fly with you in the future are watching - how happy are your previous passengers when they alight? Let's not put off future passengers who you may be waiting to get on board with you for your next adventure. Let's ensure all those God intended to travel alongside us aren't sent running because of crash landings they keep seeing when you take flight.

Finally, enjoy the view, take it all in and appreciate the rise and the fall of the process, the beauty and purpose of both ascent and descent; one doesn't work without the other.

THINK IT ━━━━━━━━━━━━━━━━

SPEAK IT ━━━━━━━━━━━━━━━━━━

BE IT ━━━━━━━━━━━━━━━━━━

EXHALE

Run in such a way as to get the prize. Everyone who competes in the games goes into strict training. They do it to get a crown that will not last, but we do it to get a crown that will last forever. Therefore I do not run like someone running aimlessly; I do not fight like a boxer beating the air. 1 Corinthians 9:24-26 (NIV)

Discipline: a word we love to hate. We rebel against it as teenagers, we try to enforce it as parents, we know it is good for us, and yet it just seems so hard. To the free spirited, discipline can feel like containment and to the legalistic, discipline can become an excuse for an over regimented way of living. Yet actually discipline used correctly is neither a container nor an enforcer, it can actually become one of your greatest tools to build your best life. It liberates time that is otherwise wasted. It adds more energy to an overwhelmed diary. Discipline tightens up and tones up areas of our lives that then enhance our ability to deliver and enjoy.

Discipline makes you accountable, it harnesses your commitment, it restricts you from the things that work against the results you want to achieve. We can see the benefit of discipline, when we may be trying to reign in that toddler tantrum or make the financial budgets balance, however we can fail to see its benefit in other areas of our lives. We can neglect spiritual disciplines, telling ourselves we are fine as we are. We can forget the discipline of controlling our words or managing our emotions and say 'that's just how I feel'. We can develop excuses for areas where actually, if we embraced discipline, no excuse would be necessary.

Discipline doesn't have to be an enemy; it can become your friend. Its results can enhance your life at every stage and every season. Today, maybe you need to start a new appreciation campaign for discipline; instead of enduring it, learn to welcome and embrace it because we all eventually love the results. We love the new set of muscles, the ability to fit in a pair of jeans, the money we save and the friendships we make. If we know its results are beneficial, we need to be willing to pay the price discipline incurs.

So what discipline could enhance your life right now? Is it in your physical world? Do you need the discipline of earlier nights, better diet, exercise or rest? How about spiritually? Reading the word, walking out the principles that lead to the promises, do you need a more disciplined approach to your commitment to God's house, His people, His values? For me discipline has made my life more manageable and less chaotic. Discipline has made me healthier in every area. Wherever I am, some things will always be part of my day; the daily disciplines sustain us in the big adventures. Fitness of mind, body and spirit - they don't just happen, so where do you need to add a daily discipline?

THINK IT ━━━━━━━━━━━━━ **30**

SPEAK IT ━━━━━━━━━━━━━━━━

BE IT ━━━━━━━━━━━━━━━━

So here's what I think: the best thing you can do right now is to finish what you started last year and not let those good intentions grow stale. Your heart's been in the right place all along. You've got what it takes to finish it up, so go to it.
2 Corinthians 8:10-11 (MSG)

Some people are the natural born planners of life, they have a list for everything (yep guilty as charged). This skill set can often be to the annoyance of the more free spirited in the group or of the teenager trying to avoid any delegated tasks. However, as life makes more demands, you soon see there are many aspects of 'the list' that we should love rather than resent. Planning is a form of intentionality, in advance of all other demands it says: this is what is going to happen. Of course things may change but without that intentional living, the likelihood is everything will change! For example, if we don't get intentional about our family nights or date nights, guess what? They are less likely to become a reality. The intentionality of saying this matters in our household means when the demands come (and they will), when weariness kicks in (and it does), the intentional choices become the way we keep what really matters from disappearing in a sea of everything else.

This is helpful in our everyday life but this skill becomes invaluable in our spiritual journey. Our ability to be intentional begins to change the dynamics of our God given destiny. We move from reactive to proactive, from unpredictable to reliable. We can all become more intentional in our speech, actions and ask. Intentionality makes decisions in the present that go ahead and help shape and even secure the future. When we are more intentional about the people we listen to and invest in, the places we go or don't go to, we remove the derailing power of reactive living, which can throw us off course with each changing situation or opinion. Intentionality targets your prayers rather than allowing circumstances to hijack them. Intentionality asks on purpose rather than waits for permission. Intentionality moves your confession from casual to careful.

We need to become those who are less casual and more intentional. Not wasting words but planting them. Not talking about actions but doing them. Caleb's daughter asked for springs of water. Jabez cried out to be blessed despite his circumstances. Job intentionally chose in his hardest times to bless God anyway. David intentionally provided for Solomon to build what he had dreamed of. Ruth intentionally took care of Naomi. What are you intentionally, deliberately, purposefully going to ask, seek and do today?

SPEAK IT ━━━━━━━━━━━━━━━

BE IT ━━━━━━━━━━━━━━━

**One generation commends Your works to another; they tell of Your mighty acts.
Psalm 145:4 (NIV)**

The more I look back the more I see miracles. They say you shouldn't spend a lot of time looking back as you can't change what has already happened. However every now and then it's good to look back not in regret but with gratitude and reflection. So often we overlook the miracles that happen in the mayhem of our lives but it is always good for the soul to take a little time and take stock of just how good God is even though at times we failed to see how much He was doing behind the scenes.

When we take a glance back, we can often see what in the midst of the situation we couldn't even recognise as a reality. The hand of God is ever with us, but sometimes it's only with hindsight that we see just how much He has gone before us. You need to create times when you recall how God held you when you felt helpless. Recall how He provided when you felt powerless. See the miracle of the lesson you learnt in the midst of the test and storm. Recall the relationship that God orchestrated in His perfect timing. How He gave you the strength where you needed to walk away and directed you by His sweet Spirit in a new way.

What about the times we didn't realise were a gift but now with hindsight we see completely differently? The change in circumstance that He orchestrated that increased your confidence and widened your horizons. The way He moved behind the scenes and took care of the smallest details that concerned your heart. God's miracle movements in your everyday moments are often something we can overlook or forget too quickly. Yet your God has been so faithful and His love and grace have followed you when even those you had come to rely on have left you.

So why not take a few moments today to pour out gratitude as you look back at the fingerprints of God that are evident all over your life. In the valleys and the mountaintops you can trace His fingerprints guiding and overshadowing. As you are about to surge forward into another day, remind your heart you have a faithful God and the God who was and who is, is the God that is to come. Let thanksgiving pave the way today and take courage in the fact that the faithfulness of God follows you into your future just as it carried you through your past.

INHALE

SPEAK IT ━━━━━━━━━━━━━━

BE IT ━━━━━━━━━━━━━━

EXHALE

When he came to his senses, he said, 'How many of my father's hired servants have food to spare, and here I am starving to death! I will set out and go back to my father and say to him: Father, I have sinned against heaven and against you. I am no longer worthy to be called your son; make me like one of your hired servants.'
Luke 15:17-19 (NIV)

We all have a quit point, for some it comes a lot sooner than for others. We end up in a place where we can feel like we aren't making progress anymore, so we think, 'what's the point, I might as well quit'. There are things we need to quit, from wrong relationships to bad habits and it can be positive if the action heightens our ability and propels us towards God's best. Quitting has its place but that's exactly what it has, a place; it shouldn't be allowed into every space of our lives.

Looking back on our childhood, we know that there were critical times when our desire to quit was overridden by a parent's wisdom to say 'quitting is not the answer, use that energy and try again'. Remember when you couldn't master riding a bike? You spent more time falling down than staying up and you just wanted to quit. Yet there was that person who got you back up on the bike and told you to try again. They knew if you pushed past this mental and physical desire to quit, a new skill would be attained and you would enjoy a newfound freedom. We have people right now in all our worlds that need us to be that voice, when one has no energy left, we step in and say 'try again'. Too many projects are left unfinished, too many breakthroughs are left unclaimed because we only heard our own inner voice saying 'quit' instead of a voice shouting 'try again'.

Several years ago, my son Noah Brave had a maths test he had convinced himself he couldn't do. My husband kept saying, 'Noah, let's try again, let's look at new ways of learning this information'. He encouraged him every day to keep going, Noah rose to the encouragement and now is in the top set for maths. If we can change that attitude from childhood into our adult years how many more skills would we realise were within us all along? The prodigal son at his worst was still able to find the best because when all his options seemed to have failed him, he decided that he should try again. At the other side was a father waiting, not to chastise him, but to welcome him home. The truth is that we would rather say we quit because that's the easier thing to do. Stop and realise you have come too far to quit - get up and hear that voice that says 'you can do it, just try again'.

SPEAK IT ━━━━━━━━━━━━━━━━━

BE IT ━━━━━━━━━━━━━━━━━━

"But I will restore you to health and heal your wounds," declares the Lord.
Jeremiah 30:17 (NIV)

A while ago I had a cut which I left untreated. I didn't take time to clean the wound, I just put a bandaid over it, saying I don't have time, it's no big deal. Needless to say the wound didn't disappear, in fact it got worse and became infected. It cost me more time in the long run sorting it out than it would have ever taken had I treated it right in the beginning. How often do we do the same in our everyday life? We think a bandaid will fix things so we attach a temporary cover over infected wounds. Offenses that we fail to clean, hurt we decide to hide, and brokenness we try to tape together with statements about how much better we feel.

The thing about hiding hurt is that eventually the wound begins to smell, the infection spreads and the body starts to feel ill because of what has been left to rot beneath the cover up. It takes more time to clean a wound and let it breath. If it's severe it may need an expert to treat it. But the time taken to fix the broken is an investment into your future and prevents the infection harming anyone else's too. It's a good daily discipline to let your hurts be healed. To bring any wounds into an air space that you create where the atmosphere flows with faith, forgiveness, hope and love, allowing time to pray and clear any potential infection. Stop feeding what is festering and start investing in your healing.

I have heard some say that time is a healer and while this can be true in certain situations, time can also be a hurter. The longer it's left, the harder it can be. The more you ignore, the bigger the elephant in the room. We need to discern between what is a healthy time to leave things and when the only healthy option is to get on and heal things. Not every hurt needs others to hear it, see it or involve in it. In fact, very few hurts need attention drawn to them but they do need the right assistance. Don't allow fear of what people may think to cause the wound to become worse than it should be and last longer than it should do.

Maybe you need to take some bandaids off today and get some air to the wound. Maybe you need to deal with what is festering so you can move forward. Take some time today to pray for God to help in an area that you know needs some healing. Allow His grace and spirit to guide you as to how to start the process of fixing what you have been hiding. Don't let another day pass with a wound that God is well able to help you mend.

THINK IT ━━━━━━━━━━━━━━━━

SPEAK IT ━━━━━━━━━━━━━━━━━━━━

BE IT ━━━━━━━━━━━━━━━━━━━━

EXHALE

Therefore, rid yourselves of all malice and all deceit, hypocrisy, envy, and slander of every kind. Like newborn babies, crave pure spiritual milk, so that by it you may grow up in your salvation, now that you have tasted that the Lord is good. 1 Peter 2:1-2 (NIV)

Did you ever get your book back at school and where the typical teacher's tick was expected, there was also a comment saying 'you can do better'. This isn't saying your work is terrible, it isn't a red pen crossing out what is more wrong than right, it is instead a statement that is appealing to you, the student, to get out the better that is already within you.

The 'you can do better' can either be seen as patronising and critical or potential awakening and helpful. You can do better used to annoy me, but the more I journey through life the more I find it is a truth we need to embrace. The better is not about being the best or winning the prize. It's not a start over, it's a let's go deeper, let's see what else is in you, let's keep exploring what is untapped and unawakened.

Sometimes we like to over complicate the situation because the more complex we make it, the less likely we are to take any responsibility to fix it. We all know that circumstances, challenges and situations will often hijack and change the terrain of our lives externally. Yet what we can always adjust and adapt is the internal terrain of our life. So instead of waiting for everything else or everyone else to improve we can decide to improve now.

If you were honest, where would you say 'I can do better'? Not in a way that is demanding or judging you but in a way that is elevating you to think better, speak better, live better. If the answer is yes, I can do better, (which in my case is always the honest answer), then the work we have before us becomes clearer. Instead of trying to fix many things, just work on your better!

Today, I want to do better as a mum, as a wife, be better with my patience and better with my caffeine intake, better at exercising and better at enjoying. Better is not striving for perfection, it's just making the small steps everyday that eventually take you a long way. We must not turn this into something we stress or strive over but rather use it like a magnetic pull over the hidden gold within. We all have more in us than we realise because God placed His very best inside each of us. We shouldn't worry about 'you can do better' or its equivalent being said or appearing on the homework of our lives. Instead, see it as a shout to your potential to wake up, see it as a cheering on to the better you were always destined to enjoy and discover.

THINK IT ━━━━━━━━━━━━━━━ 40

SPEAK IT ━━━━━━━━━━━━━━━

BE IT ━━━━━━━━━━━━━━━

EXHALE

breathe
it all in

The Lord also will be a refuge and a stronghold for the oppressed, a refuge in times of trouble; And those who know Your name [who have experienced Your precious mercy] will put their confident trust in You. Psalm 9:9 (AMP)

Don't allow your hurt to become your holding ground. The truth is, pain is part of progress, it serves a necessary purpose when it comes to building our lives in the right way. Without learning how to handle pain, we will always be in fear of its arrival, we will live in a way that tries to downplay risk so that we can restrict injury. Yet we are called to live a life that is full of adventure, exploring new heights and taking new territory. We can't do that without also enduring some pain along the way, so we need to know how best to process it.

Pain not appropriately processed will demand a name. It will want someone to centre its anger on. It will want you to chase after that which you can't get over. This unchecked pain will ask for you to feed its fury with more information. In a day and age where we are social media overloaded, pain can have more places to feed its obsession than ever before, adding more paranoia to the problem. It can scroll posts that are written by those who caused pain and become a voyager to a dangerous destination. Every time the pain gets to feed it grows and its voice becomes louder.

One of the areas where we often mishandle pain is when we make things personal. If we start to personalise every painful experience then we will feel victimised and live from a place of defensiveness instead of trust and faithfulness. Often the pain that lingers the longest is the pain we have named. A name speaks of identity and ownership, we cannot allow our pain to start shaping our identity and becoming our personal companion in life.

If we can stop the pain from being personal, we can progress instead of regress. Don't allow pain to control your conversation or hijack all your energy and attention. Don't respond in anger that will make you feel better for a moment but will not add anything to your future. Give your pain to God, give that person or situation over so you can move on. You have too much to do to stay caught up in something so small. Pain will ask for a name, it will say label me, associate me with a person, a place, give me an identity; but that doesn't mean you have to respond. Today, step away from the pain and breathe and allow your life to be shaped by a different sound, stop feeding the hurt and free yourself! Life is too short to hang around the places where pain resides.

THINK IT ━━━━━━━━━━━━━━ 42

SPEAK IT ━━━━━━━━━━━━━━━━

BE IT ━━━━━━━━━━━━━━━━

Then David said to the Philistine, "You come to me with a sword, a spear, and a javelin, but I come to you in the name of the Lord of hosts, the God of the armies of Israel, whom you have taunted." 1 Samuel 17:45 (AMP)

We have all had those people in our lives that for want of a better word are just intimidating, maybe it was a playground bully growing up or the now adult sized bully in the workplace. It could be an over opinionated in-law or a controlling partner. We can be intimidated by people's giftedness or their bullishness because no matter how old we are, we all at some point face the voice of intimidation. Therefore we have to learn at those points how to find our own voice so we can respond. The enemy loves to intimidate you and I because if he can intimidate a child of God, then the likelihood is we have forgotten whose child we are.

When David got to the front line he had to deal with the voice of intimidation. For David this voice was hard to ignore as it came booming down from a great height. The voice belonged to a giant and he came to remind David of all he wasn't and let him know all Goliath was. Intimidation seeks to downplay your worth and over play its strength, its posture is threatening and its manner is aggressive. Intimidators such as fear and shame like to speak in front of an audience.

Goliath threw out insults and laughed at David's simplicity and how ordinary he was in front of the giant's extraordinary size and impressive presence. Yet as David was invited to enter this war of words, he paused and refused the invitation. He chose not to waste his energy on a fight that did not matter. He didn't come to the front line to show off or impress. So David stood and let the voice of intimidation speak and instead chose to reply from his place of validation. It records that he simply answered, 'I come at you in the name of the God of the angel armies'. He reminded Goliath whom he served. He spoke of the One who was with him and who had gone before him. David let intimidation know: I am validated, chosen, called and backed up by my matchless God. He reminded himself in that moment that what Goliath said, had no power against what God had already said.

So friend, what is the voice of intimidation saying to you? Don't try and win the argument, just end it by speaking from the one who validates you. Let fear know I have an anchor for my soul. Let trouble know I have a peace that surpasses you. Let doubt know God is faithful. Let the lies know His truth sets you free. Don't fear Goliath, he cannot undo what God has promised He will do.

THINK IT ━━━━━━━━━━━━━━━ 44

SPEAK IT ━━━━━━━━━━━━━━━

BE IT ━━━━━━━━━━━━━━━

EXHALE

"I have the right to do anything," you say - but not everything is beneficial. "I have the right to do anything" - but not everything is constructive. 1 Corinthians 10:23 (NIV)

If I was to throw a ball at you right now what would your instinct be, to catch the ball right? You would probably be ready to grab a hold of what was heading right for you, though no one had told you to catch the ball your reactions would kick in without you asking them to. We can all live in a way that is reactionary but we have to learn how to be intentional and to discern what balls we should catch that are coming our way. Reactionary living will fill your hands with all kinds of curve balls that you would have been better letting drop to the ground rather than bringing them into your world.

Reactionary living empowers circumstances to direct your choices, the question is are you sure you want to give them that much power? It is not always easy to take a step back when everything shouts, step in. It's hard to hold your peace when everything screams, say your piece. It's difficult to ignore wrong, in order to do right. But whenever we put reactions in charge, we empower circumstances that little bit more to choose what's next. The response our reactions evoke soon become the new scenery we find ourselves living in.

Too many times we can empower reactions to be the first responder to circumstances. The problem is, often our reactions are controlled by our feelings not faith. Therefore we allow our flesh to make serious spiritual choices. Today, remember you have a choice to not react but to choose your response. You don't have to catch that ball, comment on that circumstance, attend the argument, or visit the offense. Take the time to understand what's at stake, so you don't make a worse mistake. Make space to make sense of what's next, don't rush if you need to rest first. Sometimes the gap we create changes entirely the response we give.

Maybe you need to take back a little more territory when it comes to the space called reaction and move instead to a space that first allows for reflection. Remember sometimes our short term gain can mean long term loss. So do the good work of choosing well rather than always having to choose now. Learn to appreciate the gap as much as the catch, because some balls are meant to be dropped.

THINK IT ━━━━━━━━━━━━━━━━━ 46

SPEAK IT ━━━━━━━━━━━━━━━━━

BE IT ━━━━━━━━━━━━━━━━━

EXHALE

Follow my example, as I follow the example of Christ.
1 Corinthians 11:1 (NIV)

We make many choices each morning, what to wear, eat for breakfast, priorities for the day. We can be so busy with our choices, we neglect a very important part of our day, something that requires as much if not more consideration than all the other things put together. We neglect the choice of how we will be led throughout the day.

Of the many volunteers for the job, only a few make a good guide. You decide everyday who you want to follow. Lots of feelings will put themselves forward, from weariness to anger, from hurt to hope. They will each be available to take the lead, from when you wake to when you go to sleep. But take a moment before you allow one of them to take the wheel and think about who will drive you where you want to go. We need to make sure we are choosing what we want to follow rather than letting each day be led in a myriad of unpredictable ways. Fear will freeze you, pride will push you, hurt will hinder you, grace will save you, hope will hold you.

We need to add a moment amongst the many choices we make to give thought to this choice. Who am I following today? Is it leftover anger, or is it fresh mercy? Who gets to be the filter my conversation goes through? The decider of how I listen and to where I give my attention? None of us are immune from feelings but we all have the power of choosing what we follow. I remember once travelling in a convoy of vehicles with some friends, we decided who would be the lead vehicle and off we set. It soon became apparent that maybe our choice of who to follow needed revisiting, as the friend up front seemed to forget about the people behind. The speed at which they were driving was causing the rest of the convoy to struggle to keep up and with increasing amounts of traffic it was intensifying the probability of a collision ahead. The person we had chosen to follow may have been a great driver but that didn't make for a great leader. We too have to discover the difference between just getting there and how we get there.

If you're already up and running with the wrong choice leading, pull the car over now, change driver before any collisions or wrong turns happen. You can choose and you will be amazed the difference in the journey when you have the best choices in the front seat. Take charge today of how you will travel through the day, be selective about the one who is choosing the speed and the route you take. Make a choice that doesn't just get there but it gets there in style; shift the driver from feelings to faith and you will find new scenery awaits at every turn.

THINK IT ━━━━━━━━━━ 48

SPEAK IT ━━━━━━━━━━━━━━

BE IT ━━━━━━━━━━━━━━

EXHALE

49 ━━━━━ TAKE THE TUNNEL

I press on toward the goal to win the prize for which God has called me heavenward in Christ Jesus. Philippians 3:14 (NIV)

When I was outside running recently I reached an intersection where in order to carry on my path, I needed to go through a tunnel. The park I was jogging through was so large it spanned across a busy freeway and in order to get from one side of the park to the other you had to take a tunnel. However as I was about to take the tunnel my attention was drawn to a large red and white danger sign that informed me that I should be careful, to be aware as danger was ahead. The tunnel was built to help me get to where I was going, yet the sign was warning me to not keep heading in that direction. I stood for a moment perplexed by the danger sign that made no apparent sense, as surely the much more dangerous option it would leave me with was to cross a very busy freeway. It was in that moment that I realised this sign was not forbidding me, it was simply warning me. This was not a do not enter, it was a 'be cautious when you enter'. It wasn't a stop sign, just more of a 'slow down' sign.

How many times do we avoid the adventure we need because of the danger signs we wrongly perceive? I have discovered that danger is not denial, it's advance warning to be ready for the risk. Warnings do not have to mean avoiding the path, they can be an alert for action. Risk is part of the road we have to travel. It's good to be aware of the challenges but we must not let our fear prohibit our future. The truth is, just as much as there could be danger ahead, there are also certain dangers in staying still. Stagnation is just as scary as possible confrontation. Freezing brings more jeopardy than forging forward. Today take note of the risk, be ready in case of challenge but don't reroute or derail from the path you know you're called to take.

Sometimes you just have to run a little faster through the places that are a little tougher. You may see some danger signs but they are for your benefit not your restriction. Be willing to see the danger and navigate the tough terrain, don't stop at the wrong side of the tunnel if you are supposed to go through, then get through. The disciples would often be warned by Jesus of the danger ahead from persecution, isolation and rejection. Then after telling them of the potential perils, He sent them out and told them to get on with the mission. The danger didn't change the plan but His pre-warning of what was ahead helped them to be better prepared for their own tunnel moments. So today, make sure you're not stopping because of a sign you are misreading: danger doesn't mean do not enter.

THINK IT ━━━━━━━━━━━━━━━ **50**

SPEAK IT ━━━━━━━━━━━━━━━━

BE IT ━━━━━━━━━━━━━━━━

EXHALE

"Therefore I tell you, do not worry about your life, what you will eat or drink; or about your body, what you will wear. Is not life more than food, and the body more than clothes?" Matthew 6:25 (NIV)

A while ago we got a crazy expensive electricity bill, it seemed so out of the ordinary that we chose to investigate what the extra payments had been caused by. It took months of paperwork and phone calls until we finally found we had a very overactive meter and the electricity we were being asked to pay for was not even power we had been using.

Do you know every day many of us are paying these bills? It may not be to an electricity company but we are being charged emotionally and physically for power we cannot use for anything. When we worry it eats away at possibility and destroys opportunity. Worry takes useful moments and allows fear to squander them. Worry imagines the worst and overlooks the best. So how do we stop ourselves from worrying? How do we cut off its power supply and change the use of energy in our lives? It all comes back to the power of choice you and I have; we get to choose what we meditate on, we get to choose what we discuss, we can choose where we linger and often, we will find worry has been given too much time and attention.

Every time I have to get ready to leave my home to minister overseas, I make a deliberate choice. I can pack either in peace or in stress. I can imagine the worst or the best. I can feel guilty for going or feel blessed in what we as a family are sowing. I can worry about the kids' well being or be excited about what we as a family are building. I can stay here all day and feel sorry for myself or I can pack with the attitude that this trip is going to be EPIC. It's all about reaching people and that's a good thing. Both are options and both drain energy, however one will give you nothing back in return but an exhausting bill, the other will fuel faith, dreams and anticipation for what's ahead. You see every great thing also has hard things attached. And worry just maximises the hard and even invents more problems to keep you preoccupied for wasted hours of your life. They say if you can worry then you can most definitely pray, worrying is just meditating in the wrong direction. So capture the worry and turn it into a prayer, make your anxiety list your prayer requests. Make your worry time your worship time and shift the list. Today, where do you need to stop paying worry's bills and start transferring your energy into a smarter investment?

THINK IT ━━━━━━━━━━━━━

SPEAK IT ━━━━━━━━━━━━━

BE IT ━━━━━━━━━━━━━

For God has not given us a spirit of fear, but of power and of love and of a sound mind. 2 Timothy 1:7 (NKJV)

We only need to switch on the news to see that our world is unwell. From terror attacks, to senseless shootings, hurricanes and storms wiping out whole communities, countless reports fill the airwaves that strike despair in the heart of every listener, even hopelessness and worst of all, ultimately fear. Fear is that subtle thief that comes over your heart and mind and begins to tell you that things will never get better. Fear begins to shrink what God says and magnify a bad report. Fear imagines the worse and moves you out of the neighbourhood of faith, making you a resident in the community of anxiety and hopelessness.

However, the word teaches us that He did not give us a spirit of fear but He gave us a sound mind. Therefore we need to learn how to harness the power of faith that overcomes and can overwhelm every fear. Fear will invite you to fight, it will speak to you about what could happen, it will shout at you a bad report and the more attention you give it the more established it will become. The more residency it can take in your life, the more debilitating it is to your future. Fear stops the dreams and creates nightmares, it prohibits peace and increases stress, therefore you have to know how to fight fear. It is a liar and the only way to fight a lie is with the truth of God's word. If fear is speaking, you need to commit afresh to diving deep into the word of God replacing every lie with truth. We can only silence fear when we have turned up the volume on what God says. His word illuminates what fear tries to dissipate. Fear creates doubts but truth gives us an assurance on which we can build even in the midst of adversity.

Fear is not your future. It has no place in your heart and mind. His perfect love casts out all fear and we have in those moments to lean on Him, placing our trust and hope in the one who is the Prince of Peace. We have to keep a sound mind and stop the terrorist called fear taking more victims. Today, where do you need to deal with fear? Where do you need to stop conversing with it and permitting fear to speak into things it has no business addressing.

Often fear can begin subtlty and so it creeps up in our hearts and destinies. It counsels you to shrink back, withhold but this is not a time to shrink back friends, we are the light bringers and hope givers so put your focus on Him and do not be afraid. Exhale fear today and inhale courage.

THINK IT ———————————— 54

SPEAK IT ————————————————

BE IT ————————————————

When Moses' hands grew tired, they took a stone and put it under him and he sat on it. Aaron and Hur held his hands up - one on one side, one on the other - so that his hands remained steady till sunset. So Joshua overcame the Amalekite army with the sword. Exodus 17:12-13 (NIV)

Imagine for a moment how you would feel if you were asked to stand on a hilltop and hold up your younger brother's arms all day. Your first reaction may not be excitement; maybe you would wonder why was this necessary or even feel a little put down. This was the reality for Aaron when he was asked to hold up the arms of his younger brother, Moses. God had called Moses to lift his arms in prayer to make sure Joshua won the battle against the Amalekites. If his arms were upheld, the victory was theirs, if his arms were lowered, the battle was lost.

This entire set up is the opposite to how our minds and rational works. We would think the victory was in wearing the armour and fighting on the front lines like Joshua but God set this triumph on the ability of every one to play their part. Without Moses, no arms were lifted and so no victory was possible; without Aaron and Hur, no arms were upheld and so the battle was lost; without Joshua no army were being fought. If they wanted to defeat the enemy that day they would have to be willing to play the part entrusted to them.

How we view what we do is crucial; we can rank responsibility and roles based on what we see instead of on what God has said. We see the front line as the Joshua and pay less attention to the ones that are in the background like Aaron. We need fresh appreciation for everyone on the team, this is how we are going to ensure our win. How many times have we missed our victory because we didn't want to play our part? Would you be willing to be given the job of arm holder, especially if the arm was of someone younger or with less experience?

Aaron and Hur chose to stand in the gap, they saw the Amalekites instead of focusing on what was I am sure was a sweaty armpit. It takes a bigger perspective to stay in place when others may seem to be getting all the credit but if the win for you is the win for all those alongside you, then armpits won't matter. By choosing what you see, the Amalekites will be defeated. What role do you need to shift perspective on? We need to not see the task but see what that task is achieving. Don't underplay your part - embrace the place you have been given to help the miracle happen.

SPEAK IT ▬▬▬▬▬▬▬▬▬▬▬▬

BE IT ▬▬▬▬▬▬▬▬▬▬▬▬

EXHALE

I know your deeds, that you are neither cold nor hot. I wish you were either one or the other! So, because you are lukewarm - neither hot nor cold - I am about to spit you out of my mouth. Revelation 3:15-17 (NIV)

Often we can buy into the lie that we cannot do anything to change a situation. We have no power to alter a circumstance. We begin to believe we are powerless and therefore we become motionless. We give away our power of choice and in doing so lose more of our voice. But it is simply not true, it's a lie, you always have a choice. You get to choose what you will do, say, pray, sow, forgive, love, build! You may not be able to change everything, but you can choose to do something. Don't allow life to move your power of choice.

Where are some areas that you have abdicated choosing, which are now altering and changing the way you are living? Where have you said, it will never change, and in so doing have unpacked your life in a place of dead ends and containment? We can hand over our power to choose in our careers, relationships and decision making. Who have you given the power of choice to in your world?

What choices are you delaying right now and in so doing empowering others to choose for you? Where is your hesitancy placing decisions you need to make at other people's feet? We need to get used to choosing and the more we learn to choose the better we will become at it. Examine different aspects of your life and ask, have I made a choice recently or am I just on autopilot, abdicating where I should be deciding?

Choose your company, choose your confession, choose your planting, choose your releasing. Choose your priorities, choose your people, choose your mood, choose your mountain. Just get more comfortable with the power of choice and the more you practise the better you will become at it! Stop saying I don't know, I don't care, you decide, and instead recognise each time you have a choice, however small, it's an opportunity to find your own voice and express what's in your heart. So take back the menu and just choose; you never know, you may even discover something on there you never knew you liked. Don't just keep the same thing because you are frightened to try new things; be willing to choose and embrace the options before you. Choices not only have the power to move you forward but they can widen your options and broaden your horizons. They can expose you not just to a new experience but also to a new part of you, the part that before you made a choice didn't have a voice. So seek God for wisdom, take courage and have faith today to choose well.

THINK IT ━━━━━━━━━━━━━━━ **58**

SPEAK IT ━━━━━━━━━━━━━━━

BE IT ━━━━━━━━━━━━━━━

EXHALE

**See, I am doing a new thing! Now it springs up; do you not perceive it?
Isaiah 43:19 (NIV)**

When I was little a cardboard box was magical. It had the ability to become many things: that box was a house for my dolls with windows cut out and a door at the front; it was a car my dad would push me along the kitchen floor in; it became a treasure chest when I was a pirate; an obstacle course when I had friends over. That cardboard box was full of possibilities. However, now as an adult the cardboard box is simply a box, an object to get things moved from A to B in and then something that needs removing and recycling. What happened? Where did all those other possibilities go? I now watch my youngest nieces make all the same discoveries about a cardboard box and I wonder, how long until the box loses its captivating powers and becomes just a box again?

When we first encounter many things in our lives, we see creativity and wonder but after time we just see the box. If we are not careful we will discard what we should keep and recycle what had a lot more life left in it. The box isn't the problem, it is the way we have started to see it. When you first started in that job you could see endless possibilities, now it's just a job. When you first began that relationship it was filled with wonder, now it's just become another box that you move around your life. When you first encountered God it was so intimate and exciting, every week going deeper in discovering who He is but now it's just a box you tick called Christianity.

The cardboard box syndrome can happen to us all. Of course we can come to the end of a relationship, a job can lose its purpose, the idea can be fulfilled and it's time to get on with the next. Yet in each stage of that process you can decide whether to see the wonder or the cardboard. I have at times grown fed up with something I have been handling and neglected to give it the attention I once did and then someone has picked up what I dropped and made it even better. They knew the box had more to give. That's why we need to keep that attitude of possibility and receptivity present even if we are passing on that box to someone else. Don't discard what once served you so well, instead pass it on with possibility attached. We need to keep the options open even if it's not our preference any more. Whatever you have in your world right now, from work to relationships to service, how much of that are you just handling and where are you still imagining and creating? Today, don't just move boxes, see possibilities and bring some of the joy back into the journey.

THINK IT ━━━━━━━━━━━━━ 60

SPEAK IT ━━━━━━━━━━━━━

BE IT ━━━━━━━━━━━━━

EXHALE

One of them, when he saw he was healed, came back, praising God in a loud voice. Luke 17:15 (NIV)

When Jesus healed ten lepers, they all received a miracle. Something they could never imagine possible, became possible. Their lives were forever changed. That healing did not only cleanse their disease but it gave them a road back home. The people who had previously isolated them would now be able to embrace them once more. This physical miracle held even greater healings within it relationally and emotionally.

As they rushed off to tell everyone about what had happened, the Bible informs us that one stopped. Just one! Nine carried on running towards the family they had been estranged from and the community they longed to be a part of again but one stopped. He headed back in the direction he had been so desperate to leave all these years. He went back because he decided to be the one.

He found Jesus and threw his arms around Him and with tears of gratitude, thanked Him for the miracle he had received. He did something that seemed unnecessary to the other nine, but for this one was essential before he could go on. When Jesus saw the one who had come back to do something for Him, He remarked, wasn't there another nine? He knew all had received a miracle but not all had received a breakthrough. He hadn't just been made well, he was well. He moved from a place where stigma and isolation was the norm and his first move as a healed man was to demonstrate an act of wholeness, to go and embrace, bow and thank someone. After years of being mistreated, he could have just taken the miracle and run but he did better, he went and said words of thanks before he went on with the rest of his life. Often the way we have been poorly treated can mean in a moment of blessing we hold onto what we should share in our healing. We feel justified to withhold the favour from others like they withheld things from us. But this one man started his new chapter differently than the rest and that led to his story looking different from the others. This act of gratitude towards Jesus drew from Him an extra blessing. This one leper was now not just healed but made whole.

Only one went to say thank you. Only one was willing to delay the party so he could show his gratitude. Today why don't you be the one who makes time to say thank you for all God has done? Be the one who shows gratitude to those around you. Be the one who chooses to delay the party so they can go and offer up praise. You will find, like that leper, that thanksgiving always tips you into greater blessing and moves you deeper into the presence of God.

THINK IT

SPEAK IT

BE IT

EXHALE

But grow in the grace and knowledge of our Lord and Saviour Jesus Christ. To Him be glory both now and forever! Amen. 2 Peter 3:18 (NIV)

Before the stretch is the time to get in shape! Expansion is something we can all seek. We want to increase our effectiveness, expand our future. We may pray for more opportunity, to take new ground. God wants to give us increase, yet like every good parent, He wants the growth you gain to be the growth you keep. He wants our lives to increase not just in opportunity but more importantly in maturity.

Whenever growth and expansion comes, it will create a stretch in our lives. It will stretch our attitudes, discipline, mindset and willingness. The stretch of expansion also exposes what is often hidden within us. Ambition, pride, hurt, wrong motives, insecurity, jealousy are all revealed in the intensity of increase. Jesus told His disciples, before you go out you need to look within, He challenged their priorities, rebuked their unbelief and at times questioned their motives. When Noah was told a flood was coming he had to first build an arc. We, like Noah, need to know how to build for the future. It's better to build a life now for increase than get to a place where the increase sinks you. So where can you get in shape before the stretch? Don't wait until the door opens to get your shoes. Don't wait for your moment before you deal with your motive. Don't allow expansion to expose you, let its pending arrival propel you into preparation and prayer.

Stretching is to prevent snapping. When an athlete stretches, it's to increase the muscle's ability to take more pressure, to go further, to prevent a tendon snapping, which then leads to immobility and incapacity. Spiritually, the snap is a place where we have come to the end of our grace or faith, love or patience. If we can learn in those places to stretch into the more of God, the peace that passes understanding, the joy that is strength, the love that is unending, then we can stop the snap. Jesus taught His disciples how to stretch. He asked them to love their enemies, forgive more than was comfortable, to shake the dust off their feet, to turn the other cheek. Jesus was saying, I want to identify places you may snap and teach you instead to stretch. As a disciple of Jesus today, He wants to extend you and help you apply the same lesson. So where can you stretch to avoid the snap?

THINK IT ━━━━━━━━━━━━━━ **64**

SPEAK IT ━━━━━━━━━━━━━━

BE IT ━━━━━━━━━━━━━━

EXHALE

"See, I have delivered Jericho into your hands, along with its king and its fighting men. March around the city once with all the armed men. Do this for six days. Have seven priests carry trumpets of rams' horns in front of the ark. On the seventh day, march around the city seven times, with the priests blowing the trumpets. When you hear them sound a long blast on the trumpets, have the whole army give a loud shout; then the wall of the city will collapse and the army will go up, everyone straight in." Joshua 6:2-5 (NIV)

Unity is easy to say but harder to live out. Yet God asks us to show the world what they struggle so often to see. In a world that is increasingly divided how do we truly model living in a way that's united? When we think of all the ways we are different and how many ways we can be in disagreement it seems easier to polarise than unify and simpler to stay in our own lanes rather than try and interact with one another's lane. Yet we are shown in the picture of the Trinity that God Himself is the outworking of the power that comes from unity. God the Father, the Son and the Spirit all working as one.

Unity is where God pours out special blessings. Unity is where we see atmospheres shift and walls come down. When the children of Israel went into Jericho, they were faced with a problem in the middle of their promise but God's instructions to Joshua were very clear. The way the walls would come down was not by anyone's individual strength, they wouldn't be scaled by the most able climber or struck down by the strongest defenders, they would fall when unity spoke as one. God had them walk together and rest together for seven days; they circled together and through that whole time, no one was allowed to speak. God did not want any words to be spoken that would move the people in a multitude of directions. He knew some would moan if they were able to talk, others would suggest an alternative plan, others would question the point in any of the process. So God told Joshua, no one speaks until it's time for everyone to shout. The shout brought walls down because its sound was unified. Every voice cried out at the same time for the same thing. The united shout shook the enemy camp and today we must find that same shout.

We need to learn how to come into agreement with each other, to stop mumbling and murmuring and instead save our shout for walls that need to come down. We may not always agree but even within disagreement, it is possible to remain as one in heart and spirit. We may not always want to act and move as one, but it is in our power to choose at critical points in our journey what gets to shout louder, our own agendas or the bigger picture. Today, where can you add to your shout to bring down some greater walls?

SPEAK IT ━━━━━━━━━━━━━

BE IT ━━━━━━━━━━━━━

I rejoiced with those who said to me, "Let us go to the house of the Lord." Our feet are standing in your gates, Jerusalem. Psalm 122:1 (NIV)

Nothing great comes from drifting. When you drift you are at the mercy of the waves. You are never truly sure where you will end up at any given time. The wind and the weather have more say over your destination than you do. That's why God intended that you would not drift but plant, not float but flourish. He doesn't say you should plant to contain you, but rather to awaken what's within you.

We all are created to belong. We are designed by God to be not just in union with Him, but part of His family. We aren't supposed to be aimless and homeless but we need to find a spiritual address where we can unpack our lives and put down our roots. In a world where it is seen as old fashioned to belong, this belief could be seen to go against what many others are practicing but rather than make our own version of what's best, why don't we go back to God's master plan and trust He knows best. The house of God is not perfect, no church has got it all together but God knows that we benefit from belonging. It's the process of belonging in a place where we can all help grow in our believing and becoming, that God knew we would need.

We are called to plant, not drift. It's planting that leads to flourishing. So never underestimate the power of going to His house and being at home there. King David said 'I was glad when they said to me, let's go to the house of the Lord'. David had spent his life in royal palaces and on battle grounds, he had been celebrated and rewarded greatly, yet for him the greatest and richest prize was to be found in the house of God. He preferred serving in God's house than being served in his own. The house of God, for this man after God's own heart, was not an optional extra but it was his very life.

There is no such thing as perfect church because we have no perfect people, so if we are waiting to plant until we see perfection then we will never put our roots down. Planting is a commitment that goes beyond what people will do for you and rather comes from a place of how can I help build what God says to build? To build the house of God is not some temporary thrown together place, it isn't a drop-in centre or a hostel, it's a home and homes should not be a place we occasionally visit but they should be a place we dwell, love and contribute. So how is your dwelling, where are you in need of more flourishing, can you look to a greater level of contribution? If home is truly where the heart is, do you need to do a heart check so you can do a home inspect today?

THINK IT ━━━━━━━━━━━━━━━ 68

SPEAK IT ━━━━━━━━━━━━━━━

BE IT ━━━━━━━━━━━━━━━

69 ━━ CONFUSION BREEDS COMPROMISE

"No one can serve two masters. Either you will hate the one and love the other, or you will be devoted to the one and despise the other. You cannot serve both God and money." Matthew 6:24 (NIV)

Any parent can tell you that once you start negotiating and compromising values, bedtimes, responsibilities, chores with your children, you will open the gate for lots of confusion and manipulation, which ultimately leads to a lot of misinterpretation. The same happens in all areas of our life. Being flexible and willing to change is crucial but that is very different from constantly compromising things that we ought to be establishing.

The enemy wants you to compromise on what God wants to help establish, to give up ground which God gave you to build on. He would like you to compromise your faith and settle for a partial breakthrough, believe for an average marriage, embrace a lukewarm faith. The Bible tells us choose life or death, be hot or cold, but don't sit on the fence. We have to wake up to the subtle thief of compromise. In leading and in loving, let's bring clarity not confusion. Let's not make negotiable our future and blessing. Let's be people who fight for what's right instead of compromise for what's acceptable. If you're saying I commit, then do it, don't compromise your word by your uncommitted actions. If you say I am for you, I am your friend, then don't compromise your relationship by not being there or showing you care.

Too often the confusion in our homes, churches and relationships is because what we thought was clear has become compromised and now confusion is in people's hearts and minds. Remember Eve in the garden of Eden; God was clear about what they could and couldn't eat, though He had given them so much, there was one thing they weren't to touch. The enemy came into the garden with the strategy he still uses today, if I can confuse what God made clear I can get them to compromise what should never have been open for discussion. Eve was asked, 'did God really say that?' One question started a process of confusing and second guessing, leading to decisions that would cause internal damage.

Do not underestimate the questions that come to confuse what God has made clear. Don't enter the conversations that are looking to comprise what is a non-negotiable. Today be a person of your word, be a consistent follower, a faithful friend, a trustworthy teacher. Allow your love to bring clarity, not your emotions to cause confusion. Jesus loved all, served all, and His message was clear to all. He didn't compromise salvation, direction, truth or justice, so today let's let His way guide ours and His truth be our standard.

THINK IT ━━━━━━━━━━━━━ **70**

SPEAK IT ━━━━━━━━━━━━━━━━

BE IT ━━━━━━━━━━━━━━━━

So speak encouraging words to one another. Build up hope so you'll all be together in this, no one left out, no one left behind. 1 Thessalonians 5:11 (MSG)

When I was in my early twenties I took my first role on church staff. I wasn't speaking or writing, I was simply passionate to help build and serve the church so I agreed to do whatever needed to be done. This involved a lot of admin and one of the tasks delegated to me was the church bulletin. Now, anyone who knows me will realise this was not a good fit for my skill set. Writing and checking the bulletin was a challenge, however I did my best. I would often stay late into the evening adding last minute information (usually from the youth department) and running off photocopies. Every week the church would get that bulletin and though it was not perfect, it was readable and had the information they needed.

After the first few weeks, a 'helpful' church leader would take that bulletin and red pen the mistakes they could find: a misplaced fullstop, a word that wasn't quite right or a typo. I would receive it back in the internal mailbox, the bulletin with all the red crosses and circles letting me know I could and should do better. The first week I was upset, by the twentieth week I was over it. I wondered if it was so bad why she didn't volunteer to help. She had the time and the skills but never once did she offer to come and sit with me and show me how to do it more efficiently. The red pen was the unspoken disapproval with no offer of helping me to improve.

Sometimes our lives attract red pen people; they seem to have a mission to point out all the errors and never see any potential. Red pen people don't want to help you get better, they just want to point out how you should do better. I quickly had to learn red pen people are not the problem, it's what we do in response that either becomes a problem or makes you more productive. The bulletin was not my destiny, I was not skilled for the job but my willingness to help and serve, that was my destiny. The red pen lady was actually training me for a life that would say yes in spite of the disapproval of others.

Maybe you feel red pen has been written all over your life; you are not alone, welcome to the club. Then know red pen may circle what is wrong but you are doing so much right. Let the red pen motivate you, not immobilise you. We all have areas that aren't the greatest fit but at least you tried and hey, you are reading a devotional from a girl who was weekly red penned, so don't stop writing. Just know God will honour your diligence.

SPEAK IT ━━━━━━━━━━

BE IT ━━━━━━━━━━

EXHALE

Sow your seed in the morning, and at evening let your hands not be idle, for you do not know which will succeed, whether this or that, or whether both will do equally well. Ecclesiastes 11:6 (NIV)

Have you ever given someone a gift that you thought they would adore and you got so excited to see the response when they received it? Then after giving the gift you watch as their reaction did not match what you had imagined. The display of cheers, tears and gratitude were instead replaced with a shrug of the shoulder and a less than enthusiastic thank you. In life we can make this mistake over and over when we set up a wrong expectation to a response that we cannot govern or dictate.

When we always believe and give our best, we can expect that the same will come back to us, especially from the places we sowed that seed most. Yet we cannot control the soil of people's hearts; where we sometimes expect a response of love we will find lack, instead of an embrace, we may find rejection. Yet Jesus had this situation all the time, His messages would be received by some with great gratitude and by others with great opposition and criticism.

Jesus did not allow His heart condition to be determined by those reactions. He knew the seed was good and He kept on sowing. Our example is found in Him. It isn't easy when what you had hoped for doesn't happen but that doesn't mean a harvest is not coming. Sometimes we just have to change where we are looking and we will see something new is growing from a place we weren't even expecting. Whilst we should determine to always believe for the best, we also have to grow to understand that we can't live a life that requires the best response in order to be our best.

Today, I want to encourage you: don't stop sowing because of the response you have been receiving. Just teach your heart to be patient and your expectations to be redirected to the One who is love and who is no man's debtor. Be grateful for the opportunity to bless and don't allow your heart to harden if it has been taken for granted. Give in a way that brings joy anyway, don't attach the joy to the way people respond but rather to the privilege of being able to give. God sees it all and I have found that at times when you felt nothing was happening in the fields you hoped to harvest, God has gone ahead of you and planted a harvest where you did not sow and fruit in the orchard you didn't plant. Stay obedient and trust in God's faithfulness. Keep on being generous because God can't resist blessing those who love to be a blessing.

THINK IT ━━━━━━━━━━━━━━━ 74

SPEAK IT ━━━━━━━━━━━━━━━

BE IT ━━━━━━━━━━━━━━━

EXHALE

Then He called the crowd to Him along with His disciples and said: "Whoever wants to be my disciple must deny themselves and take up their cross and follow Me." Mark 8:34 (NIV)

I have never been to a home and found a padlock and alarm system fitted to the rubbish bin or to the plastic cups and plates. These items are not guarded because they are not highly valued or desirable to steal; they are not viewed as needing that level of protection. However I have been to a home and seen a car that is alarmed, a pet that is tagged and a safe that is installed for family valuables. People insure personal high value items, both of monetary and sentimental value, because these items hold a different significance to them than anything else they may possess. The loss of those items would yield much more upset and regret, therefore they are given the highest level of security.

Similarly when it comes to handling the more valuable things in life, like people's future and destiny, leadership and increased opportunity, we ought to expect the protection of these privileges to intensify. We should be diligent to place wise security in the places of great responsibility. We want an empowerment that places Christ values over personal agendas and ambition. Jesus never hid the cost of being His disciple, He made clear the high cost to those entrusted with such great treasure. The privilege of leading others, stewarding great resources and building God's kingdom is not a career option but a beautiful honour that needs to have just enough password protection, so that its beauty is kept intact. Let's not cheapen what cost heaven its very best. Let's not handle casually the carrying of the message that leads to people's eternities. Let's be willing to do the work, to access more wisdom, more understanding, greater compassion and so much more. I have found God guards His very great promises with just enough problems, ensuring the journey is itself often the hidden gift we get to discover along the way. The problems act like extra security codes asking you to try new things, uncover new depths and in so doing, unlock more keys of wisdom and experience.

So let's not demand doors to open, instead understand if there is extra security around the things you are trying to access it is because the lessons you are about to attain are of higher value and will bring forth a greater reward for your future. Take the time to find the right way to open the things before you, rather than trying to force your way. Let's not force open what faith wants to gradually unlock. Let's not push and pull what prayer and patience will access. God may not be withholding the opportunity from you but rather choosing to grow the potential within you through this journey of unlocking what He has deemed worth protecting. Maybe He has placed in the way just enough censuring to ensure that what eventually becomes accessed, enters careful hands.

SPEAK IT ━━━━━━━━━━━━━━━

BE IT ━━━━━━━━━━━━━━━

"Come to Me, all you who are weary and burdened, and I will give you rest. Take My yoke upon you and learn from Me, for I am gentle and humble in heart, and you will find rest for your souls. For My yoke is easy and My burden is light."
Matthew 11:28-30 (NIV)

Have you ever gone to pack a suitcase but somehow the contents seem to be a lot greater than the case you are trying to stuff them into? You may have ended up enlisting the help of others to sit on top it as you try to squash everything in and zip it closed. If you are successful at this point, you have won the first part of the battle but the next is far harder as now that overstuffed, overweight bag has to be carried with you on your journey.

Some of us are compulsive adders and carry weight that is unnecessary, simply because we don't want to let something go. We place more value on the items than we do on our own energy and time. We over tire our bodies from carrying things that will never be used or worn. We can add things to our world for no other reason than a sense of obligation or a false sense of responsibility. We pick up issues, add drama, that we should not be carrying. We allow our lives to become stuffed with agendas and weight that has no bearing on our future and is detrimental to our wellbeing.

The idea is not to just keep increasing our load, you don't win medals for carrying the most weight. So what do you need to take out of your case? What have you become emotionally attached to that you need to detach from? We can often think that if we don't carry the burden, the issue, no one else will. But what if it's time for no one else to carry this? What if that season is over and the burden needs to be dropped? You're carrying keeps taking things into the future that maybe should be left in the past. On the occasions when I have overstuffed a suitcase, I have always been frustrated because when I have seen something in the next destination I want to bring home, a new pair of shoes or something for my home, I can't add it to the bag because it's already full. I left no room for the new as I brought so much of the old with me.

Our journey with God needs to have regular audit points where we go through our lives and check we are not carrying additions that have now become restrictions. So today, stop stuffing where maybe you should be unloading. God does not want you overburdened and when you pack His way, His burden is easy and His yoke is light.

THINK IT ━━━━━━━━━━━

SPEAK IT ━━━━━━━━━━━━━

BE IT ━━━━━━━━━━━━━

EXHALE

"Now what have I done?" said David. "Can't I even speak?" He then turned away to someone else and brought up the same matter. 1 Samuel 17:29-30 (NIV)

When Jesus was wrongly accused by the crowds who He had healed and blessed, He didn't waste words in worthless arguments. When His disciples were rejected, Jesus taught them the same lesson. He told them to stay silent and move on to where they would be welcomed. Jesus was teaching them how to save the fight for what matters and to leave conversations that will never further the cause. The hardest time to be quiet and not have your say, is when you have every reason to have your say. But think of it this way, will my response heal or hurt this situation?

As hard as it can be, sometimes the best response is no response. Disney made a whole lot of money from a song that said, 'let it go'. The simplicity of those words is the biggest liberator for our souls. We have to come to a place where we realise that to hold on will become our biggest hang up. We just have to let it go, knowing God sees it all and is over it all. Save your words for those who will hear your heart and see what's true. Don't allow a wrong judgement to drive you to justify, instead continue to be a blessing. Sow kindness and live in the freedom that comes when your value is not in what others say about you, but in the knowledge of what God is doing in you.

When David went to the front line to fight Goliath, he had several other fights offered to him along the way. The first invitation came from his jealous brother Eliab, who told him to get back up the hill to his sheep. The insecure older brother didn't want him stealing his spotlight. He tried to limit and shrink David with his choice of words, but David didn't get involved, he simply turned to someone else and kept on talking. He resisted the invitation to argue in a fight he knew had no meaningful outcome.

Then he had an invite from Saul to fight, wearing his armour and carrying the sword with the royal insignia. Saul was a controlling king, eager to manipulate David's future for his own advantage. Yet again, David refused the invite. He knew Goliath was going to require his focus and strength, so he decided to protect himself from pointless distractions and conversations. David let go of his need to be heard or to silence his mockers and instead focused on his God sent assignment. Today, save your breath for what matters; exit the arguments that are leading you nowhere and head to the battle that is already yours. Let's look at this more over the next devotional as God is well able to help you in the right fight, but first you must deliver yourself from the wrong fight.

THINK IT ━━━━━━━━━━━ 80

SPEAK IT ━━━━━━━━━━━━

BE IT ━━━━━━━━━━━

EXHALE

STOP DIGGING UP IN FEAR THE SEED YOU PLANTED IN FAITH. HAVE PATIENCE TRUST

THE PROCESS AND

REMEMBER NOT ALL

GROWTH IS VISIBLE

STOP DIGGING UP IN FEAR THE SEED YOU PLANTED IN FAITH HAVE PATIENCE TRUST THE PROCESS AND REMEMBER NOT ALL GROWTH IS VISIBLE

Fight the good fight of the faith. Take hold of the eternal life to which you were called when you made your good confession in the presence of many witnesses. 1 Timothy 6:12 (NIV)

So if we clarify where we need to exit the wrong fights then how do we discern the right fight? There are mountains we do need to conquer, there are battles that need to be won. Too often we can allow our vanity, pride, offense to place us in a posture that wants to throw punches. We can be tempted to fight to prove something. Yet though all of these fights may make sense in the moment, they will not serve any purpose once the anger and frustration have subsided. We must choose fights that have our future as the prize, our destiny not our opinions need to be the reason we are in the ring. The fight for our identity, the fight for the next generation, the fight for integrity, those fights matter and actually they happen less frequently. If you're forever fighting, then you need to ask yourself why.

When Nehemiah was rebuilding the walls of Jerusalem, he noticed the people were becoming weary in the fight in the places where they were exposed to the enemies' taunts. So Nehemiah began to shout to everyone helping him build, remember what this fight is all about, fight for your sons and daughters, for you wives, for your God. He wanted them to see this was the right fight and not to lose sight of the prize, as what was at stake was far too precious.

I have found there is a good fight and that's the fight of faith. The fight that propels you forward. That's the place to give your time, prayer and energy. It can be hard to discern which fight is right in the heat of a moment or the pressure of a situation. We will see things more clearly if we take more time, therefore we have to build into our own lives the discipline to hold our peace and control our tongue. If you need wisdom to pick the right fight today, begin to examine who started this fight, pain or purpose, who threw the first punch, feelings or faith?

The right fight comes from a place of stability rather than vulnerability. When you are secure in who you are and in whose you are, it changes the way you fight. You stop allowing insecurity to pick your opponent and instead save your energy for the fight that is about your destiny, rather than your vanity.

Take the time to begin to write down the places where you are assigned a good fight and then be willing to identify the fights where it's time to hang up your gloves. The only prize you want to take home is the one that glorifies God, so you don't need those trophies, you just need to work on the right victories.

THINK IT ▬▬▬▬▬▬▬▬▬▬

SPEAK IT ▬▬▬▬▬▬▬▬▬▬▬▬

BE IT ▬▬▬▬▬▬▬▬▬▬▬▬

EXHALE

Search me, God, and know my heart; test me and know my anxious thoughts. See if there is any offensive way in me, and lead me in the way everlasting. Psalm 139:24 (NIV)

A while ago I was in America with a good friend of mine. She told me she had planned a great day for us, so we set out, hit the gym, went to the store and then we went somewhere I was not expecting to be taken. She said you travel so much I thought we could go and see my chiropractor. This was an appointment I was less sure about accepting. I had never been to a chiropractor before and from the sounds coming out of his office as we sat waiting to be seen, I was pretty sure I had made the right decision in avoiding this all these years.

The chiropractor's opening line to me was, 'so let me adjust you'. Several cracks, neck pulls and twists later he was done. As I followed his instructions I began to feel the relief from some of the pressure points and tensions that I didn't even know were in need of adjusting. It didn't take long and once I got past the sound effects the adjusting was creating, it actually didn't hurt that much at all. After my treatment I thanked him and then we went about the rest of our day, which fortunately did not involve any more surprise appointments. My visit had only taken 15 minutes and no external changes from my time with the chiropractor were visible. I hadn't had a surgical procedure, I wasn't given any medication, I had just been adjusted. I had met someone, who could sense where the pressure was, which I hadn't even noticed and could bring some relief, in so doing loosening some joints and creating a little more movement.

There are times when we need to allow God to do the same to our spiritual lives. We may not have any overwhelming problems that needs confronting, we don't need extensive heart surgery but I believe more often than we realise, God wants to help adjust you. That day as I left that appointment I felt God whisper into my own spirit, ' let me adjust you'. Sometimes we neglect the small adjustments because all we are thinking about is the big change we are wanting or seeking. But I have come to understand that the more I allow God to adjust me, the less I am in need of emergency surgeries. Adjustments are the small steps that relieve the tension now. The attitude shift that changes your perspective. The confession adjustment that brings you into a place of greater peace. The relational adjust that brings some relief. The decision that lifts the weight. Maybe if you lean into Him, you may hear Him invite you into the same process. Maybe today, you could make time to invite God to adjust you.

THINK IT ━━━━━━━━━━━━

SPEAK IT ━━━━━━━━━━━━━━━━

BE IT ━━━━━━━━━━━━━━━━

EXHALE

"As for Mephibosheth," said the king, "he shall eat at my table like one of the king's sons." ...So Mephibosheth dwelt in Jerusalem, for he ate continually at the king's table. And he was lame in both his feet. 2 Samuel 9:11-13 (NKJV)

Have you ever been invited to an event that you just didn't feel good enough to attend? Maybe the dress code made you nervous that you wouldn't fit in? The invite though sincere and beautiful, somehow seemed intimidating and so you sent a polite note to decline. The truth is that you disqualified yourself from what the sender had already fully qualified you to attend. The invite was sent because they desired your company and they wanted you to feel loved and honored. We so often disqualify ourselves from what God has already invited us into because of low self esteem, or past failings that make us feel we don't deserve to be at that table. We read the invitation to His table of grace, love and favour as a wrongly addressed request.

There is a story in the Bible of a man named Mephibosheth who was lame in both feet. As a young child he had been dropped and in his fall he was permanently disabled, which left this young man living with a sense of rejection where others were accepted. Yet Mephibosheth was from the house of Saul and David, who was now king, wanted to show kindness to any of his remaining descendants to honour the memory of his friend, Jonathan. So words were sent to Mephibosheth that his presence was requested at the king's table. When the invitation reached Mephibosheth, his lameness spoke and tried to disqualify his acceptance, however David would not take no for an answer and had him sit at the royal table.

This story is just how God is with you and I; He won't take no for an answer either! He wants you to know that you are fully qualified to sit at the king's table. We have to look past the things that so often seek to disqualify what God wants to dignify. We all have areas in our life that are weak or lame. Yet don't allow what is weak to make you withdraw, instead allow what is weak to be made strong. You have a place at the King's table. Your Heavenly Father requests your presence. He loves your company. He wants to engage in your everyday. Don't believe the lie that you're not welcome. Push past the urge to stay away and be bold enough to begin to find a way forward. The beautiful thing about God's table is that it always covers your lameness under the shadow of His wholeness. So what are you waiting for? Today, no matter how you get to the place that God is inviting you to, be it limping or crawling, push past the urge to sit it out, stop dining alone and come to the table.

THINK IT ━━━━━━━━━━━━━━━ 86

SPEAK IT ━━━━━━━━━━━━━━━

BE IT ━━━━━━━━━━━━━━━

EXHALE

Above all else, guard your heart, for everything you do flows from it.
Proverbs 4:23 (NIV)

Guard your heart but don't hide it. Protect it but don't withhold it. Be careful with it but don't confine it. It's not easy to walk this balance. We give our heart to things, people, projects and sometimes our heart is broken, misunderstood or mishandled. But that's where we have to learn to guard so that God can guide. Guard is not reactive it's proactive. Guarding is not defensive, it's protective. Guarding is not to keep people out, but to cover what's within.

People often say 'don't wear your heart on your sleeve'; it sounds like good advice, but often the underlying message is saying 'don't let people in'. Guarding is not prohibiting. The idea isn't to never show your heart but that you add some security to it. When you put an alarm on your home it's not to stop people coming in, it's to stop the wrong people entering. You disable it when you know you're in good company, you know when you need to activate it, when you're sleeping or away or less alert, you can enable it in these settings and it will protect while you rest.

I don't want to live constantly armed, restricting my life and all those I do life with. I have been around people who have their heart so locked down, it leads to conversations that feel cold and an atmosphere that feels tense. I believe we can learn to live with a heart that's wide open, while having that same heart fully covered. The guarding I believe God wants is not to shut us down but to enable us to open up. I have discovered I don't need to have my alarm on all the time. I have instead chosen to learn how to put the alarm in place so that when it's needed, it can be activated. So how about you, have you learnt how to guard your heart or have you overloaded your life with so much protection, no one dare enter?

Our heart is not supposed to keep people out, don't build a fortress between you and your real feelings. Instead just add a guard that guides you away from the conversations that are unhealthy into the ones that are healthy. Add the guard of peace, trust, discernment, add the guard of wisdom, truth and prayer. These guards won't shrink your life, they will liberate it, they will increase the flow from your heart instead of restricting it. So today don't fear wearing your heart on your sleeve, just add security to your sleeve. Don't choose to withhold your heart, just add some alarms to your life. Get great at guarding so you can increase your loving.

SPEAK IT ━━━━━━━━━━━━━━━━━

BE IT ━━━━━━━━━━━━━━━━━

Do you not know that your bodies are temples of the Holy Spirit, who is in you, whom you have received from God? You are not your own. 1 Corinthians 6:19 (NIV)

You have to do what you can do and let God do what you can't. I used to be so unfit, unhealthy and overweight. I had no self esteem and no value or worth on my own wellbeing. I have learnt to love the disciplines that love me back. Exercising my mind, body and soul. Some days I hate it, other days I love it, but it always loves me back. Taking care of things like our diet and exercise may not seem spiritual but they are. A healthy you means a prepared you, a fit body means more longevity, a well maintained life, means you can sustain the greatest adventures in life.

A lot of times we can separate the spiritual from the natural but without taking care of our natural bodies we reduce our energy, flexibility and well-being to carry out our spiritual calling and destiny. The Bible makes it very clear that our bodies are a temple, yet some do a better job of taking care of this temple than others. For years I battled with my weight, no amount of diets could help me because the root of the issue was I didn't want to help myself. I had lost my confidence and with that I had lost my desire to invest any energy on me. Think about how well you are allowing you to love you, this is not about being a certain weight or looking a certain way, it is about the value you place on you. We can be so good of taking care of everybody else but we don't take care of ourselves.

I remember the day I was at the doctor's and he told me, in a very abrupt manner, I was overweight. He did not dress it up or say it sensitively. At first I was offended. I had to come to this realisation, the only reason he was telling me that truth was because he was trying to help me. I had a choice to ignore or accept the current reality and either work towards fixing it or carry on ignoring it. I had a three year battle to get in shape, but once I had embraced the discipline I began to see the results of feeling more confident, healthy, being able to do more. I had made time to love myself enough to fix something that no one else could fix for me.

We all have those areas where we neglect our own wellbeing; maybe it's that you never give yourself time, you never treat yourself, you're exhausted and you need a break. Today love yourself enough to start to fix what needs fixing, take time to do something that will improve your health. Go love yourself enough to make some changes.

SPEAK IT ━━━━━━━━━━━━━━

BE IT ━━━━━━━━━━━━━━

EXHALE

Be joyful in hope, patient in affliction, faithful in prayer.
Romans 12:12 (NIV)

Don't allow impatience to plan your future. Have you ever tried to force something into a space it clearly wasn't made to fit? I am all too familiar with this scenario from the skinny jeans I have wrestled with, that my waistline no longer wants to fit into, to the laundry basket that I refuse to admit can't hold any more dirty clothes. The action of forcing is often as a result of our impatience and frustration that what we want to happen is not happening when we wanted it too.

The delay we find ourselves in demands to be filled. It asks you to do something to speed things up. The feelings of dissatisfaction now overwhelm any previous sense of anticipation. But as any frustrated pregnant mother can tell you, no matter how tired you are carrying that baby, waddling down hallways and swelling up those ankles, you would be ill advised to force that baby to come early. Though we may not like the baby's schedule, it's there for a reason, for the baby and the mother's protection.

We can get frustrated spiritually with the time it takes for the dream within us to be birthed through us, when the answer seems to be stuck in transit. However, God's timing and perspective is completely different to ours so we need to replace our forcing with trusting. If we believe that God hears our cry and we know that He is working on our behalf, then it makes sense to trust Him with the timing. God doesn't want any premature dreams struggling to survive, He wants your frustration to be reminded of His faithfulness and for you to stop pushing what needs time and space to develop. Trust is not always easy when we are tired and weary but the harvest that comes from trust is far greater than the one that will arrive through impatience. We need to take our attention off what hasn't happened yet and take the time we have to better prepare for what is on its way.

So today, know God has got you, He has not forgotten you. In your wait make better choices; replace worry with worship. In the pause, pray and learn the lesson He is teaching you so you can embrace the place to which He is leading you. Patience is a hard quality to adopt and yet if we stop for a moment and think about the results of impatience vs patience, we realise just how much we need more of it. We don't need anymore Ishmael moments created in our lives because we got impatient waiting for Isaac. Don't allow your impatience to drive your impulses; incubate the grace to wait and in so doing you will protect the promise from being replaced with a substitute that impatience creates. Remember God is good to His word, so wait for Him.

THINK IT ▬▬▬▬▬▬▬▬▬▬▬▬

SPEAK IT ▬▬▬▬▬▬▬▬▬▬▬▬▬▬▬

BE IT ▬▬▬▬▬▬▬▬▬▬▬▬▬▬▬

EXHALE

The Lord is righteous in all His ways and faithful in all He does. The Lord is near to all who call on Him, to all who call on Him in truth. He fulfils the desires of those who fear Him; He hears their cry and saves them. Psalm 145:17-19 (NIV)

In the midst of what is temporal, let us stand on what is eternal. In a time where people are fighting for power, remember who holds the ultimate power. When many are making promises that may never be fulfilled, look to the One whose word never returns void. And in a season where much is being said in hate, pride and to degrade others, choose His way that speaks grace, honour and life. Today, remember the God you serve and the kingdom you are a part of, remember your foundations are built on something far greater than policies or persuasive arguments. We serve a higher power and our trust is in the King whose kingdom is being built on justice and truth.

It can be overwhelming at times when we hear of yet another attack or act of hatred. We can allow what is broadcast by the world to shape and shrink our own world and we may feel we don't have all the answers for the confusion around us. You may not feel skilled enough to offer solutions for such problems. Yet there is one thing you must hold fast to and that is, in times that are uncertain, you have an unchanging God. Our best response is in understanding we have a contribution to make spiritually. We can all pray for peace, we can all speak love, we can all serve our world with kindness and we can turn up the volume on hope to the hopeless and love to the unloved. As you go about your day, realise you don't need all the answers, just be an answer where you can. Look for those who you can bring strength to and represent faith in the midst of fear.

Today, look to the One who is rock solid and steadfast. The One who has kept His word for a thousand generations. The One whose only way is love and whose words are always true. The One who you can anchor your hope in through every shifting season. It is in God we trust. Where do you need to remind your soul of who your Saviour is? What are you not doing because of unnerving predictions that have been fed to you by those around you? Don't parent from fear or plan out of precaution. We serve a mighty God, let that be the basis for your decisions today. God is still in office, friends, and His name is the name above every name. His kingdom will come and His will be done and today that is good news to take into the face of any bad news you may hear.

THINK IT ━━━━━━━━━

SPEAK IT ━━━━━━━━━━

BE IT ━━━━━━━━━━

EXHALE

In the same way, let your light shine before others, that they may see your good deeds and glorify your Father in heaven. Matthew 5:16 (NIV)

A few years back I fell in love with a gift I was given for my home, a handmade wall tile that had a beautiful image and when you turned the tile over, it had a meaningful thought attached to that design. That one gift lead to a slight obsession (I will admit it). I now have a full wall (ok several walls) where these tiles make an amazing collection of imagery and meaning, from tiles that have emblems on them to hearts and words, crosses, wildlife, flowers and crests. Their meanings are vast and diverse: victory, saving, surrender, rooted, fervent, love. Every time I look at these tiles, I remember the story behind them and of finding them across the world and then carrying them home in my hand luggage.

These walls remind me that this is how we are supposed to decorate our lives. We are to be the ones who fill our walls with stories and encounters that point to something far greater than our own words can express. We are the ones who should take the time to present the pages of our lives in a way that extracts the beauty from ever difficult chapter. Turning moments into memory blocks where we display God's grace even in the times where we felt faint hearted or out of place. When people look at your life, you don't need to try and show them perfection. We don't all have to look the same or copy each other's story.

Just as I chose random tiles to place together, the beauty is even greater as each one's uniqueness contributes to make a bigger picture. And every tile is joined by one common feature, it's maker. This is how God sees you and I. We are all His handiwork and all beautiful in our own way. So let your life talk, tell of God's goodness and mercy, the times you failed and the lessons you learnt. Don't have someone else's art on the walls of your life, you are making beautiful bespoke art every time you step out, believe, trust and give yourself away.

Tell your story with blocks of wisdom, colour, romance, adventure, understanding and love. Record and journal details that otherwise you would forget. The more you etch as a memory, the more hope you frame for the future. In those moments when you are doubting, go to the memory block of His faithfulness. In the time when your trust is wavering, go look at the memory block of His greatness. Fill the walls of your life with pointers of His grace and you will find those who come to your home will leave with fresh hope.

THINK IT ━━━━━━━━━━

SPEAK IT ━━━━━━━━━━━━━

BE IT ━━━━━━━━━━━

EXHALE

Produce fruit in keeping with repentance.
Matthew 3:8 (NIV)

We have all either been guilty of or on the receiving end of an apology that seems to have a boomerang effect. No sooner is sorry said then it needs to be said again. The words somehow become less genuine the more they echo around the same issues. Just as you teach a child that they can't eternally say sorry for the same crime, eventually the guilty party has to stop asking to be pardoned and start demonstrating changed behaviour. Sorry is only one part of the remedy and change must become its travelling companion. Repentance is not a word, it's an action and when we replace the action of sorry with the word, we end up revisiting the same crime scene over again.

Saying sorry is a start for sure. Any parent will tell you once sorry becomes part of the vocabulary instead of temper tantrums and stubborn stand-offs it's a good day, but it's also just a step in the right direction. Because if sorry is good, living changed is so much better. Perhaps if we all would see apologising not as a bandaid to fix what we feel awkward about, but rather a commitment to change, then we would say sorry less flippantly and use the gateway of our apology more deliberately. Apologising is not a sign of weakness, it can actually be one of the ways we demonstrate great strength. Our moment of sorry can become the first step into new territory where we learn how to take ground instead of repeating and circling old mistakes. Sorry can become an opportunity to not just fix a problem but to find a permanent solution.

Today, where do you need to stop saying sorry and start showing it? Where do your actions need to be the demonstration of the apology you are making. Great leaders, parents, families, churches grow not because they are always right. They have discovered the determination to make what's wrong both a stopping point and a starting point; a chance to draw a line under what's past and build something better. They are aiming for the wisdom and understanding to avoid the same future mistakes. Let's not avoid the lessons that sorry extends, let's have less repeat offenders. Repentance may be an old fashioned word but it just means to make a turn in the complete opposite direction. We need to know how to make this manoeuvre, the 'repentance turn' needs to be something we teach and practice. So if you have a sorry without the turn attached, maybe it's time to get busy and put the manoeuvre into practice.

THINK IT ━━━━━━━━━ 98

SPEAK IT ━━━━━━━━━━━━━━

BE IT ━━━━━━━━━━━━━

EXHALE

And regardless of what else you put on, wear love. It's your basic, all-purpose garment. Never be without it. Colossians 3:14 (MSG)

Are you brave enough to choose love even when others don't love you well? Love is a garment that we have to choose to wear. Love fits you, more than that it suits you. We need to understand how love works so we can know how love should be worn. This garment is made for all purposes, all weathers, all occasions; it's not supposed to be an optional item in our wardrobe. You don't need to worry about it getting worn out, this love wears well. So today are you wearing His love? His love is unlimited with no end and no beginning, His love that is relentless and doesn't let go, even though we do. His love that is steadfast. That's why I know we can all learn how to wear love in greater measure. If we still find some aspects are less known to us than others then maybe we need to check how often we are choosing to wear love.

What can you do today to increase the level of love in your own life? Where would be a good place to start digging deeper and loving greater? For many our idea of love has been shaped more by the secular world than our spiritual world. Love is what we hear about through song lyrics, it's portrayed in movies and fairy tales. That love is volatile, emotional, unpredictable, therefore when it comes to defining love, we have a lot to get past before we can start to learn about real love.

His love won on the cross, His love won our freedom, His love won over hate. His love can't lose because it refuses to use love as a bargaining chip. It won't negotiate or be blackmailed. His love is for all and gives it all. His love is unable to be measured and cannot be earnt. His love is freely given and we have the privilege of not only receiving that love but being carriers of it.

How do we learn to love like He loves? How do we let love win? We have to start by letting His love in; we need to let Him love us. We can't give away what we struggle to receive, so first, let love win in you. Realise you're good enough and valued. His love wants to forgive, cover and build you. Let His love win in you and then let that love win through you. Wear love in a way that removes your limitations and list of approvals; love without need for the love of others in return but love from His overwhelming supply. Love generously and extravagantly, love over judgement, pain and what's unlovely. Love where there is no love reciprocated. Love when it feels undeserved; love when you fail, when you are weary. Let His love reshape the way in which you love. If this love is the answer you always default to, then love will win more than you thought possible. So today, let more of His love in so that you can see more of this love win.

THINK IT ━━━━━━━━━━━━ **100**

SPEAK IT ━━━━━━━━━━━━

BE IT ━━━━━━━━━━━━

EXHALE

Be kind and compassionate to one another, forgiving each other, just as in Christ God forgave you. Ephesians 4:32 (NIV)

I will never forget years ago when my husband proposed to me. It was in a tiny village in the south of France, the setting was so beautiful. As we ate dinner in a restaurant that night, we laughed and talked and I cried several times. Eventually the waiter understood we had just got engaged and said congratulations. His excitement at our news, unknown to us, had caught someone else's attention and a very expensive bottle of champagne was delivered to our table. The waiter explained a French family had heard our news and wanted to help mark the moment. They had waited until they had left the restaurant to send the gift as they didn't want any thanks. That night someone else's kindness invaded our space and helped us mark a special day; they added a wow moment to our engagement.

We will never forget that generous gesture, it marked us. We decided that day as a couple that we would carry on that tradition and whenever we had the opportunity to add a wow factor to someone's life, we would. Now over 20 years later, we have got to do some very fun things just because that's what love does. It isn't just about answering a need, it's extravagant and creative and it's about planting a seed. It's adding a God kiss to someone's world when they least expect it. It doesn't have to cost you financially, those wow moments can come in all shapes and sizes. It is simply taking the time to notice those around you and adding a wow into their world. Jesus brought a wow factor wherever He went and some people added that back into His world. The woman with the alabaster box, the boy with the loaves and fishes, the centurion who asked Jesus to just send a word. Each moment caused Jesus to say, wow, such faith I have rarely seen. The paralytic who came through the roof was a mark of his friends determination, it caused debris to fall on Jesus' head. When people went out of their way to believe, give, sacrifice, Jesus said 'wow'.

Many withhold kind words and acts because they are waiting for someone to be kind to them first but what we sow we will reap. We can live with unlocked vats of encouragement and rooms full of unused kindness that God wants us to open and allow others to enjoy. So today, why don't you decide to be the wow factor in a friend's life or mark a moment in a stranger's day? Why don't you seize the opportunity to do good and write your life into another's story by adding something unexpected, a just because act of kindness. Then walk away and you may just hear 'wow' as you leave.

THINK IT ▬▬▬▬▬▬▬▬▬▬ **102**

SPEAK IT ▬▬▬▬▬▬▬▬▬▬▬

BE IT ▬▬▬▬▬▬▬▬▬▬▬

EXHALE

It was because you, the Levites, did not bring it up the first time that the Lord our God broke out in anger against us. We did not inquire of Him about how to do it in the prescribed way. 1 Chronicles 15:13 (NIV)

Beware of hooking your life up with people that keep talking about how they are moving on, and yet show more signs of residual hurt and unresolved issues than they do of advancement and movement. Actions of clinging on to something or someone which they say they have 'moved on' from tell a different story. The constant scrolling through Instagram/Facebook posts of a past relationship let's you know it is still in their present. I have found great talkers are not always as great at walking the talk. Change is not real if it's only evidence is verbal.

If we are not careful, we can all be guilty of this virtual reality, living where what we say is not what we do; eventually that will cost both the orator and listener. Lot's wife said she was willing to move on but her attachment to her past relationships and residence told a different story and cost her everything.

True movement begins when we can embrace the future and forgive what's past - the good, bad and ugly. What you learnt, lost, gained and loved in the last season can teach you lessons in your next. When David moved the ark of God in 1 Chronicles 13, Uzzah lost his life as he touched what he was not supposed to. David was angry at God's actions, but he had to learn from his mistake and repent of his anger, in order for the ark to be moved back to Jerusalem. In 1 Chronicles 15, David this time consults God on how to move the ark with His blessing. David had to move internally in his attitude and mindset before he could move the ark externally before all the people.

Immaturity makes a lot of noise but little progress; a child can shout and cry when they are stuck in a highchair but it does not help them get out of it. We can preach, teach, comment on change, whilst actually never moving or changing! Like that infant, we need to reach up our arms and find help to get out of where we are confined. We may need someone to say - stop whining, grow up, step up, move on, voices that call more out of us. If we want out of the highchair, then we need to have behaviour that reflects our growth instead of confirming our childishness.

Today, where can you gracefully let go of the past and gain ground for the future? Instead of just talking about moving on, find ways to actually walk it out well. Unhook your life from the behaviour that is pulling you backwards and if necessary, like David, admit where it went wrong, so you and those attached to you can move on.

SPEAK IT ━━━━━━━━━━━━

BE IT ━━━━━━━━━━━━

EXHALE

Jonathan was deeply impressed with David - an immediate bond was forged between them. He became totally committed to David. From that point on he would be David's number-one advocate and friend. 1 Samuel 18:1 (MSG)

One of the sweetest things in life is being able to give the gift of friendship to one another. I don't mean Facebook friends, social media following friends or a passing acquaintance. I mean people who know you and you know them. The ones who call you up when you need talking to and sit you down when you need to be still. The friends that say what others won't say and will be there when no one else is there. Those friends, the God centred, God sent friends; we all get to be one to someone and we all get someone to be one for us. You just have to be willing to learn how to be the friend God intended and be open to receive the ones He has given you on this journey through life. God doesn't want you to be a lone ranger so let Him teach you how to be a great friend. It requires patience, kindness, forgiveness, understanding, grace, fun, time, investment, selflessness and openness. All these things we get to increase and improve when we choose to be a friend.

I love to add new friends to my world but what's more important is how many of those friends we can keep and love well. It's true some people will pass through your life, others are sent for a season, but there is also the friend that God wants you to have for the long haul, the one who becomes that safe place, a friend who does the good and bad and for that matter the plain ugly with you. We can change many things about our life but we should look to keep somethings consistent and friendship is one of the things that helps us stay steady in uncertain times.

So today, how are you doing at being a friend? What part of this gift can you give more beautifully and bless more abundantly? Let's not take for granted the friends we are entrusted with, let's celebrate them and let them know how much they matter. Jesus didn't just hang with the masses, He had friends and those friends He poured His life, wisdom and energy into. David found a friend that was closer than a brother in Jonathan and together they achieved great things. Ruth became the friend Naomi never thought was possible crossing generations and circumstances to be there for one another. Today, give thanks for your friends, let them know how much you value the investment they are making into your life and determine to be the best friend you can be. Your friendship is someone's answer to prayer. So let's aim to do friendship well.

THINK IT ━━━━━━━━━━━━━━━━

SPEAK IT ━━━━━━━━━━━━━━━━━━━━━━

BE IT ━━━━━━━━━━━━━━━━━━━━━

EXHALE

Suddenly a furious storm came up on the lake, so that the waves swept over the boat. But Jesus was sleeping. Matthew 8:24 (NIV)

I recently spent some time in the USA in a part of the country that is often hit by storms. As a visitor to that town I was amazed at just how much the weather controlled everyone's behaviour and thinking. Every person we spoke to would be watching the weather, planning for the rains, battening down in case of the storms. Each house had a weather plan of action and everyone in those homes seemed to know what that plan was including the pets. As someone from out of town I was obviously inexperienced and unprepared, I hadn't even checked the weather channel and I had not got the appropriate plans in place.

Yet this experience got me thinking how we can often become spiritual weather watchers and that's not a good thing. Living in a way that allows any pending wind, rain or storm to determine how we plan, speak, give and act. When we become spiritual storm watchers we forget where we are going because we are more aware of the weather we may be facing. We become preoccupied with outside elements and allow ourselves to live from a reaction instead of action. We choose safety more than risk and err on defensive steps rather than proactive planning. We will never be immune spiritually from storms and adverse weather but we don't have to empower passing storms by making permanent lockdown choices. Where are you hiding from a pending storm? Where have you barricaded your heart in case of bad weather? Where have you packed away things because you thought potential bad weather was ahead? We can't keep putting our lives on hold because of the changing skies above.

Don't allow life, people and circumstances, the weather, finances and family to dictate more than they should about your destiny. Instead of watching everyone else's weather predictions, why not make your own decisions? If a storm's coming then it's coming and you can't stop it but you also don't have to be scared of it. Fear does not make a good counsellor for your future. So hold onto your hope today, remind yourself of His faithfulness, sing in the face of the storm and even dance in the rain. Determine your own vibe. Don't allow looming darkness to compromise your light. Don't let the lack of joy in those that can only predict bad weather convince you to tone your joy down.

Let's not just live in response to what's around us but let's change atmospheres for the better. Who says you have to wear wellies in puddles; flip flops work too. Yes the snow is cold, but it's also great for skiing. We actually need weather changes to keep our lives well watered and heated. So just know the weather may be changing but you don't have to stop living.

THINK IT ━━━━━━━━━━━━ 108

SPEAK IT ━━━━━━━━━━━━━━━

BE IT ━━━━━━━━━━━━━━━

EXHALE

I did not go up to Jerusalem to see those who were apostles before I was, but I went into Arabia. Later I returned to Damascus. Galatians 1:17 (NIV)

God wants the growth we gain to be growth we can sustain. Recently at the gym I injured myself because I thought I could lift a weight way beyond my capability. We can do the same spiritually, picking up a calling we are ill equipped to carry, or adding others weights to our own when we are already over extended. God wants the weak to become strong. He wants our capacity to increase and our potential to be released.

God wants to build you up so that you don't feel weighed down. So don't be surprised if when you ask for more, God begins to work you out more, putting you in situations that will grow your grace, test your patience and increase your faith. God wants to build you up before He loads you up. In Galatians 1 Paul recalls how he was called into ministry. The awareness of his anointing caused him to enter a season of training out of sight of those he would later minister to. He knew that in order to be taken seriously, he had to go away and add some knowledge and training to help him navigate his calling.

I love my kids but at age 12 and 14, if they ask to drive my car, I would lovingly refuse, not out of lack of fun or restriction to their freedom, but for their own safety and the protection of others. God treats us the same as His kids. He doesn't mind you asking for the big stuff but at times He will decline because He knows it's not going to help you. Maybe there is an area where you are trying to force God to open a door and you are frustrated at the lack of response. Today, go back and examine if the request is actually something that is beneficial to your future or if it is coming from a place of impatience and striving.

You don't want the car keys before you're ready, you don't want the 50lb weight before you can lift the 15lb weight. So where do you need to go back to work so that what you are seeking can be something that you have the strength to handle? I have met a lot of people who say, I would love to travel like you and I smile politely and say are you sure? The glamour they perceive is not the reality I live with. Don't buy into a social media dream. Instead, place your energy in the right direction and know if it's worth having, it's worth working for. We all have undeveloped muscles and we need to appreciate the 'not ready yet' is not 'never' or 'no'. It's just a good coaching tip so that the muscle can build ready for when the 'not yet' becomes 'now'.

THINK IT ━━━━━━━━━━━ 110

SPEAK IT ━━━━━━━━━━━

BE IT ━━━━━━━━━━━

EXHALE

Be still before the Lord and wait patiently for Him; do not fret when people succeed in their ways, when they carry out their wicked schemes. Psalm 37:7 (NIV)

Have you ever had writers block? I have it often - the moment when you have no idea what to write next. You stare at the keyboard or the empty page and nothing comes to mind. It is made even worse if you are writing to a deadline; the time pressure adds more stress which stifles any last chance of creativity being expressed.

Some days and weeks are like that in life, whereas in other seasons, you have so much to share and you feel you have much to add and give. You can go through seasons where the page just feels blank, you feel like nothing of interest is happening and nothing of significance is worth recording. To make matters worse, the lives around you seem to be filling pages of adventures, the social media feeds have all the activity you so desperately desire and yet your feed, well, it hasn't had anything worth posting for days.

Yep we all have those times, so what do you do when you have a page before you but you feel you have nothing to write upon it? You simply breathe. Who said everyday had to be exciting, who told you every page had to be explosive? That is far too exhausting. A well told story will have moments of setting the scene interjected with moments of mystery or drama because the author knows to overload every page with activity would wear the reader out. We all need blank pages, days where nothing becomes everything. My younger, over excited self may not have believed what I am writing now, but oh how I have learnt to love those blank page days.

Days where you breathe deep, where you may just keep yourself to yourself, days when you don't give out but you just soak God in. Days where you allow yourself to rest and take all the time you need. We celebrate the full page days way more than the blank page days and the truth is, one doesn't work without the other. If every page is blank we have a problem but if every day is full we have a problem too. Don't be nervous in the silence, don't get agitated in the season called wait, don't try and write something if it is better to say nothing, don't resent the blank page, thank it for the space it created.

So if today you feel you have nothing to say, that's ok. Breathe, power down and recalibrate to prepare for the full page days there is no shortage of; make the most of this day.

THINK IT ━━━━━━━━━━━━━ 112

SPEAK IT ━━━━━━━━━━━━━

BE IT ━━━━━━━━━━━━━

Two are better than one, because they have a good return for their labour: if either of them falls down, one can help the other up. Ecclesiastes 4:9-10 (NKJV)

As a parent I am often faced with the dilemma: I need a job doing and really I should get the kids to help do it, but then I think of all the time it will take to convince them to help me, and then the added task of explaining exactly how I need them to help me. Usually after playing out these scenarios in my mind, I opt to do the task myself. Or there are times at work when the best way forward would be for each team member to make a contribution but because we are on a deadline or already over stretched, we choose to handle it on our own.

You have heard the expression, 'if you want a job doing properly, do it yourself'. While this logic is at times necessary, it is actually not the way we teach or indeed learn anything. Though the task may take longer to explain, it's the involvement of others that takes the job from a task completed to a lesson learnt. We are called to walk out our journey together, to put our efforts alongside one another and between us gain strength and wisdom. Yet when we choose to always do it alone, we also choose to uncouple from the strength that we may need further down the line, the backup that helps carry things forward. It's our willingness to work together that increases our ability to be there for one another. It brings the benefit of increasing those now trained and part of the team but it also makes us more accountable than isolation ever would.

We need to realise that asking for counsel is not a sign of weakness but one of strength. Working alongside others doesn't mean you're incapable, it means you're secure. You may prefer your own way, after all that's simpler and less confrontational. But if you want to do it God's way, it will require humility and flexibility. It will draw you into the counsel of others and can mean some may challenge you.

So today, if you need help then allow people close enough to hear how they can help. I am so very grateful for those who bring wise counsel and help to my life as a leader, mum and friend on a regular basis. Let's teach those who follow after us that asking and receiving help is not for emergencies only. Where do you need to slow down and involve others? Where can you invite others to come alongside, not just as spectators but as contributors? Welcome the iron that sharpens iron and know at times when it takes longer to travel together, that there will come a time when that companionship saves a lot more than it demands.

THINK IT ——————————————— **114**

SPEAK IT ———————————————

BE IT ———————————————

It is for freedom that Christ has set us free. Stand firm, then, and do not let yourselves be burdened again by a yoke of slavery. Galatians 5:1 (NIV)

When I was a little girl, my parents would sometimes take me to the beach and as was traditional at the English seaside, we would eat fish and chips, paddle in the water with our trousers rolled up to our ankles, have an ice cream and of course ride the donkeys. This may be something unfamiliar if you're not from the UK but here it's a common sight to have donkeys on the beach, usually with name tags and ribbons in their manes, which you can pay to ride. On my childhood rides the donkeys were clearly well trained, they knew at a certain point in the sand they all had to turn around and walk back to the place from where they had set off.

On one sunny seaside day I asked to ride the donkey and off we went. As we approached the invisible line in the sand, the other donkeys began to make the about turn to go back, except my donkey who had a completely different idea and he had planned that day his escape route. He somehow found a turbo charge and took off in the direction of the ocean. This cute docile donkey had suddenly woken up and was acting more like a racehorse with me hanging on for dear life. Eventually the donkey found the water and felt the waves on his hooves, something he had never been permitted to do, he had walked all these years by the sea but never felt the water. When the owner caught up with us, he dragged him back to the beach and as I dismounted, I watched that man beat the donkey and I began to cry.

The donkey that day may have been punished for his disobedience but as he was being told off I imagine he could still feel the water on his hooves and was thinking, you can try and break me but today, I broke free. How many times are we like that donkey, right next to the sea but too contained to put our feet in the waves? How often are we so close and yet so far? Where is the invisible line someone drew in your life that has limited you? You can live the rest of your days with sand under your feet or you can break free and feel the waves. Breaking free may be as simple as saying no or as big as facing up to a controlling situation. I will never forget that donkey and maybe he never forgot me, the little girl who in the moment of escape just held a little tighter and whispered, go donkey go.

Why not take some time today to erase some invisible lines that have limited you for too long and hear God's spirit saying over you, go child, go.

THINK IT ━━━━━━━━━━━━━━ **116**

SPEAK IT ━━━━━━━━━━━━━━━━

BE IT ━━━━━━━━━━━━━━━━

EXHALE

Everyone should be quick to listen, slow to speak and slow to become angry.
James 1:19 (NIV)

Here's some advice we often find hard to take: we need to become more intentional in improving our skill set to become quick to listen and slow to speak. Let's break this down and work on both in turn.

Quick to listen: so how are your listening skills? I have learnt that often we can be selective hearers, there are some things we want to listen to and other things we would prefer not to. This can be good when the source of the sound is not healthy or helpful but hazardous when we really need to be tuning in. Have you ever shouted for someone to come to you, maybe it was your dog who was distracted or your kids who were lost in their own world? Just like them we can turn on and off our ability to listen. Being quick to listen means that we have to lead with our ears not with our mouth and that's a whole different challenge. Have you ever started speaking while someone was still talking and the conclusion you have come to ends up being completely wrong? Had you listened to the story that you interrupted mid-sentence, you would have reached a very different conclusion. Being quick to listen is a safeguard, this wisdom puts a buffer between you and your mouth, it allows time for information to go in before any statements come out.

Slow to speak: this is the natural outcome of being quick to listen Think of it this way, if someone was talking and you were being timed, how quick would you be to add your comment? Would the clock get to a minute or would it be stopped at 20 seconds or maybe even less. If so, maybe you can add some space between your listening and speaking and see if you learn anything more by listening a little longer and speaking a little slower. Being slow to speak allows room for you to choose more intentionally the words you are going to select. Slower to speak means your pace changes and the amount you say may reduce in length but increase in weight. Some of the greatest communicators have learnt to do this well; they have made speaking an art form. Their words are weighted and their pace is measured. When you're slow to speak, anger rarely gets to take the reigns because this pace diffuses its haste. When you're slow to speak, usually what mattered in the moment becomes reframed by what will matter when the moment has past.

We all need to grow when it comes to our listening and speaking so today, pick one of these aspects and work on it. Speak less and listen more or slow down before you speak so that what you say means more. Or maybe, if you are like me, you might want to work on both.

THINK IT ━━━━━━━━━━━━━━━━━━

SPEAK IT ━━━━━━━━━━━━━━━━━━━━━━

BE IT ━━━━━━━━━━━━━━━━━━━━

EXHALE

Those who know your name trust in You, for you, Lord, have never forsaken those who seek you. Psalm 9:10 (NIV)

Where are you leaning instead of trusting? We need to check our spiritual posture on a regular basis. So often we can begin to replace trust with impatience and striving, or lean into our understanding and knowledge instead of seeking God's wisdom and timing. We can quickly forget to acknowledge the one who directs and guides our path, instead preferring our own, often more convenient and sometimes (if we are honest) selfish plan. Leaning on our own abilities and understanding will always reduce our capacity and expectations. Trusting God is a continual process, it's good work for our heart to do, to be given to the exercise of less leaning and more trusting. And it's always a good thing when the first thing we do is acknowledge Him in all our ways, before we embrace all that is within each new day. It's our awareness of His way that will adjust and align ours. His way will sometimes reroute us, grow us, protect us and usually challenge us.

So where are you right now trusting, what gap have you created where if God doesn't come through you will fall through. We can say we are trusting while installing a safety net just in case things don't work out as intended. We can say 'I trust you God' but then have a just in case plan if God doesn't answer in the way we would like Him to. Trust looks like no plan B, no lifeboat in case this goes down, no safety net in case we fall; trust looks very different than often how we act.

Today, where does your trust need a little overhaul, what can you do to actually trust more and control less? What areas can you add some action that will move your trust from a conversation to a conviction? If we are to truly stop leaning on our own ability and trust in God's inexhaustible capacity, how does that change our giving, speaking, planning or choosing? Trust will suddenly make things an option that before you would not even consider. Maybe you don't need more, you just need to believe more. Maybe you need to abandon your plan and throw yourself deeper into God.

Ask yourself, how much do I trust God with my finances, family, future? Then examine how you operate in each of those areas. Does what you believe match up with how you live? Maybe take the trust test and introduce your future to living more on the edge of trust and less in the realm of control.

THINK IT ━━━━━━━━━━━ **120**

SPEAK IT ━━━━━━━━━━━

BE IT ━━━━━━━━━━━

EXHALE

LET

YOUR

LIFE

BE

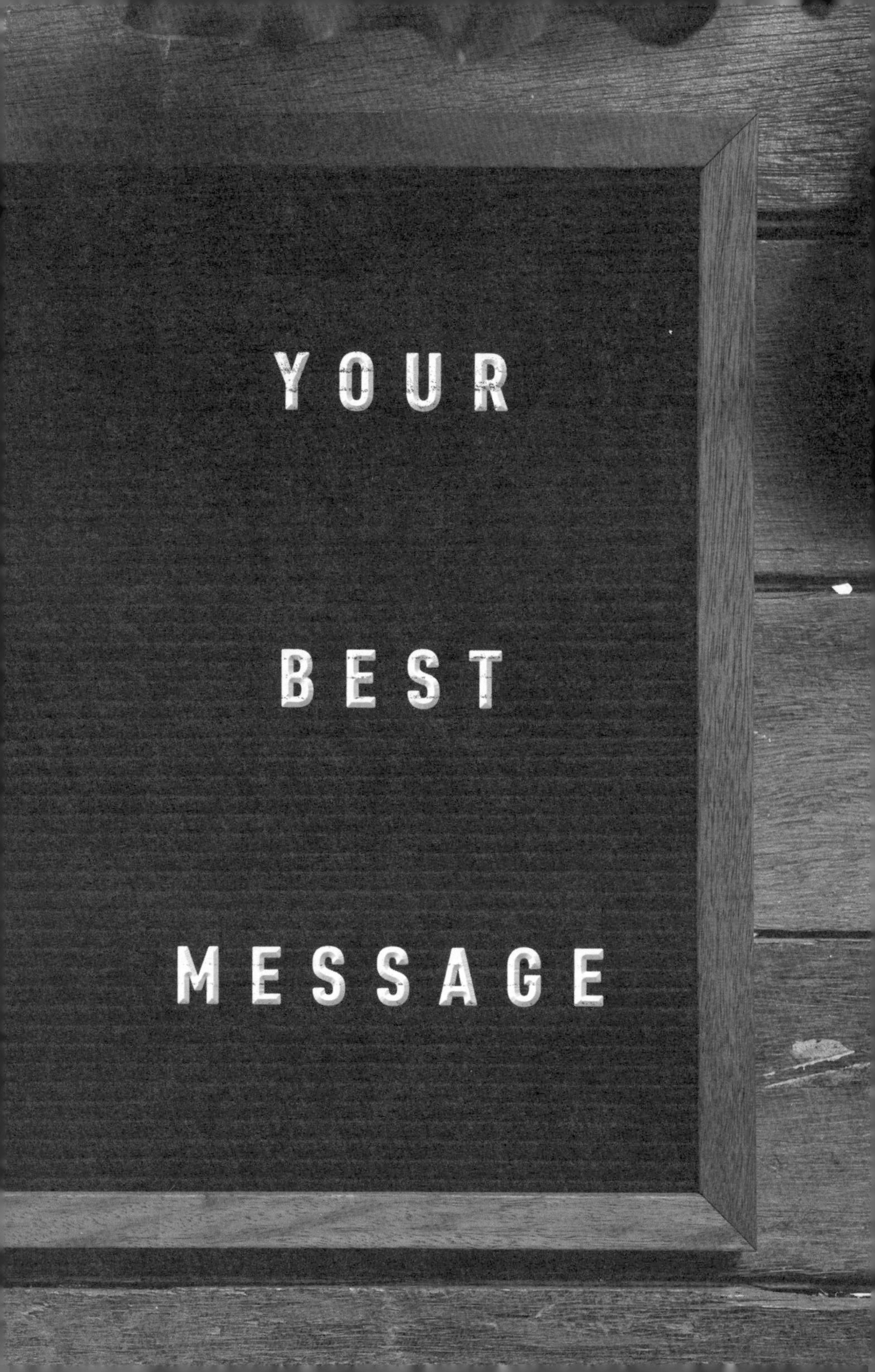
YOUR
BEST
MESSAGE

Elisha deserted the oxen, ran after Elijah, and said, "Please! Let me kiss my father and mother goodbye - then I'll follow you." "Go ahead," said Elijah, "but, mind you, don't forget what I've just done to you." 1 Kings 19:20 (MSG)

Have you ever been in a situation and just thought this is so awkward? You might be in such a scenario right now; an awkward set of circumstances that no one seems to want to address or deal with. Maybe it's a relationship that is awkward, it is ill fitting or there is an issue both parties are ignoring. Awkward is part of life and yet we don't seem able to accept or manage these encounters we all have, to learn how to handle them and even find an anointing for them.

The story of Elisha and Elijah's first meeting is nothing short of awkward. Here's a guy that is wanting to die, he's so disillusioned by ministry he lays under a tree and asks God to take his life. The reply from heaven is to get up and go and find a young guy you've never heard of and anoint him as he's going to join you in ministry. First of all the timing of this seems highly inappropriate. Why would God use Elijah's lowest point as Elisha's entry point into the ministry? Elijah eventually gets up from his place of self pity to go and do what God has asked. You would expect the first encounter to be miraculous but it was much more awkward than anointed. Elijah finds Elisha, who is busy ploughing a field, and throws his cloak on him as a sign of his anointing. In response the young man seems a little taken back and Elijah starts to walk away. No this was not what you would imagine a transitional point to look like but that's often how it can feel. It was awkward for Elijah who didn't even want to be there and for Elisha who now had to change his entire life in response.

Awkward moments happen but that doesn't mean they aren't anointed; if you can see past what's uncomfortable, then we accept what may be unusual. Just because the flow isn't there doesn't mean God can't work. Some things are just a hard fit at first but it doesn't mean they don't fit, it can take time to work new scenarios out, manage a new team, set a new course. It can be awkward to navigate some relationships and deal with some situations but we can't let awkward mean avoidance. Sometimes you just have to say, wow this is awkward, and keep on going. Elijah and Elisha moved past this and went on to do miracles. Don't panic, just keep moving forward and you may find that awkward is the stage that God is actually going to use to increase what you go on to do.

THINK IT ━━━━━━━━━━━━━━━━━ 122

SPEAK IT ━━━━━━━━━━━━━━━━

BE IT ━━━━━━━━━━━━━━━━

EXHALE

Therefore, as God's chosen people, holy and dearly loved, clothe yourselves with compassion, kindness, humility, gentleness and patience. Colossians 3:12 (NIV)

Ever heard the expression 'kindness never goes out of fashion'? Well it's true and I for one want to ensure it does not. In a world where the motto seems to be 'every man and woman for themselves' this emphasis is needed more than ever. Kindness is what makes us human. It stops us from becoming over worked, over driven, over obsessed, self-centred people. Kindness is like adding air to your lungs, wiping the mist from the lens of your life and realising we are all in the journey together. Why don't we stop and show some kindness to one another?

We all have this 'superpower'. The power to lift another's spirit with your words. The power to be kind and do good. Becoming more purposefully kind brings new awareness to our actions and words. It helps prevent us from making choices that haste and selfishness may make and it replaces choices that could feed hostility with actions that instead sow seeds of harmony. Kindness works in every language and is a currency that will always have a higher return. We may not always agree with one another but we can choose to lessen someone's pain or add to it. We can choose to sow good things or add negativity. We can choose to give or withhold.

Have you ever been in a room and someone enters that is wearing a beautiful fragrance? You can smell the aroma as they walk through the room. The fragrance fills your nostrils and changes the atmosphere; as that person moves on they leave the aroma behind them. That's exactly how it is with kindness. It holds the power to change the way things are heard and seen. It creates an atmosphere that lifts spirits and makes things sweeter. The effects of kind words or deeds linger and rest on your life long after the initial act of kindness has been expressed and experienced.

Kind people carry a beautiful aroma, it's part of what makes them so attractive to be around. This quality was never supposed to be carried by just a few, it is something we can all wear everyday. We can be vessels of kindness, we can be purveyors of this powerful fragrance. It's a choice we make as to what our life will be filled with: the problems or peace, joy or despair, stinginess or generosity, criticism or kindness. I pray we would be a reflection of our Father's heart that forgives, loves and looks for who He can bless. So what can you do for someone else that's kind today? Make someone happy, even if you feel you have no one doing that for you. Start sowing the harvest that you would want to see into the conversations and community around you. Let's use our 'superpower' of kindness to make the world a better place and you will find it makes you happy too.

THINK IT ━━━━━━━━━━━

SPEAK IT ━━━━━━━━━━━━━━━

BE IT ━━━━━━━━━━━━━━━

EXHALE

Pray at all times (on every occasion, in every season) in the Spirit, with all [manner of] prayer and entreaty. To that end keep alert and watch with strong purpose and perseverance, interceding in behalf of all the saints (God's consecrated people). Ephesians 6:18 (AMP)

A while ago I was out shopping when a man came over to speak to me. He knew I was the pastor of our church and came to ask would I pray with him. With tears in his eyes he shared very bravely some really hard things he was facing. As we talked for a few moments, my heart felt his heaviness and I was caught up in his desperate search for hope for his future. There I was simply shopping and here in the same place was this man who was hurting. That night I told my husband about the conversation and we took hold of each other's hands and began to lift up that man's situation in prayer. He was a stranger before our conversation in a busy store, but in those few moments where he was brave enough to start a conversation, he became a friend in the faith who was in the fight of his life and he needed someone to add their faith to his.

That encounter stayed with me, and every time he came to mind I would pray. I haven't met that gentleman since and that was not the point of our interaction. He needed someone to stand with him not physically, but spiritually. He asked for something not beyond my capability but something completely within my power to do, the power to pray. I wonder how many of us need that same support? We need that extra prayer cover, we can't let our hearts be so troubled that we forget to reach out for help to lift that trouble to God. We have to be willing instead to share what is too heavy for us to bear alone. It took great courage for that man to shed tears in front of a stranger but his desperation overrode his desire to keep up appearances.

Today, where do you need to ask for prayer, where can you allow another to help lift you up? We are often surrounded by the help we need and yet we choose to muddle along on our own. I think we need the liberation of asking. When you ask someone to stand with you, it isn't a burden, it's a privilege. When you say to another, will you pray for me, they don't think you're weak; they are honoured that you would invite them to add strength. Prayer is a powerful weapon, and it needs using more often. Praying and agreeing releases something that hours of talking can fail to discover. So if you need help, ask, if you need prayer, speak up and you will find when you do, you add more faith to your faith and more friends to your fight.

SPEAK IT ━━━━━━━━━━━━━━━━━━━━━

BE IT ━━━━━━━━━━━━━━━━━━━

Let the peace of Christ rule in your hearts, since as members of one body you were called to peace. And be thankful. Colossians 3:15 (NIV)

The less you respond to negative people, the more peaceful your life will become. Sometimes we can feel we have a bucket full of negativity in our life, without realising we were the ones who allowed that bucket to be filled. If we think of our lives everyday like a vessel that waits to be filled, then we should think about the things we are allowing to do the filling. Every voice we allow to fill our minds and hearts is like a tap that we have turned on and the words that are spoken from that source are now filling our bucket. Often we end a day full but not always full of what we wanted to carry.

We had a tap in our house that was constantly dripping; it's such an annoying sound. To stop that tap from dripping, we were going to have to get a plumber to help to turn it off. Until then, the drops kept falling and the bucket remained underneath and carried on filling. It was a small annoyance that I adjusted to living with, rather than being active in removing. This behaviour is not that determinantal in my home, but this type of attitude in our own spiritual lives leads to much greater problems.

Many times we allow taps to leak into our lives that need to be simply turned off. We leave the voices we don't want to deal with in the background, dripping in negativity, doubt or criticism. We don't want to have to invest in fixing the leak so we try to ignore it but while ever it is dripping, it means you are leaving out your bucket to do the collecting. We can often be too casual with the number of voices we allow to have a tap of influence into our minds and hearts. Don't become a hostage to taps that are a steady stream of bitterness or resentment, gossip or disunity. If these taps are permitted to run into your life you soon become full of the waters they hold. And the water you carry is going to become the place from which you drink and also allow others to drink from.

We eventually got that dripping tap fixed and it was only once the plumber had been that I realised just how annoying that constant sound was. I had become so adjusted to living with it, I didn't realise the relief and peace that would come when I finally removed it. Don't allow your life to adjust to what it should be addressing. Get help if you need to turn the wrong taps off. Be willing to get the tools that help sort the leaks out. Empty the bucket of negativity and fill up from taps that add faith and vitality.

THINK IT ━━━━━━━━━━━━━━ 128

SPEAK IT ━━━━━━━━━━━━━━━

BE IT ━━━━━━━━━━━━━━━

EXHALE

Let the [spoken] word of Christ have its home within you [dwelling in your heart and mind - permeating every aspect of your being] as you teach [spiritual things] and admonish and train one another with all wisdom, singing psalms and hymns and spiritual songs with thankfulness in your hearts to God. Colossians 3:16 (AMP)

A while ago I was out running errands and I ended up in a lane of traffic behind a vehicle that had a sign on the back which caught my attention. The vehicle asked a question about the driver. The question was 'how am I driving?' then underneath it was a number you could call to report the driver's capability or lack of it if you so desired. I guess it was that company's way of keeping the drivers they employed accountable. The question got me thinking - what if on the back of our lives it said 'how am I driving, leading, parenting, loving, forgiving, listening?' You can insert your own question in there but if we were open to that question being answered, would it change our behaviour?

The truth is, people are following our lives everyday, they watch how we act behind the wheel emotionally, spiritually, mentally. We are not supposed to live paranoid or trying to impress or be perfect. The driver of this vehicle was driving with an awareness that others were following and more than that, they knew who he represented. That awareness was causing him to be more cautious and mindful of how he drove. We don't often invite comments on how we are doing, usually because we are too afraid we may not like what we hear, or are too proud to feel we should have to hear what others may say. I can't help but think it is far healthier and wiser to live in a way that checks in more often with those on the road alongside us and asks, 'hey, how am I driving right now?'

Maybe if we all took that approach, we would see less collisions and more progression. Maybe if we allowed more people to answer this we would learn faster and improve in areas quicker. If our kids were asked, 'how am I parenting?' or our friends were asked, 'how am I doing as a friend?', I wonder how much more we could grow. It might be that asking others is a step too far right now, maybe just check in with yourself. Don't be so defensive you can't ask the question and don't be too sensitive to hear the answer. I have found the more you ask, the quicker you learn, the better you drive and that's good news for everyone on the road alongside us and a better representation of the one we drive with. By the way, you will more often than not find you're driving better than you think, and that's also a good reason to ask for feedback, because too often we are our own worst critics.

THINK IT ━━━━━━━━━━━━ **130**

SPEAK IT ━━━━━━━━━━━━━━━━━━━━

BE IT ━━━━━━━━━━━━━━━━━━━━

EXHALE

For this reason He says, "Awake, sleeper, and arise from the dead, and Christ will shine [as dawn] upon you and give you light." Ephesians 5:14 (AMP)

You can either view life as if your time will come some day or your time is now. You can think that at some point you will be presented with a great opportunity or you can decide that today you will seize every opportunity. One is the waiting game and the other is the awakening way. We all have seasons where we have to wait for things to happen, but there are two types of waiting, one is productive and the other ineffective. When we wait simply because we are unsure or even a little scared of what we cannot predict, then we delay the awakening of what is often hiding within our lives.

You have to decide how you live, what do you believe, either your time is now or it is sometime later to come. You either believe God is waiting for something better or you are the better right now. You are not called to wait on the bench until others exit the field. You have a part to play today. You have training to attend to, you have service to give, ideas to contribute and passion to position for the advance of His kingdom. God wants to awaken you to all He has done for you, so you can become alive to all you are called to do with Him. Stop waiting for others to position you and start out working what's already within you.

We can all get stuck in the place of waiting for someone else to do what we are equipped to do now. Don't wait until someone asks to try and find an answer. Prepare now to find wisdom that you may later be required to draw from, learn now the word that later will become the foundations on which you stand. Build into your life now stores of truth and vats of understanding. Learn to discern God's voice in the stillness so you can recognise it in the storm. If we invest wisely in the now we can sustain more in the future.

What have you put on hold that God wants you to take a hold of? We need every person fully awake and attentive, living prepared in season and out. Single people, use this season to add wisdom for the day when that status may change. Students, learn skills for when you are in the workplace. Save now for later, invest now for the future. Let's not put a delay on what can be done now. Let's not create boundaries where God wants to increase territory, let's open up a conversation that empowers and encourages one another to rise up and go further to build for the future.

Where can you move from waiting to awakening today?

SPEAK IT ▬▬▬▬▬▬▬▬▬▬▬▬

BE IT ▬▬▬▬▬▬▬▬▬▬▬▬▬

Being strengthened with all power according to His glorious might so that you may have great endurance and patience. Colossians 1:11 (NIV)

I consider myself pretty fit and active, running several miles every day, but I have learnt that there are different levels of fitness. My nemesis are the stairs (who even invented the Stairmaster - it's like a torture instrument), thankfully we live in a society that has progressed and provides lifts or escalators for the ones with an acute stair phobia (that's me). So you can imagine my agony when I see the sign in a hotel foyer that says 'lift out of order' and I am staying on the 43rd floor.

I have learnt that God seems to love stairs, I guess He thinks they are much better for us than the lift. Just in case you are tempted to spend too much time looking for the shortcut to get you to where your heart desires, can I save you some time and suggest you take the stairs? Each step you take is helping you to build strength into your story in a way the lift never could. The staircase will teach you the value of the journey and the lessons in your progress.

Anything that flings you upward can also throw you backward. Stairs keep your momentum consistent and the ground you gain becomes established. Don't waste months or years of your life trying to leap where you should learn to climb. Don't wish away your days, when you can take the same energy and take more steps. God will promote, bless and bring favour but I have found that always happens for me on the staircase that I have already committed to take. He can bring you new landings you weren't expecting, amazing opportunities at different levels, new relationships as you climb. These are all things you miss in a lift, which only has one direction and often no view of anything greater than its own confined space.

The lift only teaches you how to press a button, limiting your capacity inside its own ability; it decides your journey and limits who can get in with you at any floor without your approval. As much as I want to avoid taking the stairs at times, I ask myself, why am I avoiding them? The honest answer is usually because I am too lazy to put the effort in they require or I am too impatient to walk when the lift offers me a pain free, workout free option. Often we avoid the stairs in life for the same reason; we don't want the work or the effort they want us to invest. Yet time and experience teaches us it's these very elements that lead to the greatest achievements. So renew your commitment to those stairs; I have often seen lifts break down, but funnily enough I have never seen a staircase get stuck. Stairs win in every season. So I guess I'll see you on the staircase.

THINK IT ━━━━━━━━━━━━ 134

SPEAK IT ━━━━━━━━━━━━━

BE IT ━━━━━━━━━━━━━

EXHALE

He has told you, O man, what is good; And what does the Lord require of you except to be just, and to love [and to diligently practice] kindness (compassion), and to walk humbly with your God [setting aside any overblown sense of importance or self-righteousness]. Micah 6:8 (AMP)

Some things are just good for us, like the greens we would rather not eat, the vitamins we know we should take. The same is true spiritually; there are certain things that when added to our daily diet keep us healthy and strong. In today's verse it recommends some things that are good additions to our daily diet, a power combination that we would all benefit from.

Humility: It is a doorway we can chose to walk through. As you bend to go beneath its beautiful frame, you embrace a posture that will serve your life greatly. The doorway of humility is often missed as we walk too fast and have our head too high but lower your gaze to where your face meets His grace and you will find it easy to bow your life under this entrance.

Justice: It just helps people to be heard. Judging others can be something we do far too quickly and the results are never beneficial. When we allow God to direct our hearts and instruct our hands then our motives become about justice, not judgment. Acting justly means we view with compassion before we take any action. We search for how to bring freedom instead of locking people up in more bondage. We serve a compassionate God and by choosing to act justly everyday, the world sees just how good God is.

Mercy: It should flow through us everyday. We all need mercy shown to us and we need to add mercy to our lives and watch how it will win people over. Let mercy accompany your words and let it overshadow your thoughts; be merciful to those who you may feel don't even deserve it. The extension of mercy will add more rooms for God to fill with treasure; mercy finds beauty, that's why we need to increase its presence in our lives.

When we walk with humility, act justly and love mercy, we build more bridges to more places, we invite our world to increase and our boundaries to expand. This combination will add health to your soul and make more space in your heart. So today, take your Micah power vitamins. If you can't manage all three in one go, just choose one; maybe start to work on being more humble, or seek after a heart that is more merciful or learn from others around you how to act more justly. If you work on adding and applying these principles, you will have a better day because of their effects in your life that will enhance your posture, improve your perspective and widen your horizon.

THINK IT ▬▬▬▬▬▬▬▬▬▬▬▬▬ 136

SPEAK IT ▬▬▬▬▬▬▬▬▬▬▬▬▬▬

BE IT ▬▬▬▬▬▬▬▬▬▬▬▬▬▬

EXHALE

But each of you has your own gift from God; one has this gift, another has that.
1 Corinthians 7:7 (NIV)

So you may not live in the most beautiful location. Maybe you don't wake up to sunshine or ocean scenery (me neither). For you the days may look predictable or just endless hours of work. But can I encourage you today that whatever your life looks like, it's YOUR life. The time we so often waste wishing we had someone else's lifestyle, family, resources, location, are hours and days we render useless to our future. In a world when it has never been easier to compare and measure our lives against the posted highlights of others lives, we must be careful we don't believe that the filtered social media reflection of the worlds of others is somehow to be envied or compared to the reality of our own. The truth is, no one is immune from pain and everyone has to handle difficulties so wishing for someone else's lifestyle also means wishing for their problems too.

What you do with the place where you do life is open to your faith and creativity, passion and purpose. Often it's our inability to find fulfillment where we are that breeds a sense of resentment of where others may be. You are not a prisoner to your environment, you can make your own world as beautiful as you decide. With God you are not bound by resources or creativity, He is able. God will do incredible things where you are too. Just begin to change your outlook and your expectations. You don't need to swap lives, maybe you just need to switch your thinking. Love the life you live and you will find it will love you right back.

Don't ever feel you are competing with those you are called to be complimenting. Your beauty is not diminished by another's, our lack of self worth can lessen our ability to see true worth. So today, be confident enough to compliment others and secure enough to see the value of another's brilliance without letting it question your own validity and contribution. Beauty and happiness are not for an exclusive few, they are broad and boundless. So embrace and encourage what's around you and focus afresh on what's within you.

What a waste to spend your time wishing you were living someone else's life, when you have been entrusted right now with this life. And what an insult to your Creator who took the time to create you with all your uniqueness. He loves you, not a borrowed version of you. So commit today to less time spent on comparing and more time on exploring your life. Attitude is everything so today, pick a good one. See possibilities and speak positively, address the negative with faith and look forward with hope. Your life is happening right now, so go ahead, put this book down and make today great.

THINK IT ━━━━━━━━━━━ 138

SPEAK IT ━━━━━━━━━━━━━━━

BE IT ━━━━━━━━━━━━━━

EXHALE

"Teacher, which is the greatest commandment in the Law?" Jesus replied: "Love the Lord your God with all your heart and with all your soul and with all your mind." Matthew 22:36-37 (NIV)

When a company or business has what they call 'mission drift', experts will often talk about getting back to the reason they started in the first place. They are trying to take what has become over complicated and strip back the layers to the core of why this company exists, why it was launched, who their customers are and what their products should achieve. The truth is, what marketeers and brand analysts charge thousands to discuss with you - Jesus gave away for free. This isn't a new wisdom, it's a biblical timeless truth. Jesus was always bringing those around Him back to the reason they were following Him. He spelt out for the disciples time and time again why He had called them, why they were sent out. His mission was you and I, His driving focus was salvation for all of us. Jesus simply said go and reach people, love yourself and love one another.

Focus leads to effectiveness. Definition help us make decisions and in turn that fuels our determination. Sometimes we simply need to clarify our commitment before we get confused by all the chaos any given day can bring. We need to master the art of simple in a society of multiple options. If you have an area where you have lost passion, maybe you have forgotten your driving reason. The reason you married that person, the reason you said yes to that job, why you are planted in that place; what was most important?

The simple can so easily be lost by our overcomplicated diaries, lifestyles and demands. The when and what are all external but the why is completely internal. That is the difference that changes everything. Let's not confuse those elements. Maybe in your marriage you are frustrated about where you are but don't let that overshadow the reason you came together, your love for one another. Journey deeper into the things that you vowed would hold you together. Maybe the craziness or lack of productivity of your business or studies is frustrating, things are moving too fast or too slow. We cannot allow our temporary results to call into question our fundamental roots. Granted, not everything should remain the same but for the most part, I have found our convictions that are grounded in Christ hold fast season after changing season and coming back to those truths puts any present reality into a more eternal perspective.

So today, try answering these simple questions. Why are you building, giving, planting, loving, serving, surrendering? Let the passion that said the original yes be the filter before you say no. Let the love that motivated you speak to the weariness that is currently counselling you. Our whys can change over time but they often need to be reinforced rather than replaced, dusted off rather than discarded.

THINK IT ━━━━━━━━━━━━━━━ **140**

SPEAK IT ━━━━━━━━━━━━━━━

BE IT ━━━━━━━━━━━━━━━

EXHALE

**Praise be to the Lord, to God our Saviour, who daily bears our burdens.
Psalm 68:19 (NIV)**

Recently I was running on some trails when I past a sign that read 'No sitting. This area is for game participants only. No spectators'. I guess we all need reminding sometimes when to sit and when we need to keep moving. We often allow our circumstances to dictate our posture. Pain likes to create parking bays, delaying our healing and rerouting our purpose. Sometimes you need to signpost your soul and let it know this is not a time to sit down, give up, spectate. This isn't a place to park up, settle or let go.

We need to remove some of the benches that our burdens have built. At first the reasoning behind the invitation to sit makes sense, we are tired, the burden is heavy, we feel like it's all too much. The bench is a great option, however I have found it usually becomes not a rest spot but a full stop. It is hard to get back up once you have sat down on the bench that burdens built, it sucks you in. Instead of being a place to re-energise, you cannot contemplate one more step. Once you drop the load you also give up your momentum and what you could have carried a little further, is now stranded in the middle of the floor in the wrong place.

Our burdens need to be put down in the right place or they will create a blockage for our future. We need to resist the invitation to build a bench and use that same energy to build a bridge. Bridges are taking you somewhere, they are helping you cross from one point to another. We need to get our burdens on the bridge of truth and off the bench of troubles. We need our burdens to be carried into the arms of the One who said His burden is easy and His yoke is light. Your burdens should not be in charge of what you build; your purpose gets that privilege. So today, let purpose shout louder than burden because where burden will ask you to sit, purpose will help you stand. When burden wants a bench, purpose seeks ways to progress. It's time to get off some benches and get over some bridges.

Today, just take some more steps, you will find the trail leads us past the trial and into new territory. Where have you become a spectator instead of a participant, where are you stuck on a bench that is not helping you improve but rather is restricting you? God will give you rest and He will refresh every weary traveller, He can teach you how to build from burden instead of letting burdens build for you. So take the bridge and get off the bench. He knows where the still waters are so keep going.

THINK IT ━━━━━━━━━━━━━━━━━━━

SPEAK IT ━━━━━━━━━━━━━━━━━━━

BE IT ━━━━━━━━━━━━━━━━━━━

EXHALE

After saying this, He spit on the ground, made some mud with the saliva, and put it on the man's eyes. John 9:6 (NIV)

A blind man came to Jesus crying out for his sight to be restored. Maybe he had heard that this man Jesus spoke a word and blind eyes opened or that when Jesus touched you, you were made whole. Whatever his expectations were that day, I am not sure he was quite ready for the way in which Jesus responded when He took some mud, spat in it and then wiped it across this man's eyes. For those looking on, it must have looked as if Jesus was adding insult to injury.

What would you do if Jesus spat on you? It's worth considering because often when we say we are desperate, we have ways in which we actually want our miracle to come. I have known people who are in huge debt but their embarrassment factor has hampered their desperation for breakthrough. They want God to provide but without anyone knowing of the mess they are in. I have known marriages that are falling apart but the couple don't want to come forward for prayer as they don't want to show their life is less than perfect. What about the person with the secret addiction who wants the healing done privately and the testimony burying. Maybe we would say to Jesus if we were that blind man, I don't want my miracle that way, I want it to be clean and I want it to be done in a way that's less humiliating. In 2 Kings 5, when Naaman was told to go and dip in the filthy river if he wanted to be cleansed of his disease, he was offended but his miracle was not going to come in a way that he imagined. He had to decide to stay as he was or humble himself and get so desperate he didn't care what people would say.

Our own embarrassment levels can become our containment until we are willing to be lowered through a roof or crawl on our hands and knees just to touch the hem of His garment, until we can eat the crumbs from the table or are willing to climb out of our tree. I have had to swallow my pride when I have been in need and I have had to crawl at times to get my miracle. Sometimes it's the crawl that is the cure and the journey of humility that is the entry of the healing.

So what is the stumbling block you have to remove in order to get closer to the breakthrough you are desperately seeking? Jesus has heard your call but maybe you need to be willing to do what He is asking of you. Jesus isn't trying to make it more difficult but He wants to make sure your desperation for who He is, is greater than your embarrassment of what others may think.

THINK IT ════════════════════ **144**

SPEAK IT ━━━━━━━━━━━━━━━━

BE IT ━━━━━━━━━━━━━━━━

EXHALE

Set your minds on things above, not on earthly things.
Colossians 3:2 (NIV)

Sometimes God is doing the most incredible things yet we can't see it because we are looking in the wrong direction. A while back I saw a picture of a boat with whale watchers on one side of a boat, while the whale was jumping right behind them. The whale was stunning, impressive, powerful, it was what they had all come to see. Yet as they sat patiently waiting, they were facing the wrong way, more aware of the cold breeze and the long boat ride, than the fact the whale was right beside them. This picture is a capture of how we so often do life. We get disappointed at the small things, while we don't realise God is working right alongside us with some much bigger stuff. We get bored by the water and fail to believe in what's about to jump out. Many abort the boat trip and say it was a disaster, but if they had turned their attention they may have said, this was everything we asked for and more.

We can allow one person's weary perspective in our boat to fix our expectations in the wrong direction and in so doing lose the miracle that a more passionate perspective wouldn't have allowed you to miss. The children of Israel were never meant to circle in the wilderness for 40 years. They were supposed to enter a promised land in a few short days. How can we make days into years or a straight path into endless circling? Sometimes we need to stop blaming others, even God Himself, and ask some questions of ourselves. When did I get so focused on the small stuff that I lost sight of the big stuff? Where did I forget God's word and replace it with the opinions of others? I have witnessed this very situation many times as a parent, when the childlike immaturity speaks and wants to quit waiting in line at the theme park. My kids feel the frustration of the moment when in line to see the overpaid famous mouse (who owns an expensive kingdom), but maturity sees the realisation of a dream. Exiting the line only means re-entering right back at the beginning later.

Don't start circling issues because of wilderness scenery or weary conversations. Magnify the destination, the promise, the breakthrough and you will find renewed energy to move forward. So today, don't get locked on the wrong side of the boat. Don't give up, when you just may need to take another look. Don't allow the boredom of the place where you are currently sailing to fool you that nothing interesting is ever going to surface. God is able and He likes to bring things into our world with a splash factor. So be alert, look again and don't miss your whale!

THINK IT ══════════════════ 146

SPEAK IT ════════════════════

BE IT ══════════════════════

EXHALE

But let him ask in faith, with no doubting, for he who doubts is like a wave of the sea driven and tossed by the wind. For let not that man suppose that he will receive anything from the Lord; he is a double-minded man, unstable in all his ways. James 1:6-8 (NKJV)

Don't cry over spilt milk is a strange expression but I guess the principle it is referring to is to not get so upset about things that don't need your tears, to learn to discern between the big stuff and the little stuff. That spilt milk can't be rescued by the tears you cry and the situation is not going to change because you got upset about it. It's just milk and milk is replaceable, so why exhaust ourselves emotionally over situations that we cannot change.

So maybe we need to be more aware of the spilt milk scenarios in our lives so that we can treat them accordingly. What right now are you so upset about that if you took a step back you would think twice about giving so much energy to? What spilt milk conflict are you in or spilt milk circumstance have you become all consumed by? As a leader and as a parent I have had to learn this lesson as people spill milk all the time. I used to cry everytime someone would act mean and now I realise people are people and that behaviour is spilt milk, it doesn't need me to get so upset about it or over involved in, in fact I probably would be better just ignoring it. I have learnt with my children every crisis is not crisis and every argument doesn't need my contribution. In my marriage there have been times when I have cried about things that a day later I am laughing about. Remember when Jesus was at Mary and Martha's house? Martha was so flustered that Mary was not doing the dishes. She was angry and emotional over unwashed pots. Jesus addressed the situation by letting Martha know her energy was being wasted on what was not an issue. Martha was stressing about her chores but Mary was resting with the Saviour. One was spilt milk, as far as Jesus was concerned.

Look over your life and the things that you are giving your emotional space to, the situations that are winding you up, stressing you out, the tears you are watering a situation with and ask yourself, are any of these spilt milk? My tears won't change them and this isn't even deserving of them. Spilt milk happens but it isn't life threatening or altering so today, tell yourself not to cry over the spilt milk and move on. You will feel freer and clearer and I guarantee today will be much better without you being the milk monitor.

THINK IT ━━━━━━━━━━━━━━━ 148

SPEAK IT ━━━━━━━━━━━━━━━━━

BE IT ━━━━━━━━━━━━━━━━━

EXHALE

"And no one pours new wine into old wineskins. Otherwise, the wine will burst the skins, and both the wine and the wineskins will be ruined. No, they pour new wine into new wineskins." Mark 2:22 (NIV)

Recently I moved some things around in my home to change up the look. I hung the pictures on a different wall and the chairs and table got switched around. The end result was a new feel to the room. New seating areas were created and the rearranged accessories made it feel different, but the truth was, fundamentally nothing had really changed. No new furniture arrived and no redecoration happened. The walls were still in the same place, the table was the same, just now it had a different corner to fit in. In life we need to make sure we know the difference between rearranging and renovating.

A lot of times when we need to change things in our own lives we get confused between the two. They sound similar but the end result is completely different. Maybe our behaviour or thinking needs changing, we need to move out wrong attitudes, fixed mindsets. We may need to completely remodel our confession, relationships, patterns of choice. We need to ensure in those times we don't substitute the renovation that's needed with a far less thorough approach of rearranging. Don't move the furniture around that needs to go. Don't face the chair in a different direction if that chair needs to be removed from your space all together.

We need to discern when it's time to shift things and when it's time to completely replace them. When it's time to reorganise and when it's time to renovate. If the wall needs to go, no matter how many times you repaint it, it will still be there and it is still creating the blockage that renovating wants to fix. If the sofa has lost its purpose, new cushions won't help it. If the carpet needs pulling up so new floors can be fitted, then stop shifting around rugs and go for the renovation. There is a season when rearranging serves the exact purpose we need. But there is also a season when it's time to do some demolition, and remove what can't be rearranged anymore.

Jesus didn't want the new to be put in something that had served its purpose; the old wineskin would crack and tear and eventually the old would taint and infect the taste of the new. There are times when the cost of rearranging may seem cheaper but we need to be aware that what we may save in the immediate we may be paying for long into the future. Let's not cause the future to be tainted by our unwillingness to remove some things that have long past serving their purpose. Let's know when it's time to say out with the old and in with the new.

THINK IT ━━━━━━━━━━━━━ **150**

SPEAK IT ━━━━━━━━━━━━━━━━━━

BE IT ━━━━━━━━━━━━━━━━━━

EXHALE

You're blessed when you stay on course, walking steadily on the road revealed by God. You're blessed when you follow His directions, doing your best to find Him. That's right - you don't go off on your own; you walk straight along the road He set. You, God, prescribed the right way to live; now You expect us to live it. Oh, that my steps might be steady, keeping to the course You set. Psalms 119:1-8 (MSG)

In a world where everyone wants to make their own way, discover and explore their independence and stay away from any form of constraint or commitment, verses like this can be difficult. Staying on course, walking steadily, following instructions, all these are not exactly exciting invitations to a spirit that doesn't want to be tamed. Yet I have discovered the greatest adventure in life is when we relinquish control and choose to follow the course that the Creator of all the universe has marked out for us. When you stay on course, following Him is not boring, far from it, it is the best experience.

Too often we can become distracted or hijacked by circumstances and relinquish the controls on who sets the course for our lives. We can lose the ability to follow Him in difficult terrain and in times when we most need to hold our place. When Jesus was going to the cross, He told His disciples to wait for Him, that for three days He would be gone but to stay and hold fast. So when the disciples got nervous and started wandering down a road to Emmaus, Jesus showed up and asked, where are you going? They didn't recognise it was Jesus but by the end of the conversation their hearts burned as they were redirected back to the place where He had said to stay. Learn to tether your life to truth and stay on the path that leads you into purpose over popularity and obedience over independence.

We can feel at times somehow we are missing out, we listen to other voices who suggest many alternative routes. But the measure for where you should be has to be found in His truth and His commands. It may not always be the popular choice to stay on the path but it is always the wisest choice when it is where God is leading you. So to every restless soul and aimless wanderer, know God is calling you to come closer to Him and spend time with Him. His intention is not to restrict you but rather to save you from meaningless meanderings and unnecessary excursions. Don't despise the pace or the process, instead embrace the purpose and the privilege, be grateful for the few steps you may take that could mean more progress than the many you may run in the wrong direction. God knows where you are going better than you do, so stay close and hold fast.

THINK IT ━━━━━━━━━━━━━━━ **152**

SPEAK IT ━━━━━━━━━━━━━━━━━━━━━

BE IT ━━━━━━━━━━━━━━━━━━━━━

EXHALE

But Ruth replied "...Where you go I will go, and where you stay I will stay. Your people will be my people and your God my God." Ruth 1:16 (NIV)

Have you ever been set up by someone and it was not a blessing? Maybe a blind date or a potential new job or investment. Though someone had seemingly put a lot of work into the arrangement, it didn't reflect your own desires or preferences at all. Just imagine for a moment that the same energy and commitment was put into setting you up to win. What if everyone in your world joined forces to help you succeed, to breathe life on your dreams? Imagine how different that would make your day. With everyone out to help you win, how much greater would you dream, how much bolder would you ask? That's why the enemy is hoping we never become the ones who set each other up to succeed. He likes that our own insecurities work as others limitations and our own tendency to compete prevents us from going out of our way to help anyone else overtake us. It's sad but true that too often people can hold back from giving others opportunity or praising their ability and contribution because if we are honest, insecurity prevents us from promoting another's success. We must remember building the kingdom is not a popularity contest, it's a commission and we all get to play a part. We need more maturity in the church so we can recognise every part matters, not just the parts that matter to us.

One of my favourite examples of a life lived with this ethos is Ruth. She, in a time when Naomi had nothing, gave up her own agendas and committed to serve her mother-in-law and set her up to win. Ruth set out to take care of her and in the process, found favour from Boaz. When Boaz explained why he was being so kind to Ruth in his supplies of grain, he connected the favour to her faithfulness and explained he was blessing her because she had blessed Naomi. Her willingness to set someone up to win was now the reason he was showing her the same kindness. I love the final part of Ruth's story as this shows this principle at an even greater level. When Ruth married Boaz and had a baby, the people cried out, Naomi has a son. They accredited Ruth's baby as Naomi's win because in that moment was the celebration of both women and how they had set one another up to succeed.

When it comes to building the kingdom, that team member's win is your win. You're on the same side. When you realise we are putting the ball in the same net you stop blocking goals and start setting them up. Why not set someone up to win today, because their win is your win.

THINK IT ━━━━━━━━━━━━━ 154

SPEAK IT ━━━━━━━━━━━━━━

BE IT ━━━━━━━━━━━━━━

EXHALE

Take heed that you do not do your charitable deeds before men, to be seen by them. Otherwise you have no reward from your Father in heaven. Matthew 6:1 (NIV)

Let's be honest, we all like to feel appreciated for what we do. We thrive when we are thanked and we find renewed strength when someone takes the time to notice the effort we have invested. However, if we need the gratitude to carry on in a serving attitude, we are building our actions on shifting sands. The more you say yes to God, the more the seed you are sowing can go unnoticed. When we step into areas that are unfamiliar, we may find no recognition comes with the actions. That's why you have to know that what you are doing is part of your calling as a child of God. Your affirmation is not in the appreciation but in the knowledge that you are fulfilling the calling that God has placed on your life. I love how Jesus would perform the most incredible miracles and then say, don't tell anybody. He wasn't looking for the fame and the crowds adoration, He was simply healing and helping as many as possible because that was the work He was sent to do.

When only one leper gave thanks out of the ten, Jesus wasn't shocked they left without a thank you, the shock was that one came back and He did not retract the miracle from those who didn't thank Him. Sometimes our need to be appreciated can misguide our motives and we bless those who we think will most reciprocate and appreciate our actions. Instead learn to love where you may never be loved back, sow where you may never be thanked and give not expecting some kind of recognition. Give because your Father is a giver and if it's good enough for Him, it's good enough for you.

When we realise that every time we serve, give, bless, we are being Jesus to someone, we stop wanting the thanks as it's all for His glory. A friend of mine told me of a man in the church who for years had come to services early and would secretly leave £20 in random Bibles. He didn't want people to know who he was because he knew God knew who he was. How many of us could learn a lesson from this? If we saw how much our kindness makes God smile, I don't think we would need anyone else's praise. So today, if you have become a little fed up in serving because you feel you are not appreciated or thanked enough, maybe shift your perspective upward and sense God's smile. Some will never say thank you for the years of good you did, but God has a million ways to thank you, so trust Him.

THINK IT ━━━━━━━━━━━━━ 156

SPEAK IT ━━━━━━━━━━━━━━

BE IT ━━━━━━━━━━━━━━

EXHALE

Then I heard the voice of the Lord saying, "Whom shall I send? And who will go for us?" And I said, "Here am I. Send me!" Isaiah 6:8 (NIV)

'Here I am, send me, Lord.' I remember when I was younger praying this prayer with such passion, tears flowing, on my knees begging God to use me, send me. However, my agenda was not exactly pure. I had already predetermined how and where I would like to be sent. My willingness to go had attached to it some places where I would prefer to go and even more clearly where I didn't want to go. I remember thinking of the missions that I would like to be involved in and knowing the ones I definitely didn't want to be a part of. My seemingly generous and passionate gesture of surrender had within it a whole other agenda. So you can imagine my disappointment when, after going forward to the altar and uttering, here I am Lord, send me, I found myself going nowhere. I felt God answer me not with a new mission but reminding me instead of the current mission that I had failed to recognise I was on.

In my immaturity I was trying to escape but God knew that I needed to stay in order to grow, I wasn't ready for the mission I had in mind. Sending isn't always about far away places or missions around the world, as glamorous as they may sound. Sometimes we need to be reminded that we are sent to our families, our homes and communities. We need to see God's sending is in the things we are currently entrusted with, otherwise everytime we are struggling, we will try to get a new instruction from God about a new sending for our lives.

The prophet Jonah had a personal list of destinations he would rather not be sent, top of the list being Nineveh. He didn't want God's grace to go to people he felt didn't deserve it. But God wasn't looking for Jonah's destination choice, He was looking for his obedience. Sending isn't about requesting, it's about obeying.

I have come to discover that actually, the decision to live your life as one that is sent is far more effective and fulfilling than asking God to send you when you feel stuck in your current situation. It removes the restlessness of striving to find where we should be, of constantly questioning if we are in the right place, or in God's will. His will is that we live out our lives bringing glory to Him. So what if we stopped looking for a one off mission and lived on mission everyday? We'll talk more about this in the next devotional but for today, what if we made our prayer, here I am, send me, with a realisation that His sending is happening in our lives right now.

SPEAK IT ━━━━━━━━━━━

BE IT ━━━━━━━━━━━

Then I heard the voice of the Lord saying, "Whom shall I send? And who will go for us?" And I said, "Here am I. Send me!" Isaiah 6:8 (NIV)

Previously we thought about how being sent doesn't necessarily mean going where you want to go or even leaving where you currently are, rather it means seeing God's sending in the situation we are currently in. Today, we're going to unpack this a little more and see what living on mission means in our everyday lives.

When we are living on mission, we give God daily permission to interrupt our plans. He can send us to bring a word to someone, send us to serve, to love and to involve. How much more would be achieved if more lived as those that are sent? How many more words would be delivered, how much more kindness expressed, requests prayed and lives reached? Here I am, send me: think about that. Where are you? Where is your 'here I am' place right now? What job, town, family, church does that encompass and in your present 'here I am' location, how much more could you live as one sent?

Sometimes we can over complicate what God wants to keep simple. We can delay living as those that are sent because we feel we don't have sufficient supplies. We can make long lists of all the things we require before we can even leave the house. Things that can look like our organisation might just be procrastination. When Jesus was with His disciples, He would regularly send them out to reach people with no food and no money. He simplified the sending so that they would live unrestricted when it came to responding.

What about our lives? Where are we overcomplicating what needs simplifying? Today, what could you actually get on with instead of just saying what you need? What if you lived on mission, alert to every place where God wants to send you; the conversations He is putting your way, the new people He is bringing into your world and the places He is sending you to sow the seed that He has entrusted into only your hands. I now look at my life, which includes a lot of time going back and forth across the ocean, and realise it was when I stopped trying to be sent and instead just lived as sent that God started to expand where my time was invested. God wants to see what you do with where you are before He gives more places to go to. Stop delaying your doing because you are waiting for things that aren't even needed. You have inside of you hope, so give it. You have light, so shine it. It is time to get on with the work. The mission isn't somewhere out there, it is here and now, so go ahead and live it out, not someday but today.

THINK IT ████████████████████ 160

SPEAK IT ████████████████████████

BE IT ████████████████████████

EXHALE

When
You live
Grateful
everyday is
A gift

Therefore, [continue to] accept and welcome one another, just as Christ has accepted and welcomed us to the glory of [our great] God. Romans 15:7 (AMP)

Several times a year we have a huge party at our house. It's not unusual for our home to have a lot of people in it, we are affectionately known as the party house but there are a couple of occasions in the year we go from a few at a time to a house where every room seems to be full of people. It's organised chaos of the best possible kind. The funny thing is, I am not the most comfortable in these kind of settings. I prefer to have a conversation with a couple of people I know than mingle in a space with lots of people I know less well. However, I have learnt over the years that my comfort level can at times become unhelpful and it's good every now and then to remove the ceiling that our awkwardness or shyness can try to contain us beneath.

So these parties have become a staple part of our family calendar; we know it will be noisy and chaotic. From brand new friends arriving at the front door for the first time, to old friends who by now probably have their own keys to our home, each person comes in and immediately kicks off their shoes, they drift in from the cold outside and are embraced by the warmth. On those evenings I love to just watch each person settle in, the house becomes alive with conversation, laughter, and such a sense of family. In some corners I often see people praying for each other. In another room we have a table tennis battle going on. The kitchen is always a popular place as that's where all the food is and many stay until the night tips into the next morning.

One of the favourite captures I have in the photo album of my heart is the sight of my front porch on these occasions as it goes from a clean empty space where we hang our coats to what looks more like a shoe shop. The growing pile and variety of footwear tells its own story that speaks of so much more than shoes. It's a picture of many journeys all thrown together. Many feet that are now walking on the same path. Many opportunities for each to enter one another's shoes and by so doing, deepen our love, compassion and wisdom for one another. The shoes belong to people from multiple nations, different ages, and every stage of life who have now found themselves together sharing this part of their life.

I think we all need an entry porch that has more shoes in it, that welcomes more lives to enter and make themselves at home. We need our churches, ministries, our love and our embrace to have a large entry porch. Maybe it's time for you to invite some more people over and add more shoes to the collection.

THINK IT ━━━━━━━━━━━

SPEAK IT ━━━━━━━━━━━━━━

BE IT ━━━━━━━━━━━━━━

EXHALE

"Just as the Son of Man did not come to be served, but to serve, and to give His life as a ransom for many." Matthew 20:28 (NIV)

Have you ever been served by someone and they made you feel your presence was very much at their inconvenience? Or has someone ever extended to you an act of service but then afterwards kept reminding you of how much that cost them? What was supposed to be a blessing now becomes a burden. Service is not supposed to be about self but about sacrifice. We are not called to serve so that others give us attention or promotion. To serve is not a duty but an opportunity. When we serve for gain, we will resent tasks that don't move us closer to our own aims. Service that has an agenda is no longer surrendered. As children of the Servant King we need to constantly check our service is reflection of our heritage.

Today, maybe you can have a service check. Are we more likely to complain than contribute, are we guilty of poor service when it comes to our communities and neighbourhoods, do we expect to be served before we are willing to serve? Our homes, lives, churches and families all need a service check from time to time. Ask questions like, what is motivating me, why am I serving? Check you are serving from gratitude and overflow, not resentment and tiredness.

We should allow our servant hearts to reflect the heart of our Saviour of whom scripture records, 'He did not enter the world to be served but to serve'. Wow. The One who could demand came to humbly serve. The One who was entitled, looked for no title. Serving should not be seen as a chore, but rather it's a privilege. Consider every aspect of your life from your own family, to your friends, church, job and then see the incredible honour you have before you to be of service in each area. How you see service will change how you give your service. I remember recently making my kids feel terrible because I had been up all night sorting out things for the next school year. I complained about all the organisation I was doing while they had been sleeping. I made them feel bad for just doing what was my responsibility. The kids couldn't help out-growing their current uniform or needing new shoes but my attitude made then feel guilty. Sound familiar? I know it's not just me; if I'd done a service check that day, I would have failed.

Let's make our serving of others in every area of our life a reflection of His service towards us. Remember, you are not responsible for how people may respond to your service but you are very much responsible for the way you serve.

THINK IT ━━━━━━━━━━━━━━ 164

SPEAK IT ━━━━━━━━━━━━━━━━

BE IT ━━━━━━━━━━━━━━━━

EXHALE

The righteous will flourish like a palm tree, they will grow like a cedar of Lebanon; planted in the house of the Lord, they will flourish in the courts of our God. They will still bear fruit in old age, they will stay fresh and green, proclaiming, "The Lord is upright; He is my Rock, and there is no wickedness in Him."
Psalm 92:12-15 (NIV)

The word of God is a guide for our lives, a lamp for our feet, it instructs those who are willing to listen in how to build our best life. One of the ways God intends our lives to flourish is through the act of planting. God knows that in order for more fruit to grow, it requires more lives to be planted, however, sometimes we can mistake settling for actual planting.

Would you know how to spot the difference if this was the case? Today, maybe it's time to examine your roots, are they down or are you just taking room and board in the things God wants you to make a permanent address? Settling is when we stay, rest, even unpack our lives for a while. Yet planting is where we dig, build and sink our seed into the ground. Settling is where we are located but not committed, we are comfortable and yet not accountable, where we receive the fruit from the lives of others more than we contribute any from our own.

God's best plan is for you to move from settling to being rooted and established. Settling can subtly lead to speculating but planting leads to participating and pruning. Though settling may serve a purpose for a season, to give temporary rest or shelter, we must remember that we are not called to sit in the shade forever but to grow a life that is fruitful and becomes shelter and food for others.

Planters become providers. Their deep roots bring forth new shoots of life and resource. The beauty of planting is its consistency and productivity; it's reliable in the turmoil and fruitful in the struggle; the maturity is visible and tangible. Don't ever think working on your roots is a waste of time, it's actually ensuring you thrive for a long time.

One of the things that reveals the difference between being settled or planted is the storms that blow through our lives. The shaking often shifts the settled but it doesn't disturb what has been anchored in the deep. If you want your family to weather the storm, drop the anchor; if you want a friendship to stand firm, sink down roots of commitment. Be aware where you are settled or planted in each area of your life: friendships, work, ministry, family. Make sure you go after the fruit you want for your future.

THINK IT ━━━━━━━━━━━ 166

SPEAK IT ━━━━━━━━━━━

BE IT ━━━━━━━━━━━

EXHALE

"Enter through the narrow gate. For wide is the gate and broad is the road that leads to destruction, and many enter through it. But small is the gate and narrow the road that leads to life, and only a few find it." Matthew 7:13-14 (NIV)

A few years ago I was sat in a traffic jam with my mum, cars gridlocked, no-one moving anywhere, when the car in front pulled out of the long line and took a side street exit. Our patience was running thin so we decided that this car must know a shortcut and we would follow it. That decision was the beginning of a very bad set of subsequent choices. After following the car for a while, it suddenly took a path off to the left, so we followed. However, this route was not built for cars, it was alongside a canal where vehicles were prohibited. With no room to turn around, we were now being abused by pedestrians who looked on aghast at our vehicle coming towards them. Eventually we came to a place where it was just about wide enough to turn the vehicle around and then we had the horror of realising we would have to go back the same way, past the same angry people.

In life, the detour we think will save us time can become a very costly waste of time. We only have so much energy and so many hours in a day. The enemy sets up distractions and detours that are signposted offense, disappointment, bitterness. When you take the path they offer you, the scenery of your life changes. Detours take you away from the bigger picture, from the very thing you are called to be involved and engaged in. The big picture is lost as you get caught up in more conflicts and arguments that are only happening because of the wrong path you are now taking.

Be aware of the path you're on, avoid the disgruntled detours and determine to live in a way that continually commits to the journey and persevere even when the traffic may seem to be at a standstill. It may be tempting to exit now but what about when you have to go back into the same situation later? Better to hold your place; just because others may take a detour, it doesn't mean we should follow, because often those who exit from frustration will lead you into further confusion. The embarrassment I felt that day stayed with me for a long time. The foolishness of following someone who was just frustrated, the people we could have hurt because of our impatience and the folly of having to rejoin what we could have moved past if we had persevered. So, think twice before you take that path that may feel good in the moment but will look very different in reality. Don't let frustration be who you follow today, it rarely leads you the right way.

THINK IT ━━━━━━━━━━━━━ 168

SPEAK IT ━━━━━━━━━━━━━━

BE IT ━━━━━━━━━━━━━━

EXHALE

The Lord will make you the head, not the tail. If you pay attention to the commands of the Lord your God that I give you this day and carefully follow them, you will always be at the top, never at the bottom. Deuteronomy 28:13 (NIV)

How much of our life is more the wagging tail than the leading head? So often we shrink ourselves because of feelings of inadequacy or awareness of deficiencies. Yet God says, you are the head and not the tail. The head makes decisions, sees, hears, speaks, leads and activates. The head thinks and plans to act, it is crowned, anointed and noticed. Yet more often than not these descriptions, this sense of worth, we can think is only for a special few. So we act more like a tail, wagging for affection, we hesitate on speaking up or stepping out, thinking our contribution lacks any significance.

If we, the Church, live more as the tail of our communities and societies, the world will never truly hear, see or experience Jesus. That's why no matter what our personality, our sense of confidence or amount of courage, we can't keep exercising tail behaviour. We need to become comfortable with taking leadership across our lives, not abdicating responsibility but instead embracing each opportunity. We need to learn to find our voice, to speak our heart, build our families and lead in our workplaces and communities. This verse is asking you and I to magnify the beauty of Christ by being those who lead, speak and act well.

In the book of Esther, we read of the journey of this young orphan. She had a moment where she understood: I can just stay in the king's harem and hide or I can begin to act in accordance with my calling. She knew she could just be another person who was there to entertain the king, blending into the backdrop of history or she could step up and be a spokesperson for her people and in so doing change other people's destinies. Her role as queen didn't start with a title; it began when she acted as one whose head was ready to carry the authority that came with that crown. We don't need any more tiaras on tail like behaviour. Instead we need to walk in the authority our Heavenly Father has already given to each of us. We need every generation to awaken to the reality that it is our time to wear the crown as royal sons and daughters. We are positioned by God to fulfil the purposes of God and that requires way more people to lift their heads instead of chase their tails.

Today, examine where you need to be more head and less tail. Someone is waiting for you to take the place that God is calling you into, you are born for such a time as this so go ahead and make your time count.

THINK IT ━━━━━━━━━━━━━━━━━━━ 170

SPEAK IT ━━━━━━━━━━━━━━━━━━━

BE IT ━━━━━━━━━━━━━━━━━━━

With the tongue we praise our Lord and Father, and with it we curse human beings, who have been made in God's likeness. Out of the same mouth come praise and cursing. My brothers and sisters, this should not be. James 3:9-10 (NIV)

The words we are speaking are consistently affecting the way we see. Every confession will either clarify or confuse the lens of your life. Each declaration will add depth or distortion. We begin to take a hold of our confession when we sense the circumstances are against us, our words get more attention when we feel pressed, but what about the rest of the time? Your words have power everyday, they are a weapon even when you don't feel you need to fight. Words shape our world and therefore we shouldn't have a day where we are careless with something so powerful.

We need to be more mindful of both the outbursts we have and the things we have spoken quietly, even whispered silently. Maybe we need to be more deliberate about what we are saying everyday, so we can avoid the disasters that sometimes our confessions have been incubating unchecked. This week, be more aware of your words. I know it can be hard especially if you use a lot of them each day (guilty as charged). Your confession, your intonation, they matter. Be mindful that speaking about it will change your perspective of it, for better or worse.

Words frame our world. They act as a lens that either shrinks or widens our vantage point. They open or close doors and they welcome or ward off things that approach our lives. James is very clear about the power of the tongue and also about our responsibility to take a hold of that tongue and direct it well.

Today, where can you be more aware of your words? Stop saying you're not good enough, pretty enough, stop saying you will always be single, sick, broke, alone. Even the most innocent of comments carries an impact in your world so don't overlook what you can use to your advantage; we may not be able to control what others say but we can take a hold of what we say. Be wise in your words. Choose the words that give you the best window through which to view your current circumstances.

Take a little time today and do a confession check up. What are you declaring over your destiny, family, future? Line up your words with His word. Let your confession be faith filled and your vantage point will become more God filled. Speak some things out today that create new possibilities instead of reinforcing present difficulties. Your words matter so much more than you realise; they are shaping your world and the lives of those in your world too. Let's make time to examine our words so that when we use them, we use them well.

THINK IT ━━━━━━━━━━━━━ **172**

SPEAK IT ━━━━━━━━━━━━━━

BE IT ━━━━━━━━━━━━━━

EXHALE

Do not merely listen to the word, and so deceive yourselves. Do what it says. Anyone who listens to the word but does not do what it says is like someone who looks at his face in a mirror and, after looking at himself, goes away and immediately forgets what he looks like. James 1:22-24 (NIV)

As great as quotes about change may be, they won't change you. As good as the thought on love is, its power is in the action not the statement. We have to be continually mindful that what we post does not change who we are. What we actually live out, our daily disciplines and practices, shape who we are. If you're posting about forgiveness that's not a bad thing, but the better thing would be that the post has come out of your life practices, not from Pinterest. We can all sound good in our virtual world, but the fruit of what we quote needs fruit in the lives we lead.

Today, take some time to be honest with yourself about the gaps that need closing between the world you post and the life you live. Let's not give into pressure to boast-post or insta-impress. Just be willing to journal your journey, they are usually the most inspiring stories. Post the wisdom that is in your weekly wardrobe, those well worn garments of truth that you have learnt to wear well.

In Acts 26, the apostle Paul stands before King Agrippa and begins to speak in such a way that everyone knows his words are not head knowledge but his lived out experience. The passion and conviction made even the King say, 'keep this up much longer and you'll make a Christian out of me!' Paul's authority was his authenticity. The arguments he made were convictions he had come to in the many trials and tests he had faced. He wasn't speaking of an unknown god but a very real and known God.

I don't want to quote verses instead of living them. I don't want to pretend to be something I am not. It's exhausting to keep up an act. It's easy over time to think we become what we post. But our behaviour defines our growth, not through posting but processing and the hard work of changing. We have all heard the gospel preacher who says just because you live in a chicken coup doesn't make you a chicken, illustrating the point that just because you attend a church service, it doesn't make you a follower of Jesus.

We need to post less snap shots of what we want people to see and just get busy living what we say. Honesty is always the best policy. We are all a work in progress, so don't try and fake a life when you can discover the unfolding beauty of building a life.

THINK IT ━━━━━━━━━━━━━━━ 174

SPEAK IT ━━━━━━━━━━━━━━━━

BE IT ━━━━━━━━━━━━━━━━

EXHALE

See what great love the Father has lavished on us, that we should be called children of God! And that is what we are! The reason the world does not know us is that it did not know Him. 1 John 3:1 (NIV)

Have you ever played 'how much do I love you'? The arms begin to stretch out, this much, this much, until the arms are fully extended and an embrace is the only appropriate response. You realise that what you are communicating is that your love for that person, or their love for you, is more than you can ever describe. I used to play that game with my children over and over. Whether you've ever had that said to you or not, the truth is, that's what God says to us all. In fact, His love has no end and no expiration point, His love for us is without measure. It was stretched out on a cross and it is the love that He holds out to you in this very moment.

So how much of that love have you let in? We can talk about the depths and the endless nature of God's love but talking, singing and reading about it does not mean we are actually receiving it. This love is not going to run out so we don't need to conserve the love of God. Imagine if you gave your loved ones a cheque and said, I really want you to be blessed with this money, treat yourself, then every time you checked your bank statement, the cheque had yet to be cashed. You would look for when the withdrawal would leave your account but there it sits, untouched. Not only are the ones you want to bless missing out, but now you feel that you are also being denied the opportunity to be the blessing you wanted to be.

That's how it is with God's love; you have a blank cheque but some of us are very slow to make a withdrawal. We have access to this limitless love but we put limits on the love. God wants you to cash the cheque, let Him love you, learn how to be loved by His Father's heart, lean into the love of God. When your own love is running low, let His love overflow. His love is lavish, it's unconditional, His love covers and doesn't judge, His love forgives and holds no record of wrongs, His love is gentle and His love is strong.

His love changes everything. God couldn't help Himself, when He saw you and I. Love sent its very best so we could be found, included, changed and transformed. His love couldn't leave us, it was always going to seek and embrace us. Don't ever wonder, do I matter, do I count? You are loved so much that heaven came to earth. And with that love coming down, everything, absolutely everything, can change. So when you need something changing, my suggestion is just let His love in.

THINK IT ━━━━━━━━━━━━

SPEAK IT ━━━━━━━━━━━━

BE IT ━━━━━━━━━━━━

EXHALE

You do not have because you do not ask God. When you ask, you do not receive, because you ask with wrong motives, that you may spend what you get on your pleasures. James 4:2-3 (NIV)

We often spend more time lost than we need to. More time searching than necessary and more time struggling than makes sense. The reason we can prolong our situation is because we have lost the art of asking. We feel to ask is somehow embarrassing. Our pride tells us to persevere on our own. Our struggle says no one will want to help. Yet asking is an essential part to growing. At school asking was encouraged in order to learn more. We grew through our ask. But the older we become the more we try to make it happen on our own and we feel to ask would almost be a waste of time, a sign of weakness.

Yet asking is inviting, it says enter my world, help me, advise me. When we ask we acknowledge where we are at and we find answers that are hidden within other people's stories. We dignify the wisdom within one another and we listen more intentionally so we can move more purposefully. What do you need to ask? Ask for help, ask for wisdom. Ask for directions, ask people over, ask that person on a date. Ask for the promotion, ask for prayer.

The Bible teaches us we should ask often. And it also tells us in James 'we have not because we ask not and when we do ask we have the wrong motive'. So keep your motive pure, let's make sure our asking is not about need. But what about some seed asking, possibility asking. Jesus' mother asked for Jesus to fix the wine situation at a wedding. A strange and out of time ask but the ask provoked a miracle that I am not sure Jesus planned on doing that day. Asks open possibilities. Maybe you could see more growth not just from working or striving but from some more honest asking.

Asking, however, needs a new reputation; it's not embarrassing its actually a sign that you are smart. It's the ones who ask that get, it's the ones who ask that learn and it's the ones who ask that also help others ask. Asking is powerful and it's empowering. We need more asking. You never know your ask could be the start of the miracle you have been searching for. And if the answer you get isn't the one you expected, then you will also benefit from the ask. It will resolve what wasn't clear and stop you wasting time in the wrong direction.

Why not make today an asking day? Ask lots of questions until it becomes more and more comfortable and feels more natural. Let's ask more because God wants to answer more.

THINK IT ━━━━━━━━━━━━━━━━

SPEAK IT ━━━━━━━━━━━━━━━━

BE IT ━━━━━━━━━━━━━━━━

EXHALE

What a wildly wonderful world, God! You made it all, with Wisdom at Your side, made earth overflow with Your wonderful creations. Psalm 104:24 (MSG)

Have you ever heard kids or sometimes adults say, I'm bored, there's nothing to do. They make this statement while surrounded by beautiful countryside, bikes in the yard, books to read, games that could be played, conversations that could be had. Boredom is not something that happens to us, it's something we happen to choose. I have heard people say my friends are boring, my town, church, marriage, job is boring, as if boredom moved into an area of their life like an unwanted guest. So if that's true, maybe a better question would be, how can others in the same circumstances find life anything but boring?

Often boredom is a result of a lack of imagination; when we stop dreaming and creating we start accepting and regressing. A marriage that becomes boring is simply a relationship that has been neglected, a couple that stopped initiating adventures and surprising one another. The marriage went from dreaming together to just doing life with one another. At any stage in our lives, we can allow boredom to take over, from our parenting to our own careers and aspirations. I want to encourage you today to deal with the boredom factor; why not decide to do something about it and turn the bore into something more?

If we serve the Creator of the universe, then surely we can reflect some of that creativity as His kids. If our God is filled with endless answers, then maybe we too can start looking for something greater. We get bored when we allow limitation to dictate our expectations and lack to be our life coach. Let's get back to the place we used to spend hours in as children; just because we are grown up doesn't mean we have to give up dreaming and creating. Take a picnic to the park, start a new hobby, have a dance party, invite over new neighbours, dream up some new ideas. Love your life again and do things your life will love.

Often we don't need to get away to find excitement, we need to stop giving way to boredom. We need to add passion back and stop accepting beige as the only colour option for your future. God is the God of possibility so we too need to start to imagine and create, from the possibility hidden in your problem, to the potential in your new ideas. Don't miss the opportunity tucked away in the obstacles or the new adventure within the familiar. Be a possibility finder, dreamer, thinker and doer and kick boredom to the curb.

Often the truth is we are not bored, we have become boring. When we realise that, we also realise the cure is closer than we think. If we change it all changes, so today, instead of being a bore, be bold and reach for more.

THINK IT ━━━━━━━━━━━━ 180

SPEAK IT ━━━━━━━━━━━

BE IT ━━━━━━━━━━━━━

EXHALE

Here a dinner was given in Jesus' honour. Martha served, while Lazarus was among those reclining at the table with Him. John 12:2 (NIV)

I have always loved setting a table. Something about the table is so inviting, it's a place that says, sit a while, stop rushing past me and wait a while with me. In a world where we seem to do everything whilst moving, the table creates a welcome break from the constant motion and instead offers an opportunity that will require a little more time and devotion. In our home, the most comfortable seats are at the dining table; I want those who sit there to stay awhile and relax.

Jesus would go in the midst of the chaos and recline with His friends at the table. He would sit and eat in the home of Mary and Martha and catch up with His friend, Lazarus. He would take time at the table with His disciples, sharing stories and enjoying their company. Jesus was at home at the table and I love that we can create Jesus moments in all our homes when we set a table. Once He invited Himself into the home of Zacchaeus, knowing how much he was despised. Jesus chose to eat with him and sit at the table where the conversations were unhindered by the comments of others and Zacchaeus could open his heart in his own home. That table time led to Zacchaeus turning his life around.

Often we underestimate the power that's in connection and rush past places that seem far too ordinary to bring forth something extraordinary. It was at a table that Jesus performed His first miracle turning water into wine, it was at a table He was anointed with the contents of an alabaster box, it was at a table He broke the bread and poured the wine. It was at a table He predicted the denial and foretold the betrayal. We all need table time when we sit and take stock, time when we lean in and learn, time when we drop the mask and focus on what matters. If your life looks more like a fast food marathon, then maybe it's time for the addition of a table, a let's stop the hustle and breathe space, a no work, no devices or distractions zone. A time and place where life gets shared. It's not about what's on the table, it's who's around the table, it's not about fancy food but open hearts.

Set an environment that says, you are expected, prepared for. It can be hard when you live alone to open up your home, it can also be hard when your house is full to get everyone to sit still. Setting a table can be paper plates and plastic feeding cups if that's your stage of life. Just take a moment to create an environment, one that invites little and big people alike to calm down, sit down and and stay awhile.

SPEAK IT ━━━━━━━━━━━━━━━━━

BE IT ━━━━━━━━━━━━━━━━━

I went past the field of a sluggard, past the vineyard of someone who has no sense; thorns had come up everywhere, the ground was covered with weeds, and the stone wall was in ruins. I applied my heart to what I observed and learned a lesson from what I saw: A little sleep, a little slumber, a little folding of the hands to rest - and poverty will come on you like a thief and scarcity like an armed man. Proverbs 24:30-34 (NIV)

Doing nothing is not neutral. Where we fold our arms weeds will grow. Where we fall asleep walls get broken down. Sometimes we need to stop wishing we had someone else's life and just wake up and look after the one we have been entrusted with. It's not the easiest truth to accept but the work that neglect will accrue is often much more expensive than the work diligence will require.

This proverb paints a picture of a person who has simply crossed their arms and closed their eyes for a moment, yet that moment of neglect has led to a lifestyle of regret. We can think an outside attack will destroy what we have laboured to build and yet we fail to be aware of the internal damage that can be caused when we allow what we have been entrusted with to be ignored or unprotected.

Our apathy is not neutral, it creates an access point for the ground we have previously taken to be placed in jeopardy. Once when my son was sick, I sent him to bed to sleep it off (no, I'm not the best nurse). Later I went to check in on him and the fever was worse; now a little more concerned I prayed a 'short and sweet' prayer over him. As I left his room I felt the Holy Spirit speak to me, 'Is that it? Is that the kind of prayer you are praying? Go back and take authority over this situation'. Those words awakened what had become apathetic and dormant in me. I realised nothing changes if it is not challenged, I went back in that bedroom and prayed with passion and authority that no sickness was welcome in my zone. To my surprise the fever broke and my son even said from his deep sleep, 'Amen'. It seems his body was asleep but his spirit was wide awake and waiting for me to wake up too.

Later we will look more at the importance of owning our zone. For today, look around at what has been entrusted to you. It may be a ministry, a relationship, a job. Don't take these things for granted, don't sleep on the job, doing nothing is not neutral, it's a backward step. Nurture your heart into a beautiful garden and when weeds are found, pull them out of the ground so something more purposeful can grow.

THINK IT ━━━━━━━━━━━ 184

SPEAK IT ━━━━━━━━━━━━━

BE IT ━━━━━━━━━━━━━━━━

EXHALE

Then Abigail made haste and took two hundred loaves of bread, two skins of wine, five sheep already dressed, five seahs of roasted grain, one hundred clusters of raisins, and two hundred cakes of figs, and loaded them on donkeys. And she said to her servants, "Go on before me; see, I am coming after you." But she did not tell her husband Nabal. 1 Samuel 25:18-19 (NKJV)

Previously, we looked at how quickly a little neglect can turn into an access point for decay. We have to own the zone of our relational world if we want to keep it from thistle and thorn. We must wake up and own our zone financially, emotionally, physically. Today, identify your zone, the places and people you get to do life with and ask, am I growing what I have been given or have I folded my arms in neglect?

There is a story about a woman named Abigail; she was married to a mean, hard hearted man named Nabal. When David asked for Nabal's help, he refused and in fear of David destroying Nabal's land, the women came to ask Abigail to own her zone. She didn't know how she could help but she knew she had to do something. She saddled a donkey with a basket of cakes and saved the day. She owned what Nabal ignored. Own your zone today and save what folly and laziness will spoil.

We can't afford to allow our minds and hearts to become disengaged when it comes to the seeds that are being placed in the soil of our lives. It's much easier to stop the wrong things being planted in the beginning than having to tackle foliage that has roots because it's had time to grow unchallenged. We are in a battle for our minds, fighting the temptation for lethargy, taking a break, taking a back seat. When we are not vigilant, our passion fades and our priorities change. So take back the ground God has given you, tend the soil of your family and marriage, pull up the weeds of discontent and disharmony.

Distance doesn't happen overnight between two people, it grows steadily every time the things that separate are allowed to take root, when you allow love to drift, passion to become an unattended fire and complacency to make the choices that commitment used to make. Don't wait for the big disaster to wake up to what's been growing in your zone. Regularly tend the garden and own what is yours to grow.

Today, make a decision about some things that are adrift and begin to close the gap to stop things falling through the cracks.

THINK IT ━━━━━━━━━━━━━ 186

SPEAK IT ━━━━━━━━━━━━━━━━━━

BE IT ━━━━━━━━━━━━━━━━━━

EXHALE

Then she gave the king one hundred and twenty talents of gold, spices in great quantity, and precious stones. There never again came such abundance of spices as the queen of Sheba gave to King Solomon. 1 Kings 10:10 (NIV)

In all our asking, needing, searching and seeking, I pray we have also made time for thanking. If you have ever been on the receiving end of many demands that came with little thanks, you know it's not a nice feeling. We never serve for the gratitude but we never forget the ones who do say thank you. When the Queen of Sheba came to visit King Solomon, it is recorded how she was overwhelmed by his wisdom and generosity. She was so thankful for what she saw and received, she gave Solomon more than anyone had ever given a king. She didn't have to give anything, she was the Queen of Sheba, yet even in her riches she had kept an attitude of generosity and gratitude. That made her visit leave a lasting deposit. Her gratitude wrote her into Solomon's story.

The greedy monster of comparison often steals or displaces our gratitude, it tells us we have no need to be thankful as we are not as blessed as others around us. Yet gratefulness is a seed you cannot afford to withhold, when it is planted it grows such beauty in your heart and always has food for the soul, even in the leanest of times.

Several years ago in the middle of our Christmas gathering, I remember being overwhelmed not by the gifts but by the beauty of my family and realising afresh how rich we truly were to have one another. I stopped the present opening and we took hands and prayed and gave thanks. Suddenly the whole atmosphere in the room changed, the kids stopped ripping paper off presents and thanked God and then thanked us as parents. Ever since then that has become our tradition; we need to model a life that stops to say thank you.

I pray we never forget the simplicity and yet the power that rests in gratitude. 'Thank you' should not just be a word we say, but a spirit we live by, it's a magnet for miracles. When we live in an awareness of God's goodness, we constantly fill our mouths with words that say thanks and our hands with actions that want to give back. Take some time out to make a thankful list: write down five things that you are grateful for, maybe it's a relationship, a job, your health. Give thanks each time you ponder something on the list. When was the last time you sent a thank you card to someone and took the time to express what you feel? Maybe you can let someone know how grateful you are. I guarantee by focusing on that list it will prioritise your day and line up your confession to be more magnetic to future miracles.

THINK IT ━━━━━━━━━━━━━━━ 188

SPEAK IT ━━━━━━━━━━━━━━━

BE IT ━━━━━━━━━━━━━━━

EXHALE

And do not forget to do good and to share with others, for with such sacrifices God is pleased. Hebrews 13:16 (NIV)

As a mum of two kids and an auntie to many, one thing you find yourself teaching over and over again is how to share. Toys, food, even friends, it seems from our youngest years we have an aversion to sharing. We can carry that underlying attitude into our adult years; though we may not like to admit it, we all have some things we are definitely less keen to share with others. You may not mind sharing your food, but what about your friends? You may not mind sharing your stuff but what about your space? Being generous is different to sharing. Generosity is giving out of what we have but sharing means we are actually creating a space for someone to share an experience with us. It's easier to give someone money to go for a meal than it is to share dinner with them in your own home.

When we started pastoring the church, I realised I was going to have to share my life, share our home and be willing to share as a family so we could build God's family. If we don't understand the difference between giving and sharing, then we will continually be frustrated. When Hannah begged God for a son after years of barrenness and torment, she was given Samuel. But Hannah made an arrangement with God, this child would be a gift she shared and so after weaning the boy, Hannah took him to the temple to serve God for the rest of his days. Hannah knew the difference between giving and sharing. She still stayed in Samuel's life but he was the gift she chose to share.

Sharing isn't easy to navigate, there are a lot of unspoken rules and that's why we need to always work on our attitude. If you agree to share, you can't control what the other person will do with what you are sharing. I often ask my friend to share a muffin with me if we have a coffee stop on a trip and that friend knows what I mean is, I want the top of the muffin and you can have the bottom, it's an unspoken agreement. But when I ask my husband to share the muffin, he has the audacity to eat half of the top as well as the bottom. Sharing sometimes can be with an unspoken understanding but often times it's not. All you can do is hope they love and care for what you are sharing in the way you do. Yet sharing is often one of the greatest ways we grow and one of the fastest ways we learn. We all need to be told every now and again, you need to share because a possessive life is a contained life. Sharing isn't just for little kids to learn, it's for big kids too.

THINK IT ━━━━━━━━━━━━━ 190

SPEAK IT ━━━━━━━━━━━━━

BE IT ━━━━━━━━━━━━━

EXHALE

He heals the brokenhearted and binds up their wounds.
Psalm 147:3 (NIV)

When I was a teenager, I had an amazing group of friends. We would hang out every weekend and circulate between each other's homes so we always had a place to go and sleep over on the Saturday night before church on Sunday. One weekend we were staying at a friend's and the usual fun and games started. We were trying to do cartwheels in our friend's front lounge; it was not the smartest of ideas especially as we were in the smallest of lounges. I remember my very tall and long legged friend volunteering herself to go first and as she sprung into the air we could all see her landing was going to mean something was breaking, either her leg or one of the ornaments. Sure enough her leg came down onto a glass bowl, a favourite of our friend's mum, and it shattered into not a few but what looked like hundreds of pieces.

Our friend went into panic; she knew she was going to be in serious trouble. My friend who had caused the accident came up with what in her mind was a genius idea, she decided we should fix the bowl. The only thing we could find to put the bowl back together was sellotape. Yes, we sellotaped the pieces of crystal onto each other and used enough tape to get it to resemble the shape of a bowl. We then put the bowl back in the window and went upstairs hoping no one would ever notice. As you can imagine, it wasn't long before we were busted. Sellotape was an inadequate material to fix our mess.

We laugh at this in the natural but what about when we do it spiritually? When we know something is broken but instead of getting the right help we use sellotape to hold it together. We know we need to get someone else to help us fix what is complex but we instead use the tape we use for everything else, then we wonder why it keeps coming apart. When David messed up with Bathsheba, he started to try and tape together the bowl his poor choices had broken. He called Bathsheba's husband back from the front lines and when that plan didn't work, he sent orders to have him put up front where he would lose his life on the battlefield. David's sin led to a lot of sellotape and God sent a prophet to address what David and Bathsheba had tried to mask. God doesn't do sticky tape because He knows eventually it will lose its stick. So where is it time to deal with the tape and admit the mistake?

THINK IT ━━━━━━━━━━━━━━━ 192

SPEAK IT ━━━━━━━━━━━━━━━━━━

BE IT ━━━━━━━━━━━━━━━━━━━━

EXHALE

And the Lord answered me, and said, "Write the vision, and make it plain upon tables, that he may run that readeth it." Habakkuk 2:2 (KJV)

"Dream big, work hard, stay focused and surround yourself with good people." I saw this quote and I remember thinking how true it is, in a world that often separates out all these elements, this statement ties them all back together. The truth is that on their own, each can make a contribution but together they trigger movement. Have you ever met a dreamer? Maybe you fall in that category yourself, seeing possibility everywhere but with little time for the facts in case they try to deflate the dream. They love to colour in the vision, they are creative and impulsive. However, left alone the dreamer can become discouraged; all the dreams in the world don't actually build a world. Every dreamer needs to partner with a planner for the dream to become a reality.

Maybe you're a hard worker, a planner, you have invaluable skills, you see the possibility but you also have a plan of how to break it down into workable parts. Planners are the ones that want less time talking and more time doing, they don't want to colour in a dream, they want to build it. However, left on their own, planners become obsessed with detail and lose sight of the big picture, they can see more problems than solutions. Planners can start to limit the future to fit the size of their own ability whereas dreamers seem to have endless possibilities to increase territory.

We often can go to the extremes in life, polarising what others have to offer. So I love this statement because it invites the dreamer to become a doer and the doer to start dreaming. God told Habakkuk to write down the vision and make it plain so others can run with it. Not only does God want dreaming and doing to come together, He also wants others to get on board. David had a dream to build God's house but he also had a plan of what that house would look like. He wrote it with such focus that even the size and length of nails was recorded. His commitment led to the right workmen being employed and craftsmen knowing where they were needed. His clarity meant when he had to pass that dream on to his son, the focus wasn't lost because the detail was there. The longevity of our dreams relies on our willingness to combine dream, plan and focus so more people can make it happen.

Today, be aware of the elements not just within you, but around you. Let's make more dreams a reality, ensuring what we say becomes what we see. Let's look for the partners we need to make the plans happen. Dream big, work hard and stay focused, that way we all get to play our part in making dreams a reality.

THINK IT ━━━━━━━━━━━ 194

SPEAK IT ━━━━━━━━━━━━━

BE IT ━━━━━━━━━━━━━

EXHALE

Like one who grabs a stray dog by the ears is someone who rushes into a quarrel not their own. Proverbs 26:17 (NIV)

Some invitations require us to be more discerning with our RSVP. We must learn where our attendance can make a positive difference and where our contribution will be counterproductive. When conflict comes to your life, you don't have to let it move in or become your tenant. Imagine for a moment someone showed up on your front steps, agitated, aggressive and wanting to fight. I think we would all agree we would not invite into our home hostility we knew didn't belong to us. What we can understand so clearly in this illustration, we often fail to comprehend in our everyday realities. Many of the tensions that we end up entertaining could have been turned away if we had chosen to answer differently.

You and I are the gatekeepers to our hearts and minds and we need to remember that not everyone or everything should be allowed over the threshold of our thinking and conversing. At times, our desire to be helpful can be misinformed and also misused. Hold off in always volunteering to handle the hostility. You can't be a referee when no one is seeking a healthy resolve. Solomon was once asked to become involved in a disagreement between two women with two babies, one that was dead and one that was alive. Both claimed their child was the living one as they insisted their case but Solomon refused to go any further with their fight. So wisdom spoke as he said, let's cut the living baby in two and you can both have half. His seemingly crazy suggestion soon settled the argument as the real mum spoke up. Solomon's wisdom was to not get into something that was pointless and instead silence all the foolish arguments.

When you take care of your response, you will find that your name will drop off the invite list; you have moved from always available to respond responsible. And that may be one of the greatest gifts you give yourself. Many people are tired from spending too much time with the wrong house guests so serve notice on negativity and make some new space for a different kind of conversation. If you find it hard to evict the wrong tenants from your life, then make things simpler by stopping them from ever getting as far as unpacking.

So here's some steps to check before you RSVP: what has this conversation got to do with me? Can I help in this conflict? Is this conversation looking to resolve or vent? Is this coming from a positive spirit or offence? Sometimes, the best reply is to pray for them and redirect them from your door to God's. Remember, it's better to be misunderstood now than to be implicated in something damaging later. Create some boundaries now that your future self will thank you for and be at peace.

THINK IT ▬▬▬▬▬▬▬

SPEAK IT ▬▬▬▬▬▬▬▬▬▬▬▬▬▬

BE IT ▬▬▬▬▬▬▬▬▬▬▬▬▬▬▬▬

EXHALE

Therefore submit to God. Resist the devil and he will flee from you. Draw near to God and He will draw near to you. James 4:7-8 (NKJV)

Pull or push? They sound similar but they cause two very different postures within us. If you have ever moved a large cumbersome piece of furniture up a narrow awkward staircase, you will understand what I mean. You have to choose which side you're taking: either you're the one that goes first, navigating backwards or you are the one beneath the furniture, who can't see what's next. The one who is pulling has a completely different perspective and posture from the one who is pushing. Both have limitations and neither has the full weight or the big picture.

Often we can spend time trying to push our teams, family, circumstances around us into where we feel they need to go. Pushing requires a lot of pressure, taking on the often dead weight of a situation you are trying to move. Push means your vision is restricted as all you see is the obstacle, be that the circumstance or person that is in front of you. Push means you lean into the problem trying to convince it to move. I have spent too many hours trying to push the immovable or shove the reluctant.

I have found that pull is a much better way to lead your life, team, family. Pull moves you from behind the problem to being ahead of it. Pull means your thoughts and actions are more from your future than from what is stuck in the past. Pull is drawing you out, instead of forcing you forward. Pull says take my hand it's going to be great, where push says I will shove you there. Push tries to convince you. Pull compels you. Push is coming from being under pressure, pull is calling something higher.

I have been led in worship by those who push you to engage and challenge you by saying you need to worship deeper, more passionately. It feels like it is shoving rather than leading. The worship leader who comes from pull has already been where they want you to go, they have already set a table for the worship, therefore they are less forceful and more inviting. Equally I have been taught lessons by pushers but been inspired to climb by others pull. The end result of arriving in the destination may look the same but the way we get there is very different for both the teacher and the student. Today, check where your effort is being expended. What end of the furniture do you have? Are you using the right technique for the current situation, maybe it's not that the furniture is too heavy or won't fit, maybe it's that you are at the wrong side of the situation. Become one who learns when to push and when to pull and maybe more things will get moved with less damage all around.

THINK IT =============== **198**

SPEAK IT ================

BE IT ================

We find ourselves standing where we always hoped we might stand - out in the wide open spaces of God's grace and glory, standing tall and shouting our praise. Romans 5.1-2 (MSG)

Too often we can get caught in a prison that we allow to be built around us. A holding cell that confines our dreams and contains our thoughts. The walls we allow to be constructed are often made up of people's opinions, insecurities and judgments. Not wanting to upset the norm or step on anyone's toes, we choose the path of least resistance. We downsize dreams so as not to attract criticism and we live a life that fits in rather than risk standing out. I have found my playing small may appease some for a while, but it will never allow me to reach the ones God had placed outside those walls.

We need to regularly remember, we were made in the image of our amazing, vast and great God. He doesn't place you behind bars, but He puts you in wide open spaces. He is not restricted on how big or expansive your life can become, in fact He wants you to ask bigger, reach higher, He is the God of the impossible. Some people will always make themselves the planning permission department for your future but you have to stop submitting your plans to the wrong people and step into your freedom.

Trust God's voice over the many voices and opinions. Love how He loves and go for the great, because your great God is with you. Look for the wide open spaces and start to fill them with creativity and confidence. You can't help others be more secure by playing it small. You can however help many more by living a life that loves beyond those walls. So if you need to do some demolition, what are you waiting for? Liberate your life to start looking like God's design, a future that is flourishing, growing and fruit bearing.

Jacob was told all his life how to build. His mother constructed walls that isolated him from the rest of the family through her own vanity. Jacob eventually became so contained by these actions that he had to break away and leave home and in doing so found fields in which he could rebuild his own future. He worked hard for years demolishing his old life so he could build his new one. Jacob had to wrestle to find his own identity and he was renamed by God in his struggle. God invites us all into the same wrestle, to demolish the walls He never asked you to live within, the wrestle to find your voice, your source, perhaps even as Jacob did, your own limp.

Today, what walls do you need to start to see fall? There will never be a better day to begin so welcome the wrestle that will redefine your destiny and cause you to walk differently.

THINK IT ━━━━━━━━━━━ **200**

SPEAK IT ━━━━━━━━━

BE IT ━━━━━━━━━

EXHALE

DON'T

LET

YOUR

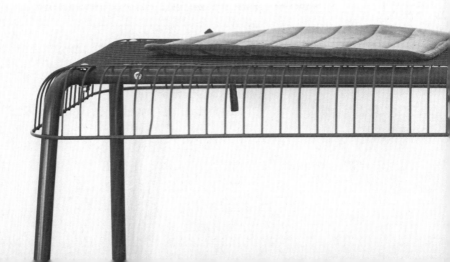

BURDENS

BUILD

BENCHES

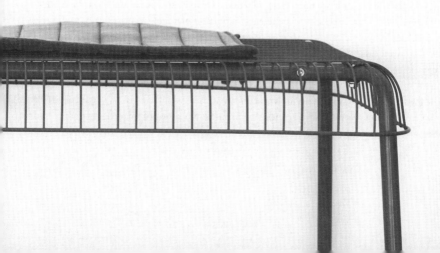

I appeal to you, brothers and sisters, in the name of our Lord Jesus Christ, that all of you agree with one another in what you say and that there be no divisions among you, but that you be perfectly united in mind and thought. 1 Corinthians 1:10 (NIV)

When was the last time you held someone's hand to let them know, I am here for you? When were you last shoulder to shoulder to help lift another's burden that would be too much for them to carry alone? Where are your prayers right now attached with focus and joined in faith with others to intercede for a miracle that may not benefit your world but will forever change theirs? When did you last use your words to add to someone else's world, bringing oxygen to their dreams? Where did you last walk a mile in someone else's shoes so you could help understand more of what they are going through?

God designed you and I to fit together, our journey is not one where we are to remain solitary but it is a journey of discovering the real power of unity. There is no greater joy than a victory won for each other, no sweeter sound than words that build and unite what the world would love to trouble and divide. God's best work is seen when His creation brings out the beauty in each other by uniting across every potential difference and divide. When Jonathan committed to serve David he did it at great risk to his own life. Jonathan was uniting his heart and soul with David. That commitment took Jonathan to battlegrounds that placed him in danger; he sacrificed his own authority to unite with God's priorities. Unity is not for the cautious or fearful, it's fierce. Unity is not a speech or a nice thought, it's a fight to die to self and remove all possible division. When God urges us to unite, it's a call to action and often an invitation for a lot of hard conversations.

We need to be the ones who fight more for unity. It won't just happen or appear; marriages are not just united by a ceremony but by people agreeing to the homework of uniting dreams and ideals, uniting purposes and values. Unity is the place where we surrender our selfishness and instead pick up a different language of togetherness. Unity is the refusal to go alone when we can go together. It's the persistence to win as a team instead of fight for the individual prize. Unity is not an automatic product of Christianity, we have to become more proactive in making it happen.

Today, where is the unity you are working to attain? What are you doing to unite more in your personal world and beyond? Are you known as a uniter or a divider? Set some goals for more unity because God said where we unite, there He commands His blessing.

THINK IT ━━━━━━━━━━━━━━━ 202

SPEAK IT ━━━━━━━━━━━━━━━

BE IT ━━━━━━━━━━━━━━━

EXHALE

A heart at peace gives life to the body, but envy rots the bones.
Proverbs 14:30 (NIV)

I remember some years ago, our friends brought their children over and as it was a nice day they had packed up several toys for the kids to play with outside. They played well and our friends' children gladly shared their new toys, which my kids seemed to take ownership of all afternoon. When our friends left however, rather than talking about what a great day they had, a monologue of grumbling began - it isn't fair they have those things, my scooter is rubbish compared to his, I wanted that toy, everyone has it apart from me. If you are a parent you will understand, unless your kids are more angelic than mine. What my kids didn't realise was that their behaviour was not convincing me of their need; I didn't want to buy them what they so desperately wanted because their asking came from a place of jealousy.

Spiritually, jealousy can cause us to resent another's blessing, as if God is not big enough to bless all of His kids! When our natural kids envy their friends' gifts rather than enjoying the moment with them, we as parents do not wish to feed a sense of entitlement where we should see contentment and enjoyment. Don't allow your jealousy of another's blessing to cancel out the delivery of your own. A jealous heart is like a return to sender memo. It says I am not ready to receive because I am too caught up in a place called resent. Let's not redirect our own deliveries because we cannot confront our inner enemies.

Sometimes we are strong for people in the struggle and stingy in their success. We can find it easier to be supportive when their circumstances seem harder, but what about when they are doing better or have better? Can we also be present then? If we restrict our support and celebration to those who have less, then we will never gain the joy and experience that comes from being around those who can teach us and encourage us from their more. God loves to bless all His kids but He also knows what's best for us; He grows and blesses our lives according to our faith and our own generosity.

We are all on a journey, but at times when your path intersects with another's blessing - throw a party for them! I did just that when I was told I couldn't conceive; instead of envying others pregnancies, which was the easiest and more tempting path to take, I decided to start throwing baby showers for everybody! It blessed the new mum, but the thing it blessed even more was my own soul because I was denying my flesh and feeding my faith. So take your jealousy to God. Saul lost everything because jealousy devoured his destiny. Repent, refocus and let's not allow jealousy to redirect any more deliveries.

THINK IT ━━━━━━━━━━━━━━━━━━━━ 204

SPEAK IT ━━━━━━━━━━━━━━━━━━━━

BE IT ━━━━━━━━━━━━━━━━━━━━

For all the promises of God in Him are Yes, and in Him Amen, to the glory of God through us. 2 Corinthians 1:20 (NKJV)

One of the first words most children seem to adopt is the word no. Maybe it's the ease in which it can be said or maybe it's the way it helps feed that stubborn toddler streak. Whatever the reason, no becomes a staple part of the child's limited vocabulary. Yes, however, seems to take a while longer to be adopted even though it's also just a short word. As we grow up, we all need to learn the value of a no and use it when necessary but what about if our top pick became yes.

Yes is a much more pleasant word to hear. Yes is welcoming and inclusive. Yes is willing. Finding our yes is an important addition to our vocabulary as we grow up. I have discovered that it's the simplicity of a yes that leads you into the most beautiful of places. Often we have no idea just how much our yes is about to achieve; helping, giving, serving, hosting, increasing and investing. The prophet Elijah told a woman to go and ask her neighbours for jars. Every neighbour who said yes to this widow added to her miracle. Each jar became the increase of God's provision.

It's the yes in our lives that becomes the 'so be it' in another's life. Think about the people whose yes has become your amen. The house helper, babysitter, gift giver. The wisdom sharer, encouraging note writer, perspective bringer. The prayer partner, food deliverer, way maker. People so often underestimate the power of a yes and so say it less frequently than maybe they should. Of course we all need to be careful we don't overburden ourselves to commit to more than we are able to fulfill; let grace and God's peace guide you with your yes. However I think I would rather edit my yes than live with the full stops of my no. Jesus says yes to all. Heaven is God's yes to human kind. Yes you are all included, yes you are all forgiven, His yes just needs our yes.

I want to remind you today to look for the places where your yes can become life to someone who is overwhelmed by too many who have said no. Mary and Joseph had a no from every innkeeper until there came a yes. The stable provider was the yes that allowed the 'so be it' of heaven to have a place to be delivered. What yes can you offer to allow possibility, provision and generosity to live? Someone right now may be praying for the miracle that your yes is the vehicle for. Don't withhold what God wants to unfold. Let your yes become someone else's amen.

THINK IT ━━━━━━━━━━━━━━ 206

SPEAK IT ━━━━━━━━━━━━━━━

BE IT ━━━━━━━━━━━━━━━

EXHALE

God is our refuge and strength, an ever-present help in trouble. Therefore we will not fear, though the earth give way and the mountains fall into the heart of the sea. Psalm 46:1-2 (NIV)

Think about this for a moment; God is on your side, He is working on your behalf. He is your very present help, right now He is with you. Our God is constant, in a world where all else is changing. This is an incredible truth and one which, if we hold on to, will change our perspective in so many ways.

Remember the story of Elisha in 2 Kings 6, surrounded by the enemy his servant was gripped with fear. All he could see was all those who were against him. Then Elisha prayed, Lord open his eyes. Suddenly his vision shifted as he saw the hills full of the Lord's army. Now instead of feeling outnumbered he was overwhelmed with God's faithfulness. Maybe you need one of those moments. A spiritual eye opening to see what you have missed because your focus is in the wrong place. God is on your side, which means some of the options you were considering need to be re-examined.

How would you now choose, act, plan differently if your eyes began to see God move clearly? God's provision and power consistently surrounds us. God doesn't have an agenda, He isn't going to move on once you have served your purpose. He is an unchanging God and therefore, He won't ever change His mind about you, you can't do anything to make Him turn away.

Today, are you placing too much importance on someone's opinion when God wants to renew your perspective? Have you allowed someone to hurt you and in doing so, have you forgotten the God who is for you? People can be unkind and often it can seem things are done that side swipe you for no real reason. But people are people, none of us are perfect and so in those times you have to remember, God is God. His decision to stay by your side has never altered. He is not leaving or forsaking any one of us. So where people are fickle, lean into God's faithfulness.

You don't need to over concern yourself with the side people may take at times when God is always on your side. Open your eyes and see.

THINK IT ━━━━━━━━━━━━━━━━ 208

SPEAK IT ━━━━━━━━━━━━━━━━

BE IT ━━━━━━━━━━━━━━━━

EXHALE

"The younger said to his father, 'Father, I want right now what's coming to me.' So the father divided the property between them. It wasn't long before the younger son packed his bags and left for a distant country." Luke 15:11-13 (MSG)

I used to work in the recruitment industry and I discovered something that has stuck with me for years. People who slammed doors, struggled to find open doors. People who caused a mess on the way out of one place, rarely found a new employer who wanted to invite them into their workplace.

We are often taught to make a good first impression, but what about our last impression? We often remember what people say as they leave, rather than when they first arrive. It's the dinner guest, friend, employee that leaves you well that you want to go on and help do well. The Bible is full of examples of this truth, in fact, God often sent those who exited poorly on a long detour to fix the mess before they could embrace the next miracle.

The prodigal left in haste and ended in a mess, but he re-entered in humility and found grace. David had to go back to the troops he left in anger over his son Absalom's death, so he could ensure they were with him for future success. Joseph's family would have to navigate reconciliation with the one they discarded in jealousy. Don't allow anger to be in charge of your exit if you want peace to be in the next entry way. Don't let unkindness speak on the way out or it may become the echo you hear on the next way in.

What mess needs to be addressed so the future can be embraced? Let the references from your past excite your future. Let what you left, call out with joy to what is to come, writing a reference that speaks of good endings and therefore encourages even greater beginnings. We need to look past the moment and remember with every exit, we are writing the resume for our future. As an employer, in a new team member I am not just looking for how well they did on the last job but the way they left the job. We may outgrow a place, a job, a relationship but that doesn't mean we discard it as if it never served a useful purpose. We need to be grateful for the place that it filled in our lives, even if the last period of time was testing. We need to try as hard as possible to let our last words be ones of blessing.

Remember the lessons the last season taught you and be thankful for the way they grew you. Don't slam the door you simply need to shut and don't walk out with an attitude if you want to enter the next season with gratitude.

THINK IT ━━━━━━━━━━━━━ 210

SPEAK IT ━━━━━━━━━━━━━

BE IT ━━━━━━━━━━━━━

EXHALE

But you need to stick it out, staying with God's plan so you'll be there for the promised completion. Hebrews 10:36 (MSG)

Have you ever watched a Formula One race? It's a series of very fast noisy cars going round in circles and occasionally pulling into a side lane to get a tyre change or refuel. This combination of doing laps and taking pit stops is not dissimilar from how we do life. One needs the other and vice a versa, they facilitate each other going the distance.

If you just take laps you will eventually burn out. If you stay too long in the pitstop you will lose momentum and find it too hard to rejoin the race. Our lives, ministry, family, careers involve learning to love the laps and not just living for the checkered flags. Loving the laps means understanding progress isn't always in the next thing, but a lot of times it's in doing the same thing in different seasons with the same passion. Building relationships, character, stability, something that will last, means alongside the new, we also have a lot of the same.

The ability to lap is a dying skill. Yet the benefit of lapping leads to a lot more checkered flags being attained. The apostle Paul took laps, he went back and forth teaching and establishing the early churches, correcting and often times repeating what still needed establishing. His laps led to foundations being laid on which the church continues to build.

All that back and forth means that laps are exhausting and so need the addition of pit stops, times when we come off the lap into a lane and get the time and investment we need to make sure we aren't running on empty or check to see if we need to make any changes. The energy, alignment, refuelling and sometimes change of drivers happens at the pit stop. You need the crew in your pit to be ready, prepared, able to add energy, bring change, efficient in their skill sets at pivotal moments. Pit stops are prepared and planned moments when the crew know what needs attention so we can sustain the laps we are assigned.

Celebrate the laps, not just the new and exciting, but applaud and support the faithful and familiar. Look after the pit crew, not just the visitors or spectators or star drivers. Where do you need to take another lap and where do you need to work on your pit stops and invest in more pit crew? Let's model a life that has longevity and speed, adventure and stature, checkered flags and well taken laps.

THINK IT ━━━━━━━━━━━━━━ 212

SPEAK IT ━━━━━━━━━━━━━━━━━

BE IT ━━━━━━━━━━━━━━━━━

EXHALE

I'm asking God for one thing, only one thing: to live with Him in His house my whole life long. I'll contemplate His beauty; I'll study at His feet. Psalm 24:4 (MSG)

Learning how to read the word of God is a skill we have to apply our hearts and minds to if we want to get all we can from the wisdom that lies within its pages. For some the Bible is daunting, for others it can be confusing but being in His word is something we can all grow in. No one wants to endure study; the Bible should be a place of life and adventure and so the way we read it matters. We all approach God's word differently. Some like to study with lots of books and concordances, others prefer to study with music and worship. There is no right or wrong way, you just have to find a way. We have often over complicated something that Jesus worked so hard to make simple. He taught in a way we could all understand and His messages were made so clear through stories and parables that from scholars to servants, they could take truth out of His teachings.

The Bible was written for you, within the pages He placed wisdom and truth just for you. So let's consider a few ways we can all get a little more out of our study.

1. Pray before you read. The Holy Spirit wants to guide you and read along with you. When we learnt to read, the books had only a few words each page to sound out; often the same words would repeat over and over because the goal of the book was not to tell you a story as much as it was to add to your vocabulary. The Holy Spirit is a great guide when it comes to reading the word. Invite Him into that space and don't rush on if He keeps holding you in one place.

2. Make notes. This whole devotional asks you to journal what you see and hear. That's because the more we put on paper what is being written on our hearts, the more potential it has to come alive. Writing down helps you clarify thoughts, so when you study, bring your paper and pen. Yes I am old school, somehow it's just not the same if it involves a keyboard but hey, each to their own.

3. Apply the word. When you read a story about giants, apply it to the giant you face. When you read about the Prince of Peace, look for the application in your everyday life. You may have deodorant in your cupboard but that's not going to keep you fresh unless it's applied. It's the same with the word of God. Slow down and take time for applying.

The word of God is living and active, we'll look at this more in the next devotional but for now, get your pen and paper out and invite the reading guide in.

THINK IT ━━━━━━━━━━━━ 214

SPEAK IT ━━━━━━━━━━━━

BE IT ━━━━━━━━━━━━

For the word of God is alive and active. Sharper than any double-edged sword, it penetrates even to dividing soul and spirit, joints and marrow; it judges the thoughts and attitudes of the heart. Hebrews 4:12 (NIV)

Let's look a little more at how we make God's word come alive in our lives. When the early church was seeing more and more new believers added, the Bible says that those who became followers in the faith 'devoted themselves', they made a choice to not rely on handouts but to find the truth for themselves. God's best plan for your life is that you too would devote yourself to the truth of His word, so here's a few more ways you can enhance your studies.

4. Know where to go. Perhaps you are reading the word over a year or you have a favourite few books of the Bible you like to read over and over. One of the ways I have found the word comes to life is by taking what's happening in my everyday world and then searching for where that's happening in God's word. That way, my life in the present is being shaped by those who have already journeyed it in the past. The wisdom they left becomes my lifeline now. So journal what is overwhelming you or where you need help; perhaps it's relational, maybe a financial call you need to make. Go to the Bible and look for those examples with intention. When we read not out of regime but out of necessity, that can make all the difference.

5. Don't quit. Sometimes we don't like to study the word because we feel we don't understand enough of what we read. Don't worry, we have all tried to move quickly through Leviticus. The Bible is truth in season, it comes alive alongside your life, so what you don't understand, write it down, put it to one side and come back to it at a later time. Whatever you do, don't get stuck. I have read passages that made no sense to me at one time and yet years later, they were exactly what I needed to hear. Revelation doesn't come all at once so keep going.

6. See and hear. When you study, listen for God's heart for you. Hear His compassion in the parables and hear David's love for God in the psalms. Listen for Job's frustration that he then tethers in faithfulness, hear how Jesus spoke to the disciples. You can only do that if you allow the word to consume you instead of just inform you.

So my friend, where is it time to fall back in love with His word? Be not just a hearer but a doer of the word. Don't take sound bites when God has written you a symphony of His love and wisdom. I pray this devotional will awaken what maybe has fallen asleep when it comes to the power of studying His word.

THINK IT ━━━━━━━━━━━━━ **216**

SPEAK IT ━━━━━━━━━━━━

BE IT ━━━━━━━━━━━━━━

EXHALE

There is a time for everything, and a season for every activity under the heavens. Ecclesiastes 3:1 (NIV)

Have you ever been to a large changing room where there are no private cubicles, it's just a free for all? For some this seems no problem at all, they walk around in their birthday suit without any apology for how that may make you feel. For others they try to find a corner that's out of sight to change as fast as possible without drawing attention to themselves. The communal changing room is not the easiest place to be. I often think when you do life with others, especially when you are in a local church, anytime you change it's a communal experience. I have been in the same church all my life and I know first hand that changing in front of people who have known you for years is very difficult; it's almost easier if it's strangers.

Every changing room has rules of conduct to limit your exposure and also to stop any bad behaviour. I think we need the same rules posting in the church and wherever we have to spiritually change in front of each other, so let's examine them.

Limit your changes
When you go to get changed, they will always limit how many things you can take in, they will have a maximum allowance of changes that can happen in one go. The reason for this is that they don't want you spending longer than necessary in a state of undress. We need to learn that changing shouldn't be a once in a lifetime experience, that's too much for one trip to the changing room. Changing is overwhelming if you are trying to change everything in one go, so it's better and easier for all concerned if we go and change more regularly. Change should be frequent not rare, you should go and change things when you know they are not a fit for you anymore and the more you go, the quicker the changes become.

No cameras
In changing rooms, especially at the gym, you'll see signs stating that no cameras are allowed, no photographs can be taken. They are protecting people from being exposed when they are in the middle of a change and we need the same rule for our life. We need to protect each other, not expose one another. When we repeat what was going on in a changing room to someone who wasn't in that space, we spread around images that should never have been taken. Let's stop taking photos of one another in the seasons when we are changing and allow each other the space to make the change.

Let's carry on looking at these rules in a couple of days. For now be encouraged, change happens to us all so let's all commit to make changing easier for all.

THINK IT ━━━━━━━━━━ 218

SPEAK IT ━━━━━━━━━━━

BE IT ━━━━━━━━━━━

There is a time for everything, and a season for every activity under the heavens. Ecclesiastes 3:1 (NIV)

So let's revisit the changing room; maybe you're mid-change right now or maybe you need to help someone make a change. Let's look at how we can learn to change in a way that keeps people intact rather than leaving them feeling exposed.

Accept assistance
Changing rooms have staff to help you. We all at times need assistance in our changing process; maybe we need advice on how to get something to fit or what to do next. We need to allow those who are good with change to speak into our change. Don't try and muddle through if there is help available, take it and make the change less painful. Jesus helped His disciples change, He didn't let them struggle when He knew He could intervene. Steve and I have asked for assistance sometimes when we have had to make big changes in either our marriage or ministry or just in managing our world. We have sought out the changing room assistance and you may need to do the same.

Time limit
Changing rooms are not a place where you live, they are a place you visit, so don't move in. Know that this is a point I need to pass through in order to get to where I need to be. Changing rooms have a lot of footfall because at any given time, we are all coming in and out of those doors. Maybe you are stuck in the changing room between where you were and where you need to be. The only way you exit is to make the decision that time is up, I have been here too long, I need to make a decision and get dressed in the attire that my next season requires.

Everyone is in the same boat
Always remember, if you are in the changing room than anyone else that's in the same space is there for the same reason, they are changing too. You are not alone and just as much as you may feel awkward, they probably feel awkward too. Changing rooms aren't easy for anyone but they happen to everyone. And for those who are in the changing room space but not changing, that's not ok. You are violating the reason that space is for. So let's not loiter in a place where people need to be left alone to make the changes. Your presence is not helping but hindering.

Maybe if we can be better about our changing room behaviour we can see transitions made simpler and people helped instead of exposed. Let's not avoid the changing rooms but rather become better at our use of them. So today, if you need to change go ahead, chances are I won't be far behind you.

THINK IT ━━━━━━━━━━━ **220**

SPEAK IT ━━━━━━━━━━━━━━━━━━━

BE IT ━━━━━━━━━━━━━━━━━━

EXHALE

We hear that some among you are idle and disruptive. They are not busy; they are busybodies. 2 Thessalonians 3:11 (NIV)

Have you ever heard the expression 'not my circus, not my monkeys'? When we allow someone else's drama to cast us in a leading role, we can feel we have been drafted as an extra into a circus of chaos. Instead of making for the exit we often try to contain it, when our best response would be to say: this is not my circus and these are not my monkeys.

Sometimes my children will tell me about one of their friend's teenage meltdowns, the drama they are in between them and a person who they have fallen out with. I can see how my kids feel a sense of obligation to get involved and try to bring resolution but more often than not I have to let them see that in this scenario, their words are just added background noise; they would only be wasting their time getting in the ring that was already overcrowded with other cast members.

We as adults can be guilty of the same problem. We are too easily drawn into drama and often when you get into someone else's circus you will become the clown of the act rather than the ringmaster. You don't have time to waste juggling what was never yours to juggle. Don't be fooled by the invitation to enter the stage show in people's lives if the show is not going to edify you or anyone else that happens to be ring side. Sometimes our ego likes to guide in these scenarios, flattered that your opinion has been asked for or your presence has been requested. Don't be flattered by the invitation to speak, if the speaking will only mean more confusion and complication. Check the reasons why you are responding.

Often the religious Pharisees would try to drag Jesus into the ring where they wanted to argue with Him over the way that He performed miracles. They would set up a show to discredit Jesus but He shut the circus of religiosity and legalism down. He refused to join the drama when He was called to be peace. If the circus comes to town, you need to remember that doesn't mean you have to attend, and you certainly don't need to perform or sell tickets for others to go. What you feed is what will gain strength, so if the drama is becoming larger than it should be, then we need to starve it of time and space. Maybe it will decide it can get a better audience elsewhere and not come to your town after all.

THINK IT ━━━━━━━━━━ **222**

SPEAK IT ━━━━━━━━━━━━━━

BE IT ━━━━━━━━━━━━━

When you tell God you'll do something, do it - now. God takes no pleasure in foolish gabble. Vow it, then do it. Ecclesiastes 5:4 (MSG)

When I was a student at university I used to hate it when assignments were set. There seemed to be these never ending projects that I had no idea how I would get completed on time. However, I knew that the assignments were not a suggestion, they were an expectation and if not completed, the grades would not be added. The assignment was a responsibility that I had to fulfill in order to graduate.

Like it or loathe it, you and I have assignments that we are responsible before God to complete. We have assignments to our home, our community and God's family. We have an assigned life, however often we fail to live assigned. We see some things that are ours to fulfil as more of a multiple choice or an optional addition. We need to comprehend that if we don't fulfill our assignment, then something is going to fail. If we have an assignment from our boss who is going to pay us a bonus, I wonder if our commitment would suddenly get a little clearer and we would work a lot harder.

When we said yes to following Jesus, He gave us assignments to be part of the body, to save His family, to reach the community. They weren't suggestions, they were assignments that came with a life that was handed over to Jesus. Ecclesiastes warns us to be careful what we vow before God because what we sow is what we have to fulfill. We can't get mad at God for the assignment we vowed to take. We can't pick and choose what assignment we will do, too many never graduate because they fail to complete what they are well able to achieve. The great commission is not called the great suggestion because it is not a good idea, it's an assignment that God set for all our lives and that includes you. He assigned you and I to go reach, to disciple, to be messengers of life. So how's the assignment going?

My assignments at university were not beyond me but they demanded a lot from me. They made me prioritise and focus my choice of activities. However, the assignments were part of what I signed up for; an incomplete assignment would possibly lead to a fail so that got my focus back. Maybe you just got distracted and needed a reminder of the assignment in front of you. Maybe you are asking God for a new assignment but He isn't responding until you complete the current one. Today, live assigned, don't back down, step up and get some more of the assignment done.

THINK IT ━━━━━━━━━━━━━━ **224**

SPEAK IT ━━━━━━━━━━━━━━━

BE IT ━━━━━━━━━━━━━━━

EXHALE

Praise the Lord, my soul and forget not all His benefits.
Psalm 103:4 (NIV)

There is a standing joke in our home that if you don't know what to do or where someone is, go to the fridge. Not because my family are constantly eating, although that would be a reason to try the fridge, but because that is the famous posting point for mum's list of things to know. With lots of activities and people coming and going, it seemed helpful to have a place where we could all go and see what was going on. The fridge has been for many years our orientation point. I chose the fridge because I knew that was the one place where everyone was bound to visit at least once a day.

I am a self confessed list lover. If I can put it on a list, it helps me somehow move it out of my mind and into a place of action. However, an over obsession with lists can also turn a home into a military posting point and take the fun and spontaneity out of the day because the list has already claimed every hour. So somewhere between list mania and listless living I would like to think is a good balance. But I have also learnt that those lists can all too often be all about the 'to dos' and less of the 'to bes'. We have to do the groceries, homework, practice, study but where on the list is we need to eat together, be together, have fun and take time out.

Maybe we need to have a new list that overwhelms all the others. A list that reminds us to never lose sight of the real priorities. Less doing stuff and more doing the stuff that matters. We will always have an endless list of jobs but we don't have a limitless amount of time. Time is restricted and therefore our priorities need to be constantly adjusted. What worked in one season may shift in the next; what was enough time before may be too little time now.

I don't want to run an orderly home at the expense of a happy home. I am not after some military efficiency, I want to leave room for the crazy and the messy but actually, the busier life gets, that's usually the first thing we lose or replace. So maybe you, like me, need to adjust some lists and think of new things that need adding. Time for yourself, a catch up with friends, watching a funny movie, going on an adventure.

We serve a God who is order and creator, who asks for discipline and for dreaming. I now often write love notes on my list too. I write things that make each reader smile, yep we still have a list but we run the list, the list doesn't run us and that makes all the difference in the world. Today, maybe you need to start some new lists.

THINK IT ━━━━━━━━━━━━━ **226**

SPEAK IT ━━━━━━━━━━━━━━━━━━

BE IT ━━━━━━━━━━━━━━━━━━━

Your very lives are a letter that anyone can read by just looking at you. Christ Himself wrote it - not with ink, but with God's living Spirit; not chiseled into stone, but carved into human lives - and we publish it. 2 Corinthians 3:1-3 (MSG)

We are all writing some kind of script for our lives everyday. Each decision sets us up for the next conversation or commitment. Everytime we engage our thoughts and give them permission to make choices or mould conversations, we are adding to the script of our lives. I think if our job was one of a screenwriter, we would take this concept much more seriously and think much harder about the lines we were wanting others to learn or listen to. In our everyday lives we are unconsciously allowing many things to write our script. We give the editorial privilege to stress or worries and that scripts our lives into directions and decisions that if we had edited more carefully, would never have been allowed to have a say.

So today, take some time and think about how and who gets to dominate your script. Did you give your offences the pen yesterday? Maybe you liberated the resentment you held to script hours of your thoughts and therefore your words. Maybe you let someone's inconsiderate nature direct your next few conversations and then you used hours going over how they had wasted your time, instead of making the best use of the time remaining. When Adam and Eve were in the garden, the enemy came to change the script. He suggested lies to Eve that she then passed on to Adam. The script of humankind was forever altered because where they should have taken a hold of the pen, they let sin speak. Don't give the enemy that power, cut off the conversation before it goes to print. You can edit your script.

I often notice my script gets hijacked at times when I feel emotionally overloaded. In a normal, more steady headspace, I would have more editorial control but we all have those areas where we know our hearts are more sensitive and therefore our decisions can be less well scripted. For me, I know when I am going away to minister, the script of my life can quickly turn negative if I don't get proactive. Guilt will tell me I shouldn't leave my kids, then I will feel like I am failing as a wife. No one in my family has ever said anything to make me write my script that way but the enemy knows exactly where you and I are most vulnerable.

Perhaps it's time to go back to your script and make sure you like what you read and if not, you have the power to make the edits.

THINK IT ━━━━━━━━━━━━━━━━ 228

SPEAK IT ━━━━━━━━━━━━━━━━

BE IT ━━━━━━━━━━━━━━━━

EXHALE

Cultivate these things. Immerse yourself in them. The people will all see you mature right before their eyes! Keep a firm grasp on both your character and your teaching. Don't be diverted. Just keep at it. 1 Timothy 4:15-16 (MSG)

For something new to emerge we need to be willing to immerse. Often we try new ideas. We launch projects and make plans, yet before we emerge we need to take time to be those who have immersed themselves. To be immersed means to plunge yourself under, to throw yourself deeply into, to be covered completely. At times we are so focused on our emerging idea that we have missed a step. Our word or plan can feel dry because we didn't soak in it first.

When we immerse in God's love, word, grace, wisdom, how we emerge changes. A person who is immersed will always emerge with greater understanding, you won't just hear where they are going but you can see it. Immersed leaders don't drag you along, they help you dive in. They are not dripping with stress but are overflowing with life. Immersed people are presence people, you know when they enter a room and you can hear them above the crowd when they speak.

When you walk through life, what kind of footprints do you leave? Is what's on you flowing through you so that people can see its mark even before they hear its voice? Are you spiritually dry because you have lost that place where you are immersed in devotion and instead are simply going through the motions? Immersion is the oil and lubrication to our lives, it's the place where anointing meets effort and presence overwhelms our best practice. The people knew when Moses had been with God. His whole appearance changed as God's power covered his life. Do people say the same about our lives?

A few years ago my husband and I went to the Great Barrier Reef. I was so excited to see this beautiful place that I had admired on many TV shows; I wanted to see the incredible coral and fish. However when I got there, I realised the only way I would see all these things was to go way down deep in the water. My fear was suddenly an obstacle to my dream. The guide explained you can see some things on the top layers but if you want the real experience, you have to go deeper and get fully immersed. The same is true spiritually; you can see His grace or know it; feel His love or live from its overflow.

Let your words and your thoughts be immersed, identify the areas that are dry and go deeper. Where you are stressing, allow God to saturate. Get your worry under the water. Go deeper today so you can build from a place where you have been immersed in something greater.

THINK IT ━━━━━━━━━━━ **230**

SPEAK IT ━━━━━━━━━━━━━━━━

BE IT ━━━━━━━━━━━━━━━━

Enlarge the place of your tent, stretch your tent curtains wide, do not hold back; lengthen your cords, strengthen your stakes. Isaiah 54:2 (NIV)

Recently, I felt God speak strongly to my heart from Isaiah 54, to get ready for a season of enlargement. While I was excited about the thought of what that could look like, I was instantly sobered and aware of the commitment and work that would also bring. Enlargement requires our engagement. It calls for a willingness to work and a humility to serve and surrender.

Maybe this recent experience I had can help add another layer of understanding for those who are saying 'enlarge me, Lord'. I recently ordered a lot of very pretty furniture online. It didn't arrive as I saw it on the internet. It wasn't pretty at all when it was delivered to my door. It looked like a big pile of boxes. The enlargement of each item would require engagement: opening the box, reading the instructions (a step most want to miss by the way), building each section, rebuilding the parts I built incorrectly the first time due to haste. What seemed a good idea and a cheaper way to get the furniture turned out to be time consuming, frustrating and costly. I had failed to budget into this plan the patience to build what I had ordered and the tools that I would need. Enlargement isn't cheap; there is no shortcut, if you try and cut corners it will cost you more in the long run.

Enlargement calls for personal commitment and willingness to go back to school to gain the skills that the expansion will demand. I used to pray often, enlarge me, now I pray more carefully for the increase that I know will first ask for me to increase. So, as I felt God speak this to my spirit, I found myself whispering back 'I get it, God, I'll go get my tool kit'. Let's pray for the things we are willing to build, so that every box delivered gets unpacked and finds its full potential.

Today, think about the new things you want to see happen. Articulate the dream you want to build, then start to get the inventory ready of what that may require. Get ahead of the demand by working on the supply. Pray more, read more, change quicker, remove the things that could hinder. After our delivery of what felt like a thousand boxes, my husband said, that's it, no more, if you order it then you are building it. Sometimes we need to say that to ourselves and to one another too. It's ok to help people build but doing it for them is not the idea.

I pray your season of enlargement finds a heart that is ready for all the expansion and engagement it will require. Yes, I'm preaching to myself, but hopefully helping someone else on the journey too.

SPEAK IT ━━━━━━━━━━━━━━━

BE IT ━━━━━━━━━━━━━━━

The wise woman builds her house, but with her own hands the foolish one tears hers down. Proverbs 14:1 (NIV)

If I was to listen in on your conversations this week, would I learn more about your struggle than your strength? Would I walk away with more awareness of your problem or your provision? One of the hardest things about being a writer is the dreaded word count, trying to fit your thoughts into a limited allowance on a page but the process soon teaches you how to be more selective and actually become a better communicator. We need to adopt this same exercise in our own lives on a regular basis.

We all have a part of us that wants to analyse our circumstances, breakdown the relationships, dissect the problems, assess where things began to go wrong or finally went right. Yet if we are not careful we will over analyse the issue and under value the resolution. We will over discuss the problem leaving no air space for the provision to be heard. Proverbs 14 says 'the wise woman builds her house, but with her own hands the foolish one tears hers down.' Maybe it's time to stop tearing things apart and instead start building things up.

Don't live with a spirit that seeks to critique each scenario; it's not ultimately helpful or enjoyable. In Mark 5, a servant from Jarius' household came to tell him to stop bothering Jesus because his daughter was dead. Jesus took a hold of the situation and spoke straight to Jarius and told him not to fear, just to believe. Then He said, your child is asleep. Jesus renames the situation from death to sleeping. Those who had seen the girl's condition gave the verdict, but Jesus instead wrote His own ending, one filled with possibility. When we are more aware of the bad than the good, then we have to try and convert every negative into a positive. If you choose to start by seeing the best, it is not long until you find a strength and sense of momentum from which to deal with problems.

Today, take a moment, breathe in the air, see the horizon, be thankful. Be in awe of your Father God. See the beauty even in the chaos and allow a little more wonder instead of analysis to shape your situation. Don't miss what you have now because you're overthinking what may or may not happen later. Use your words wisely and edit out what ultimately won't edify your soul. Build up instead of tearing down and you may find you make more progress than you thought was possible.

THINK IT ━━━━━━━━━━ 234

SPEAK IT ━━━━━━━━━━━━━

BE IT ━━━━━━━━━━━━━━

EXHALE

Walk with the wise and become wise, for a companion of fools suffers harm.
Proverbs 13:20 (NIV)

We often are too casual about things that are essential, while being over focused on things that are inconsequential. I have always believed friendships are some of the most important decisions you can make.

We are called to love all and embrace the many but within that we must choose a few to take the hand of and travel with on this life journey. If you are a parent you will know only too well how important this becomes as your children begin school and start to make friends. You pray they make good choices, you guide them gently away from the bad influences. If we understand this with our children, why do we often seem to misunderstand or neglect this as adults? We can give less time to being deliberate in our company as we grow older, we get stuck in the familiar and lose the energy to address relationships that are well overdue for some changes.

Friendship is a partnership and however casual or serious you make that commitment, it still involves a point of connection and a level of attachment. I have lots of friends, in fact they are my favourite thing to collect. Friends make life the best adventure. However, I have also learnt that not all friendships fill the same space in our lives. Some are fun to be with but others are fundamental to your journey; some visit our lives, some are permanent residents. Discerning the level of input and entrustment we give to our friends takes time, however it is always good to make sure you are heading in the same direction.

In Amos 3:3 it says, 'do two join hands unless they have first agreed where they are going?' The hand you hold is also determining the path you walk. Therefore do you need to check some of these decisions? Maybe more conversations should be had before we take just anybody's hand. We can't complain that we don't like where we have ended up if we took the hands of people whose destination had always been set to arrive there. Sometimes we can think we can convince others to change where they are heading part way into the journey but that discussion has to happen before we take hold of their hand. It's better to be clear at the start than have to try and navigate these conversations when the journey is well under way.

If you want to go to where wisdom lives, walk with the wise. This same principle works with the foolish too. So ask today, do I like where I am heading? Then look at the hands that you are holding.

THINK IT ━━━━━━━━━━━━━ 236

SPEAK IT ━━━━━━━━━━━━━

BE IT ━━━━━━━━━━━━━

"My son, do not make light of the Lord's discipline, and do not lose heart when He rebukes you, because the Lord disciplines the one He loves, and He chastens everyone He accepts as His son." Hebrews 12:6 (NIV)

If you have ever tried to bring discipline to a naughty child you may have adopted a few supernanny techniques. When all else has failed, you may opt for the time out corner. You send the emotionally spent child to sit and reflect on their behaviour; the severity of the crime will determine the longevity of the time out. Maybe we all need some time out corner moments. Maybe we have grown older but there are definitely times when we really need to grow up.

I often put myself in the time out corner. I have learnt that actually it's the best gift I can at times give myself and others. If I will go into time out, I can stop things being said that don't need to be heard and even save myself from embarrassment that didn't need to be witnessed. When Jonah was holding a pity party, he went off to sulk, he went to a time out corner, but instead of the time out making him reflect, he just sat resenting. So God sent a worm to eat the vine he was shading under because He wanted Jonah's time out to bring repentance not resentment. Our time outs need not to just be about our calming down but about growing up. When my perspective has been lost because of something I feel that has been handled wrongly, then it's time for my time out. When my frustration has the microphone, when my weariness is expressing itself through grumpiness, it's time for a time out.

Just as the child may have to be dragged to the time out corner, you may at times have to drag yourself. Though you won't get any thanks from the child that you place there, you will be thankful later that the time out created a space to redirect some misdirected energy. You will thank yourself later that you called time out before you acted out. You don't need to vent in public what should be dealt with in private. Don't use God to justify what's not coming from a God-centered place. Let's be wise when we are weary and rest instead of responding. Let's listen to our true narrative before we post a fake one. Time outs are not just for kids, they are actually a good idea for all of us. Time to reflect, pause, check ourselves.

Why not build your own personal time out corner, no one needs to know it's there, it's between you and God. You can set the time of how long you sit there, you may come to find that actually you want to linger there longer because often God does some of His best work in us when we volunteer a time out with Him.

THINK IT ━━━━━━━━━━

SPEAK IT ━━━━━━━━━━━━━━━━━━━

BE IT ━━━━━━━━━━━━━━━━━━━

EXHALE

Be still before the Lord and wait patiently for Him.
Psalm 37:7 (NIV)

Why is the pause button often one of the hardest things to use when it comes to our words? Why do we forget that we can at any time just wait and take a breath? It's like we can get caught up in a conversation or expressing an opinion and we forget the pause button is our friend. The Bible says even the fool seems wise when they don't say anything and at times we can allow the fool to appear smarter than us because we can't stop talking. Often we say more than we should, we get in too deep with our words, commit too quickly, over react or respond prematurely. It's not always easy to pause, especially when we may feel passionate. Often we just want to say what we feel needs saying without taking a moment to think about it.

I am a great believer in sharing your story, being someone open to conversations. It is healthy to communicate and connect with others and voicing concerns or questions is a part of the growth journey. But what keeps us healthy and our conversations wholesome is knowing how to press pause when what comes next is more detrimental than beneficial. Today, examine your ability to pause, have you discovered how to hold information as well as share it?

Here's a little tip that keeps what we say more healthy than hurtful and more hopeful than doubtful. The best pause you can insert is to take it to God first. A gap that makes you aware of His presence, which will then have a filter effect on what you say next. Remember Job and his comforting friends? Turned out they were not so good at the comforting. They all needed a pause button. Each one added their own opinions. They tried to judge why Job was being judged. They made assumptions that were so far removed from the actual truth. However, Job in his frustration kept a God filter. In his plan he allowed a pause that kept his heart pure even in his hardest moments. Job's pause led to his provision and so can yours.

The pause of taking it to God first doesn't have to delay you forever but maybe it can help your life read better. God is always available, He's a great listener, He doesn't get upset when you're upset. He will never add fuel to a fire that needs putting out. He may not even reply to your question or your concern but time just talking with Him will always alter your tone and often diffuse your dilemma. Pause is a great button for our conversations and confessions. So create some God gaps, you may find if you pause long enough, He will give you something better to say anyway.

THINK IT ━━━━━━━━━━━━━━ **240**

SPEAK IT ━━━━━━━━━━━━━━━

BE IT ━━━━━━━━━━━━━━━

EXHALE

BECOME

SOMEONE'S

AMEN

Peter replied, "Even if all fall away on account of you, I never will."
Matthew 26:33 (NIV)

Why is it so hard sometimes to actually say what we mean? We have all been in the scenario when someone asks, how are you, and what you mean to reply is, not well, but we say, I'm fine. Someone asks, do you need some help, and we say, no, but what we should say is, yes. We often don't say what we mean because we are too aware of what we perceive people want us to say. We filter our answer until it is well and truly diluted. Of course we all have times when we need to think before we speak but overthinking leads to not saying what needs to be said. If you say you are fine when you are actually not enough times, then you begin to convince yourself of that story and live in a way that doesn't help you with your present reality.

Remember when Jesus told Peter he would deny Him? He pre-warned him this is what's going to happen, you are going to deny Me three times. Peter couldn't accept what he was hearing because he knew in his heart he would never betray Jesus in this way. Yet under pressure and in circumstances that disorientated him, Peter found himself saying something that he didn't mean. His denial was not how his heart felt towards Jesus, whom he loved deeply, but under pressure he said what he felt would make his life easier. Jesus later restored Peter by asking him three times if he loved Him and Peter answered each time with deep conviction, he said what he meant over and over. Jesus knew Peter was going to say something he didn't mean and He knew that he needed the opportunity to say what he really meant.

Where do you need to do the same? Where do you need to hear yourself say what you really mean and mean what you say. Where do you need to be more honest about where you are at instead of saying you are somewhere you have never been. God knows what we really mean even when we don't say it, we shouldn't try to hide from God what He is more than able to handle. Maybe the first place to say what you mean is to yourself. We can so often fake our feelings but maybe it's time to face them. Sometimes you need to say I'm not ok, or ask someone for help. At times you may need to say, I can't do that as I need some time for myself or maybe you need to say yes to the opportunity because your no was simply to keep someone's insecurity appeased. Proverbs 24:26 says an honest answer is like a kiss on the lips. Maybe you need to kiss your life with some honesty and have a better day because you mean what you say.

THINK IT ━━━━━━━━━━━━━━ 242

SPEAK IT ━━━━━━━━━━━━━━

BE IT ━━━━━━━━━━━━━━

EXHALE

"The master was furious. 'That's a terrible way to live! It's criminal to live cautiously like that! If you knew I was after the best, why did you do less than the least? The least you could have done would have been to invest the sum with the bankers, where at least I would have gotten a little interest.'" Matthew 25:26-27 (MSG)

You are full of untapped potential right now. You may not believe it, but that doesn't mean it's not true. You have seeds of potential within you, they were placed there by your Heavenly Father; the potential for new ideas, new skills and talents, new initiatives and new areas of growth. That potential is in you but in order to truly be awakened, it needs its travelling partner and that is called purpose. Purpose is the activating agent, it ignites the fuse that moves a seed of possibility into a reality.

Think of it this way: a lightbulb has great potential to illuminate places, it can change the entire atmosphere and ambience of a space. However, though the lightbulb has that amazing potential, none of it can be realised unless it's placed in the setting for which it was designed. It needs a lamp to fit into, otherwise the bulb is just a piece of glass. Without being used for the purpose it was designed, it offers no light and is fragile.

Where have you got some attaching to do, what potential needs to find a purpose? Maybe you have untapped potential to teach or care for others, maybe it's time to serve in an area that can awaken it. Start volunteering in kids or youth ministry, start a Bible study; we can sit around all day talking about our potential but we need to identify how we can shine. Don't be a potential light source, be purposeful. Plug your gifts and talents into a place where you can illuminate the darkness. If you're a floating Christian try planting this year, it will help you unlock something that disconnection will never trigger. If you're between jobs, find a company to attach yourself to and allow the setting to help you shine and increase your capacity. If you're uncommitted relationally, take the next step and find people you can do life with.

Don't leave your potential in a place of vulnerability this year, fragile to the elements and changing circumstances. Why not bring your potential wattage into a setting that will harness your power and then use it for a much bigger purpose? Don't allow yourself to be distant, instead determine to make some more purposeful connections. Remember the parable of the servants who were given bags of money to invest; the one who buried the potential in the ground was reprimanded by the master. The money wasn't given to be hidden, it was entrusted so it could be expanded. Your potential needs to go to work, so stop burying and start shining.

THINK IT ━━━━━━━━━━━━━ 244

SPEAK IT ━━━━━━━━━━━━━

BE IT ━━━━━━━━━━━━━

EXHALE

"Well done, my good servant!' his master replied. 'Because you have been trustworthy in a very small matter, take charge of ten cities." Luke 19:17 (NIV)

Offence, hurt, misunderstanding, they happen to us all but they can actually be used to grow and improve each one of us in our call. Often, what began as a small problem is quickly escalated by unchecked emotions. Yet I have found the times I have grown the most have frequently been in the hardest of places where I have had to choose faithfulness over feelings, committing to let my anchor not my anger direct me. You see faithfulness is easy in the good times but it often becomes the ground the enemy is most after in the hard times. He loves to divide what you have worked so hard to unite, knocking down what faithfulness and longevity has laboured to leave. However some of the best growth and greatest breakthroughs happen when we place faithfulness over feelings.

Faithfulness is a key ingredient to growth. It's the ability to remain faithful that increases capacity. Think about Mary, just a young girl who was asked to carry this most incredible baby out of wedlock, a virgin birth. The questions, the emotions, yet she said yes. That yes led her to be faithful to carry what would literally increase her capacity. She was a faithful servant who became a faithful mother who was in faithful surrender at the cross when feelings would have called it all loss.

Faithfulness is not a fashionable word in today's culture but it is the secret ingredient to taking something from good to great. It's faithfulness in the marriage that builds far more than feelings ever will; it's faithfulness as a family that keeps you stronger than anything else can and its faithfulness in your walk with God that will lead you deeper into all He has for you. Faithfulness may not seem exciting but its rewards are outstanding. Where can you put more focus today on faithfulness and less on feelings? Where do you need to revisit vows you have made to help redress feelings that maybe have had things too much their own way?

Where would we be without the faithfulness of God? It has held us when we have let go, His faithfulness has been good to us on the worst of days and surrounded us in the hardest of places. His faithfulness has lasted a thousand generations and we are now the recipients of that great faithfulness so let us also be those who pass along what we have so freely received. If you are going to be known for something, faithfulness is a great place to start, so today, where can you work a little more on being faithful?

THINK IT ━━━━━━━━━━━━━ **246**

SPEAK IT ━━━━━━━━━━━━━

BE IT ━━━━━━━━━━━━━

EXHALE

**And Abraham said to God, "If only Ishmael might live under your blessing!"
Genesis 17:18 (NIV)**

We have all been guilty of it, trying to make things happen in our own strength. Maybe you thought you would get the position and you didn't so you repositioned yourself. Maybe God told you to wait for the right connection but you went ahead and forced something different. You would think by now we would be wiser but we all still have those moments when we feel somehow God's timing is off. We wonder if He has got distracted by other more pressing issues. We reason that we are helping Him not hindering Him and so we go ahead and make things happen in our own efforts, rather than resting and trusting in God's ways.

Ishmael is used time and time again as an example of how when we don't wait we produce something that is not God's best for our lives. We all have Ishmaels that we have forced into existence. We created a replacement for what God had said was going to happen as we felt it may never happen. Too many times I've seen Ishmaels be produced but then worse than that, Ishmaels be abused; embarrassed by what impatience created we try and distance ourselves from the mistake. But Ishmael was not at fault, it was Abram, Sarai and Hagar that had made poor choices and Ishmael was now inheriting the consequences.

Ishmael did nothing wrong. When he was born he wasn't trying to take someone else's place, he was the innocent result of impatience. When Hagar cried out to God about the baby she was now carrying, God gave Ishmael his name. He didn't name him mistake or accident, He did not identify him with the set of circumstances that led to his birth but He called him a name that means God hears. God knew this child would be overlooked and in many cases ignored and so He wanted the child not to be labelled in a way that he didn't deserve.

If it isn't bad enough making Ishmaels happen, what's worse is the way we treat them. What we insisted we needed, we now treat with disdain and embarrassment. When we project our guilt onto the guiltless, when we disapprove of Ishmaels instead of confronting our own shortcomings, we are failing all over again. In Genesis 17 when God renames Abraham, it's then that he finally speaks up for his son and asks God to bless the mistake he made. God says not only will I bless him but I will make him greatly increase and be fruitful. God wasn't going to discard Ishmael and as Abraham heard those words he too adopted his son back into his household.

Where are you treating an Ishmael poorly? Maybe there needs to be a change of heart so that you can help restart not just your future but the Ishmaels too.

THINK IT ━━━━━━━━━━━━━━━

SPEAK IT ━━━━━━━━━━━━━━━

BE IT ━━━━━━━━━━━━━━━

EXHALE

Greater love has no one than this: to lay down one's life for one's friends.
John 15:13 (NIV)

The lyrics 'I found my life when I laid it down' are from one of my favourite worship songs and they are a truth I have read and heard taught many times. They are so liberating and yet at first glance they can seem more containing than empowering. It is suggesting what you want needs to die in order for what you really need to live. It is asking for a sense of surrender in the way we determine what we are going to serve. God's word is a constant challenge to not just sing these words but live them. Where the world would say go and get what you can for your life, God's way is the exact opposite and says to find your life, give it away. That means we have to consistently analyse if we are living life the world's way or God's way.

If we allow this to become the standard for our decisions and the guide for our goals, then it will not only transform our world but it will renew and revive our entire perspective and purpose. Jesus came and laid down His life as the greatest demonstration of love and in so doing gave us the ultimate example of how to truly live. Why? Because what we lay down doesn't own us, where we let go and release control we are able to embrace change and growth. Lose your ambition inside His compassion, let your desires be overwhelmed by delighting in Him.

This may seem a big ask but I have found when you allow this to become a daily guide, it starts to help you discern the difference between the life you are driving, even forcing and the life that you are sharing and finding a flow in. I remember experiencing this so clearly when I was a student, I had so many decisions to make from what to major in, where to work, what time I had to give to the church. I remember in all those decisions having to find that place of surrender and check in with myself as to what was the main force behind the choice. I began to find great comfort and strength in being able to filter the many choices through this God given principle: Lord, I lay down my life so I can discover real life.

Today, as you go about your day, position your life in a way that allows things to be laid down that may have taken up the wrong space. Be bold and allow God to show you how to find more life through the beauty of surrender. Let's not just speak or sing words, let's everyday take another step towards living and embracing the power these truths hold. Find your life not through what you win, but what you are willing to lose.

THINK IT ━━━━━━━━━━━ **250**

SPEAK IT ━━━━━━━━━━━

BE IT ━━━━━━━━━━━

EXHALE

The Lord is gracious and compassionate, slow to anger and rich in love.
Psalm 145:8 (NIV)

Have you ever received a gift that was so beautifully wrapped it told a story of its own - this gift was given with love and care. Recently I was in a store where they offered gift wrapping; the line was full mainly, I have to say, of men but they seemed to feel they needed this service. I am sure they could have wrapped the gift themselves if they wanted, they had just been selective in not learning that skill. If there's one thing we do need to learn, it's how to gift wrap things God's way

Thoughtfulness is God's gift wrap, He doesn't just do things, He wraps things. He gives with love and compassion. He doesn't just meet a need, He gift wraps that answer in a personal way. Maybe some of us just need to practice thoughtfulness a little more in our everyday. It makes a huge difference. Jesus wrapped his message in a parable that would help as many as possible. He would at times not just teach the crowds but also feed them. Thoughtfulness doesn't just do the task, it gift wraps it, making a moment into an experience.

Before you speak or act, take some time and think on some good things. One of my favourite things to do is lay the table and have people we love around for dinner. I am not a great cook but I can set a beautiful table. I have found that the time invested into place settings, flowers and candles changes the simplest of food into the most special of dinners. The thoughtfulness creates an environment where weary souls come and unpack their daily cares, where laughter echoes in the conversations that happen as candlelight flickers; hours pass by and that gift wrapped space becomes something we all get to enjoy. Parenting is better with gift wrapping, it says I see you and I thought of you. A few years back I started the routine of setting up the breakfast bar with a note written to the kids telling them how great they are, alongside the cereals and juice. It isn't any special breakfast but they leave knowing they are special every morning.

Thoughtfulness adds warmth and depth to your world, it makes a message carry more meaning and takes your everyday and wraps it in a way that captures the best, even in the worst times. Thoughtfulness may not be a popular trait but I think we would all benefit from adding more of it to our lives. Today, apply thoughtfulness to your busyness. Gift wrap your world, the good news is it doesn't involve paper and sticky tape, just time and a little extra love and we can all do that.

THINK IT ━━━━━━━━━━━━ **252**

SPEAK IT ━━━━━━━━━━━━━━━━━━━

BE IT ━━━━━━━━━━━━━━━━━━━

EXHALE

"You do not want to leave too, do you?" Jesus asked the Twelve. Simon Peter answered Him, "Lord, to whom shall we go? You have the words of eternal life. We have come to believe and to know that You are the Holy One of God." John 6:67-69 (NIV)

I have never been known for my handy work. I don't know how to use a tool kit and I am not any better with a needle and thread. I do know if you are going to try and stitch something up then you need to make sure you tie up the loose end, otherwise your work will quickly unravel. I learnt this when I attempted to darn a sock; one wear later and the hole was back, bigger than ever. We have loose ends in life and just like my thread, they can create problems if they are left to unravel.

Have you ever felt you keep having the same conversation about the same problem? You feel year after year the same hole appears that you thought had been fixed, you see things unravel that were supposed to be sorted, that's a sign that some loose ends have been left. Today, maybe it's time to trace where your loose ends are so you don't keep repeating things that should be finished with. Ask yourself, what do I need to do to seal this up so that I don't keep coming back to this spot? We need to grab hold of any thinking that is unloosening what God wants gathering. In John 6, when a lot of followers had left Jesus, He turned and asked the twelve, do you want to go too? Jesus was checking for loose ends. He had no intention of dragging the reluctant or undecided.

Loose ends need to be addressed in life. The unspoken situation needs to be dealt with, the awkward silence needs to be ended, the unforgiveness needs to be cleared up, the guilt needs to be resolved. Sometimes the only way you can tie up that loose end is by closing a door instead of leaving it open, it's saying no instead of maybe. It's saying yes instead of I'll think about it. Tying up loose ends is far more definite and deliberate than at times we want it to be, however life is too short to keep darning the same sock so some different decisions need to be made.

See this as a gift to yourself. Though we can't resolve every situation, we can decide for our future some things we are not going to keep revisiting. Put more focus on some things that need ending in order to propel you into some new beginnings. Be brave and write a few things down that need the loose ends sorting. Then begin to think of what would make that situation one that stops repeating, what you could do to make sure that you don't have to redo this over and over again.

THINK IT ━━━━━━━━━━━ **254**

SPEAK IT ━━━━━━━━━━━

BE IT ━━━━━━━━━━━

EXHALE

Then I will go to the altar of God, to God, my joy and my delight. I will praise You with the lyre, O God, my God. Psalm 43:4 (NIV)

Altar is a word we don't use much. It can conjure up an image of a sterile place where you go and confess your sins or where you stand for a ceremony. Yet to come to the altar is a beautiful thing. We all need to know that we can come to a place of divine exchange. We are all invited to the altar of surrender and the more we journey there, the more we leave what is not ours to carry and gain what only God can bestow upon us.

In the last few years, I have fallen more in love with these moments when there has been people flood to the altar. I have become more and more convinced it is an invitation we must never stop extending. I have heard some say altar calls are hype or an emotional moment that doesn't last. Here's what I see each time I have the privilege of praying with those who have come forward in one of those moments. That walk from the chair to the front was for many not easy, even uncomfortable, exposing at times. Their mind may have tried to talk them out of it, yet the heart nudged them, go ahead, walk to freedom. Instead of staying hurt and hidden, the heart longed to come closer and lean into a moment that would mark a milestone on the journey.

I think when our altars are full, our aisles should be filled with praying believers cheering on every brave responder. One day maybe your sister, brother, child, friend, even you, will be in that moment, so pray over those you don't know seeds of faith for the day it's someone you do know. No, it doesn't fix everything, yes, there is a whole walk of obedience and healing to follow. But someone took a step, a step away from what was and towards what can be, surely that's worth celebrating.

So today, I am wondering, do you need to come to the altar? Maybe this week you will walk something out in a church service somewhere, but you can come now, right where you are and kneel before Him and ask for an altar of exchange. It says in Isaiah 61 He wants to give you beauty for ashes, the oil of joy instead of mourning, a garment of praise instead of a spirit of despair. There is an altar of exchange and it awaits your transaction. Create a place in your busy life that becomes a sacred space for you and God to make a divine exchange. Don't stay as you are when you can come right now to the altar, as the song lyrics so beautifully say: 'oh come to the altar, the Father's arms are open wide'. Let's never lose the wonder in every surrender.

THINK IT ━━━━━━━━━━━━━ **256**

SPEAK IT ━━━━━━━━━━━━━━

BE IT ━━━━━━━━━━━━━━

EXHALE

You also, like living stones, are being built into a spiritual house to be a holy priesthood, offering spiritual sacrifices acceptable to God through Jesus Christ. 1 Peter 2:5 (NIV)

Just one of the many reasons why you will find me and my family in church this weekend is because I know that being in the family of God is not just a good idea, it's God's very best plan for your life and mine. My family is better because of God's family and for me that's something I am committed to keep outworking.

I don't go to church because I have to, though I guess technically it would be strange if the pastor stopped showing up. That aside, I have all my life been convicted in my commitment to the church. She is not perfect, the church is a family with many things still to work out and sort out but it's God's family, I am one of His kids and that means I belong within what He is building. I go because He is a faithful God, He placed me in His family. The church God is building is unlike any other structure for its bricks are not made of mortar but they are living stones. We are the very material God fashioned to build with. Therefore we have to make sure we don't keep moving our stones out of the wall, but instead see His example of faithfulness as our motivation and willingness to love what He loves.

Have you lost sight, fallen a little out of love with the family of God? We can all have seasons when it seems harder to show up than others. We can all have times when we would like to leave the family or even disown them for a while. Don't allow your church attendance to be based on emotions, circumstances, diaries, bad past experiences. Find a house you can call home and let your life be built there. Let's not treat casually or make optional what Christ made foundational. The world needs the church to arise and be strong and we all get to be a part of making that happen. Let's build it up, not tear it down. It's time to belong, believe, play your part.

Today, what can you do to bless the house of God? Pray for the church, speak well of her, the Bible tells us to put our seed in the soil of God's house and to pray for those who lead in the family of God. Maybe if we all took care of the house, we would find less things that divide and more things that unite. Let's all do something that blesses God's house. This week turn your mind to how you can add more bricks to what God said to build.

THINK IT ━━━━━━━━━━━━━━━ **258**

SPEAK IT ━━━━━━━━━━━━━━━━

BE IT ━━━━━━━━━━━━━━━━

You know well enough from your own experience that there are some acts of so - called freedom that destroy freedom. Offer yourselves to sin, for instance, and it's your last free act. But offer yourselves to the ways of God and the freedom never quits. All your lives you've let sin tell you what to do. But thank God you've started listening to a new master, one whose commands set you free to live openly in his freedom! Romans 6:16 (MSG)

For a very short season in our lives, the Gambills owned a hamster. It was I now realise a moment of weakness on my part; it was that stage every family has to navigate when the incessant demands for a pet are being made by the youngest members and the adults are being slowly worn down. It started with the ask for a dog, we tried to settle at a goldfish and somewhere between those extremes we clearly landed on a hamster. They live in a cage, they don't need walking, it was a good compromise. We bought Harry (that was our hamster's name) a hamster wheel and he would spend all his energy with his very short legs running around that wheel, going nowhere.

We upgraded Harry from the wheel to one of those plastic balls; he would get inside his ball and the world, well at least our kitchen, was his oyster. We got a lot of hilarity from Harry in his new toy. He was very confused and clearly directionally challenged. All of a sudden he wasn't in the confines of his cage and now his running meant he was moving. Harry hit every wall in our kitchen, I was convinced we did that poor hamster damage and he should have been fitted with a helmet first but the difference in experience for the same movement was a world apart. How many times are we exerting energy on a hamster wheel that never takes us anywhere? We can exert our time, gifts and talents but if we are in the wheel, for all the running you really are not moving. We end up right back where we began. We can get in hamster wheel conversations that are exhausting but never seem to find resolve or any sense of progress. We can be working on hamster wheel projects that don't gain any new ground. We can get stuck in hamster wheel relationships that are not going anywhere.

Ask yourself these questions today: what new scenery am I seeing; what new idea am I incubating; what challenge am I setting myself to grow new skills; what new conversation am I starting that will explore new possibilities around me? We need to ask the things that will activate the change. Stop getting on the wheel and start looking for the ball. A new way to do things, a new way to use the same energy but get to new destinations. Yep you may bump your head a little more often but if my hamster could talk he would let you know every bump was worth it. One day he actually hit the corner of the skirting board so hard the ball came apart and Harry was really free - he had the best time running and pooping around the kitchen. Maybe the new idea will break something free within.

THINK IT ━━━━━━━━━━━━━━━ 260

SPEAK IT ━━━━━━━━━━━━━━━━

BE IT ━━━━━━━━━━━━━━━

EXHALE

For I am the Lord your God who takes hold of your right hand and says to you, do not fear; I will help you. Isaiah 41:13 (NIV)

Have you ever had a hug from someone who maybe held on a little longer than was actually comfortable. They seemed to want to let you know they were really happy to see you even if you didn't really reciprocate the same enthusiasm. Maybe you have had a moment as a parent when you have held on to your child when they needed to know everything was going to be ok, past the wriggling and past the pushing away until finally they surrender and give in. They suddenly loosen up and relax into the hug. That's how God at times wants to hold you and I. He wants you to get past your wrestling, past your rushing and allow Him to hold you. He wants you to find that place where you just let go and let God be God.

We can all identify with those moments when we have avoided that kind of closeness with God, when we don't want to get into the kind of posture that makes it hard to ignore what we know we need to confront. We can get good at being close to God but not letting God any closer than we are comfortable with. There are times when shame will keep you at arm's length from God's presence, when failures will say you're not welcome, when comparison can say your're not deserving of the affection He is extending. For many of us, we are so busy being there for everyone, we don't realise we need to allow God to be that someone for us too.

In 2 Samuel 12, David's soul is in agony as his sin had caused his son with Bathsheba to be fatally ill. He begs and laments before God, he sobs in sackcloth. When he hears the child has died, he gets up, washes himself and goes to worship. David knew he needed to be held again by God and for him, worship was his place of holding. His grief and shame had created distance but worship closed the gap.

Maybe you need to put some worship music on and just let His presence overwhelm you. God doesn't just want to lift burdens off you, He wants to hold you as a parent holds a child, in a way that lets you know, everything is going to be ok. We all have a wriggle point where we feel uncomfortable to let the embrace go on, we have a point where we say, that's all I need or even as long as I deserve. Yet in this area we need more childlike faith, trust and understanding. Being held is not a sign of weakness, rather it's a picture of someone strong enough to know you don't have to try and be a hero on your own. So go ahead and be held today.

THINK IT ━━━━━━━━━━━━━━━ 262

SPEAK IT ━━━━━━━━━━━━━━━

BE IT ━━━━━━━━━━━━━━━

EXHALE

"She will give birth to a Son, and you are to give Him the name Jesus, because He will save His people from their sins." All this took place to fulfill what the Lord had said through the prophet: "The virgin will conceive and give birth to a Son, and they will call Him Immanuel" (which means "God with us"). Matthew 1:21-23 (NIV)

Immanuel God with us is one of the most beautiful ways to describe our Saviour. This name He is given is a name we often don't refer to unless it's December. Then you see it written everywhere from songs we sing to cards we receive, as if He is suddenly with us in a different way. But Immanuel is who He was yesterday and who He will be tomorrow; Immanuel is with you right now as you read this and in every step you will take when you put this book down.

Maybe we need to use this name more when we talk and think of our Saviour. Maybe we need a constant reminder that He is constantly with us. How often do we forget this truth? How many times do we act as if God isn't right there in the situation with us. We pray as if He didn't know what had happened and we refer at times to God in a way that suggests He is far away, distant or otherwise engaged. God is with you, that is a mind blowing truth.

Imagine for a moment you decide you are going to be joined 24/7 to someone, so you arrange to be handcuffed to them and throw away the key so there is no backing out of the decision. Everywhere they go, you are there. Everything you said, or did, every struggle, every victory, all is shared. But imagine if the person you were handcuffed to acted as if you weren't there. They carried on with no acknowledgement of your presence. Not only would it seem strange but it would also be insulting to you who have made such a big commitment to be with them, and they didn't even seem that bothered about your presence.

I think we can do this with God a lot. We forget Immanuel God with us is who He is in our day to day; we forget He is already right there in it with us. How differently would you live if you were constantly mindful of God being attached to you? Maybe you would change faster and easier if you lived more aware Immanuel is here. Maybe you wouldn't go to some places and would choose some different conversations, you would be kinder and think twice when it came to your behaviour. Awareness changes things, it makes you more responsible and intentional. How aware are your actions and decisions that Immanuel God is with you right now as you sit and read this text? Today, maybe involve a little more Immanuel in your decisions and choices; as He has decided to attach Himself to you, you might as well take full advantage of having Immanuel alongside you.

THINK IT ━━━━━━━━━━━ 264

SPEAK IT ━━━━━━━━━━━

BE IT ━━━━━━━━━━━

EXHALE

No discipline seems pleasant at the time, but painful. Later on, however, it produces a harvest of righteousness and peace for those who have been trained by it.
Hebrews 12:11 (NIV)

Every morning I have a routine. It's not exciting, it doesn't make me jump out of bed, yet I stick to it because I like the results. It starts with coffee (that bit I do like), then I take time to pray and focus on my day - most days I love this part too! Some days though are harder, my soul is weary or my mind distracted, yet I chose to take the time to focus my faith and fill my mind with what I know is good for me. Often, this is when I will get a thought or word that I share or read a verse that stirs my spirit. Then I head to my treadmill and run, no matter what I feel like. For years I never exercised or had this kind of routine, but I didn't like the results of that lifestyle as much as I do this one. Though the routine asks me to wake up, be alert and do some work, it also gives back - I get energy, wisdom, health and a readiness for the day ahead.

Discipline is a word we love to hate. We want the results but hate the routine, it is boring, monotonous, even painful. I have had to change my perspective on many occasions when it comes to the daily commitments that discipline demands. I have had to stop calling things tiresome that are actually life saving. It's the discipline that took me to a place of better health, it's the commitment that gave me the new found confidence, it's the study that caused the moment of success. Imagine what Noah must have felt like every day, another piece of wood to hammer on a structure that could only sail on water and they had never even seen rain fall. Everyday the monotony and the ridicule from those looking on as he spent hours, days, months, years committed to this project. There must have been so many days when he wanted to give up but his commitment to the discipline was the only thing that was going to get the job done.

So whatever discipline you are struggling to embrace, be it exercise, diet, prayer, chores, study, music or other commitments, think today of all the ways other people's disciplines have made a way for you. Think of the ones who consistently showed up, gave, encouraged, taught, inspired. The teachers, the trainers, experts, counsellors. The ones whose discipline helped you get through and whose hard work became your answer to prayer. Allow your appreciation for the discipline of others to grow, and in so doing begin to express gratitude for what it brings to your life.

The discipline you express today can be a gift for your tomorrow, so let's go!

THINK IT ━━━━━━━━━━━━━━ 266

SPEAK IT ━━━━━━━━━━━━━━━━

BE IT ━━━━━━━━━━━━━━━━

EXHALE

Even the sparrow has found a home, and the swallow a nest for herself, where she may have her young - a place near your altar, Lord Almighty, my King and my God. Psalm 84:3 (NIV)

Maybe because of the hours I spend travelling, this word means more to me than most. Home is something my heart longs for and it is my favorite place to be. I have stayed in beautiful hotels and been blessed to see amazing places around the world but nothing makes me as happy as home. I even love being in other people's homes and often if I am away speaking, I will cancel the hotel booking if I know I have a friend in the area with a spare room. Home creates an atmosphere, it's personal, it's individual, home is messy in the best possible way. Home is come as you are, stay as long as you want.

You may have a very different idea of home; some may have grown up with home not being a place you enjoyed being or maybe it was a home with so many rules it was hard to relax in. Though we may not have the best start, we all get the opportunity to explore what home could be. You don't have to build what your parents built, you can dream and build what your heart desires. You can make any space large or small a place that is home for you and for others. When Joshua sent spies to Jericho they met a woman called Rahab who was a prostitute. Her upbringing had caused her idea of a home to be distorted. But Rahab now had a chance to dream again with the arrival of these spies and in exchange for her help, Rahab asked for her family to be saved. Rahab wanted to try again and build what she had never been given: a home, belonging, safety and family.

Home matters and if you have lived your life with no sense of belonging, I pray today you would begin to dream about the kind of home you want to have. God's house teaches us how to build home well. It is a safe place, a place of beauty and blessing, God's house is a place where everyone can belong and where His presence is felt. Maybe no one taught you how to make a house a home. You can start by looking at God's model and then get around some homes that make you feel that sense of belonging.

Home is somewhere we all need to find. That address that is not just physical but also spiritual. That place where we belong and learn to become all God intends us to be. So to every drifter, I pray you find home, to every builder, keep building and to every homeless heart, I pray you will see God's house has a huge doormat saying, welcome home. Maybe it is time for you to start to build the home of your dreams.

THINK IT ━━━━━━━━━━━━ 268

SPEAK IT ━━━━━━━━━━━━

BE IT ━━━━━━━━━━━━

EXHALE

Then Peter came to Jesus and asked, "Lord, how many times shall I forgive my brother or sister who sins against me? Up to seven times?" Jesus answered, "I tell you, not seven times, but seventy-seven times." Matthew 18:21-35 (NIV)

When our patience runs thin and our grace is tested. When we feel hurt by those close or distant. When we are the victim of other people's poor choices. Remember, we all hold the greatest gift of freedom and that comes in often the hardest choice called forgiveness. Forgiveness that moves past feelings or facts. Forgiveness that is grace given and mercy driven. When Jesus was asked by His disciples how often they should forgive, they suggested seven as a sufficient number. I mean if someone has wronged you and you are willing to go past that seven times, that is something worth celebrating right? However, Jesus instantly replied, not seven but seventy times seven. In other words, you have got a long way to go.

In this journey of living free we often have to start at the place of knowing how to be truly free. Forgiveness is by no means a popular or even desired choice; it presents the greatest personal pain and yet actually its results are much more of a gain. Therefore we must keep allowing forgiveness to flow or we will actually stop our own growth. It's not always easy to do, but it is a gift you give yourself to unshackle from the pain in the present moment and instead welcome the new horizons forgiveness will bring in your future. Jesus chose a number He knew we would all have to do the maths on. We would all have to display a lot more forgiveness than we would have chosen but that's the way grace works. We have to remember the times when we needed that seventy times seven extended to our lives and realise what we have so often received we are now responsible to return into the lives of others. No one wants to forgive, we are always more mindful of the hurt than the healing and yet forgiveness is just as much the thing that frees us as the thing that also liberates the perpetrator. None of us deserves the forgiveness Christ died to give us. So if He is our example, we need to stop excusing what we need to address and forgive.

So where is it time for this principle of seventy times seven to override your own principles? Where do you need to let this standard become your standard? Today, walk free from the prison that unforgiveness has kept you locked in for too many years. Try this idea over all those others that suggest themselves as the best way forward. Seventy times seven will never be the favourite but its ability to liberate is second to none.

THINK IT ━━━━━━━━━━ **270**

SPEAK IT ━━━━━━━━━━━

BE IT ━━━━━━━━━━━

EXHALE

Put to death, therefore, whatever belongs to your earthly nature: sexual immorality, impurity, lust, evil desires and greed, which is idolatry...rid yourselves of all such things as these: anger, rage, malice, slander, and filthy language from your lips. Colossians 3:5-8 (NIV)

Have you ever been around someone who is overflowing with life and you feel you are barely holding onto it? Or have you spent time with people who radiate peace and yet you feel like peace is a distant memory? Why is it sometimes we feel as if we have caught none of what others are full to the brim with?

If God wants us all to have life in all its fullness, an overflowing abundant life, that means you and I. He wants to pour His life into us so maybe it's time to look at the vessel its being poured into. Maybe your life has a hole or a lid issue. A drainer or container situation. Let's examine both of these potential problems that could be causing your life to be limited in some ways; today we'll examine if you have any holes to fill, then we'll look at lifting some lids.

Have you ever poured water into a vessel that has a hole in it? What should have been contained instead starts to leak out. The more holes, the less you keep. Holes mean what we could have had to overflowing can't even begin to start filling. Holes are those things that we leave unattended that work against what God has for us. Holes like doubt that let faith slip away, holes like offense that keeps us away from community, holes of disappointment that stop us from truly being able to believe.

The only way to fix a hole problem is to work on filling them in. You have to start somewhere and today is a good a day as any. Colossians lists some of the things that can lead to holes that will drain God's best from your life. It mentions things such as impurity, greed, anger, slander, they become a drainage point sucking out what is good and leaving us void of the life that is ours to have. These verses, however, also go on to give ways in which those holes can be filled; it lists attributes like kindness, humility, gentleness and patience. Humility blocks the hole pride wants to create and kindness fills the hole that slander wants to make. These hole fillers are available for our lives and when we start to close up the holes, we start to live life with the fullness that God wants to pour out into our lives. So today, maybe it's time to fill some holes so you can attain more of that overflowing life. Why not write down the holes that need to go and then pray for God to give you the best filler for every place where life is leaking instead of overflowing.

THINK IT ━━━━━━━━━━━━ 272

SPEAK IT ━━━━━━━━━━━━━━━━━━━

BE IT ━━━━━━━━━━━━━━━━━━━

"A good measure, pressed down, shaken together and running over, will be poured into your lap." Luke 6:38 (NIV)

We have looked at the life that God wants to pour out into us, the overflowing life that is ours to take a hold of. However, we can have leakage problems through holes that are in our lives, holes that need filling. We also can have a lid issue; lids are limiters to the overflow that God has for us. Lids are the ceilings we create when we say we are ok as we are, when we remove the faith factor and replace it with the lid called self-sufficiency. Lids are when our mind can't stretch to what God says is possible, sealing what God has done and saying He doesn't need to do any more. Lids cause the waters to become stagnant, leaving no opportunity for the water to flow or be renewed.

When the rich young ruler asked to enter God's kingdom, Jesus went for his lid, his money had become his container. When Jesus said give all your money to the poor, the young ruler walked away. He couldn't lift that lid so he lost eternal life. Trust is a lid lifter; it creates room for God to be God and for Him to move how and when He wants. When we choose to trust, we choose to not contain God within the four walls we have created but we allow room for His answers and His ways, which are often beyond our own. God's word is also a lid lifter; when we open the word we allow the truth to widen our believing. His word becomes stronger than ours and the lid that our own limited confession creates is removed.

If we have a lid on our lives in the area of finances, then we can lift that lid with actions that make us live more generously. Giving moves us from a place of containment to being a vessel that pours out to others. When we give we lift the lid of lack and also the lid of control; when we liberate our giving we also remove the limitation from our receiving.

Identifying where the lids are helps locate what actions are required to lift these off your life. Today, where are you stagnant? Is there a lid on your life when it comes to correction, have you put a lid on the voices that can shape you and mould you? Is there a lid on your faith? Have you stopped believing for something that is beyond you own ability to make happen? We can allow fear of failing, fear of losing or being let down to put lids on our love, trust, faith. Those over time remove the ability to receive God's overflowing life.

Lift some lids so you can live beyond where limitation wants to keep you. Take a risk, ask big and trust that God has more than enough for you.

SPEAK IT ━━━━━━━━━━━━━━━

BE IT ━━━━━━━━━━━━━━━

EXHALE

Do nothing out of selfish ambition or vain conceit. Rather, in humility value others above yourselves, not looking to your own interests but each of you to the interests of the others. Philippians 2:3-4 (NIV)

We have all seen those films when the enemy is pursuing a depleted opponent, where all the attempts to win the battle have failed. So in a last ditch attempt to not lose any more lives, someone bravely appears from behind the defense line, waving a white flag - it's time to surrender. In that moment you can think one of two things: that the losing side gave up too easily, or they did what they could to save the little they had left, instead of lose everything they have.

White flag moments, however you view them, are a part of life. We will all come to a place where we recognise, if I don't surrender, then the chances are I will not survive but if I do surrender, I am going to be embarrassed and have to do a lot of apologising. There are times when we need to realise we are fighting the wrong battle, we are arguing for the wrong reasons. We need to call a truce before any more damage is done and we need to humble ourselves so that we can save ourselves. Sometimes we need to make this decision on behalf of others too, those who jumped on the same bandwagon with us and perhaps look to us for leadership. We need to show them that sometimes, it's better to be the one coming over the top with the white flag than the one digging our heels in until the bitter end.

No one wants to admit defeat and yet if we just stopped and thought about what we are sacrificing by not surrendering, I think we would get the white flag out. Some battles you need to fight but others you need to quit; some fights the win is noble, others to win is pure foolishness. Maybe we should issue a white flag at every wedding and say there are times when you just need to use this and save what pride would sacrifice. White flags may seem weak but if you are waving them to save what stubbornness would choose to lose, then the white flag is not a fail, it's a win.

So where do you need to get your white flag out? Where do you need to stop fighting with God and say, I get it, I quit? Where do you need to say to someone you love, I'm sorry I created a fight that there is no gain in winning? Where does humility need to wave the flag and in so doing put pride in its place? For some your white flag will look weak but for those it's about to save from more heartache, it will be the best thing you have ever done.

SPEAK IT ▬▬▬▬▬▬▬▬▬▬

BE IT ▬▬▬▬▬▬▬▬▬▬

Your word is a lamp for my feet, a light on my path.
Psalm 119:105 (NIV)

Years ago I had the most horrible experience. I was coming home from my weekend job and on the way from the car to the house I dropped my front door key. It was dark outside and no street lamps were near enough to help me in my search. Instead of doing the sensible thing and knocking on the door to get a torch, I chose the Charlotte option, which was to feel around on the pavement. That decision scarred me for life; rummaging around on the floor I finally felt something I assumed was the keys and went in for the grab only to my horror to find it was a slug that I had decided to pick up, yes a big fat slimy slug. When I finally got into the house and had scrubbed my hands, my mum made me creamed mushrooms on toast which looked like the very slug I had picked up. I have never eaten creamed mushrooms since. This whole escapade could have been avoided if I had simply gone and got some light for the path. I would have quickly known the difference between my keys and a big ugly slug.

This same scenario plays out over and over again in our lives. We are constantly dropping things we need, losing our peace, faltering in our faith. The word of God tells us exactly what to do in this scenario, we often choose the more foolish option, we rummage around in the dark, and we pick up a counterfeit when we could have got the real thing. All we had to do was go and get the torch to bring some much needed light to the path.

The Bible puts it this way: Thy word is a lamp unto my feet and light unto my path. God gave us all a torch, He knew we would drop things we needed, He knew we would get confused where to step. We pick up a lie instead of the truth, we take something that is not God's best because we fail to see things through His perspective. We all need to get better at using this torchlight, we all need to stop having slugs in place of keys.

If you're in a dark season, open up the word that gives light. If you feel you can't see a way, give time to read of His ways. If your feet are stumbling, stand on the rock that doesn't move. If your words are failing, meditate on the words that are faith filled. His words always shape our words if we let them. This word wants to be your torch so write down some verses that can help illuminate the place you are struggling to see. Meditate on scriptures that will help you discern and take time to take it in before you pick anything back up.

INHALE

THINK IT ━━━━━━━━━━━ 278

SPEAK IT ━━━━━━━━━━━

BE IT ━━━━━━━━━━━

EXHALE

Do not let any unwholesome talk come out of your mouths, but only what is helpful for building others up according to their needs, that it may benefit those who listen. Ephesians 4:29 (NIV)

Have you ever heard someone talk about being well, but come away sensing that they are still sick? Maybe it is a conversation you witnessed, a dialogue you had, even a post you read. Though it may have been eloquent in word, it just sounded unhealthy in tone. The truth is healing is not one dimensional. Even if the wound is closed and the cut is healed, the memory of how it happened and the scar tissue is still there. Healing your mind may be one part, but what about your heart, your soul? The healthiest life is one that doesn't just look well, but it sounds well and lives well.

Sometimes we are more aware of looking healthy than sounding healthy. We at times need to ask those around us to tell us how we sound. Healing has a sound, it sounds free not resentful. It sounds clear not confused. It sounds beautiful not bitter, victorious not defeated. It sounds honest and whole. When we have been through a season that tests us, we need to allow time to fix the parts of our lives that have been wounded. When David's wife Michal watched him dance before the Lord, it says she despised him in her heart. Even though a party was happening, the ark was returning, Michal instead spoke words that revealed wounds that had never healed. David went straight to the issue of her hurt over the demise of her father, Saul and his ascendancy as king. She had acted as if she was whole but inside she was hateful.

Let's be aware of the sound of our story, it's tone, it's pitch, it's volume. Maybe you are saying you are over the betrayal but the conversations you keep having about the mistrust you feel and the doubts you have make the restoration of the relationship a very hard mountain to scale. When we say we are healed but we still speak our hurt, it has the same effect as an out of time lip sync, the confession and the conviction are out of sync. The only way you can fix that is to stop faking it and go back and start the track over again, only this time actually mean what you sing.

It can take a while for our heart and our head to sync up and in those areas where we know we still have a way to go, we need to be even more cautious. Maybe you have a lip sync area that needs some attention. Be brave today, and be willing to do the work so that your healing is not just seen but heard.

THINK IT ━━━━━━━━━━━━━━ **280**

SPEAK IT ━━━━━━━━━━━━━━━━━

BE IT ━━━━━━━━━━━━━━━━━

EXHALE

You Are
LOVED

Brothers and sisters, do not be children [immature, childlike] in your thinking; be infants in [matters of] evil [completely innocent and inexperienced], but in your minds be mature [adults]. 1 Corinthians 14:20 (AMP)

Can you tie my shoe, can you iron my top, can you pick me up, can you sort out this problem? These may be familiar asks in your world, or I am sure you can replace them with similar. None of these are bad asks and the world won't be a worse place if you respond. However, just because we could doesn't always mean we should.

These scenarios are innocent enough, but what if we replace them with other asks. Asks that if you answer will end up over burdening your life and actually setting someone else's progress back. Tying a shoe for a three year old may be ok but a 13 year old less so. If you keep tying the shoe because you can, how will they ever learn that they can too. So at times we need to stop and think, just because I could, should I? Should you sort out that person's problem again? Should you address that issue that's not yours to address? Should you do that for them or could they do it themselves?

Knowing when help becomes a hindrance is not always easy to discern. Understanding that sometimes the kindest response is, I think you can do that yourself now, is something we all have to learn. Recently I was stressing about how I would get my kids where they needed to be and trying at the same time to make an appointment I had for myself. As I was clearly speaking the stress out loud, my beautiful daughter, Hope, came over to me and said, mum, why are you trying to drive me to my friend's, I'm fine, I can take the bus. Suddenly I realised I was trying to sort something she wasn't even asking me to sort for her, she was very capable of catching a bus but that had been something I hadn't even considered because I assumed I needed to sort this out for her. I was clearly over mothering and her helpful interruption was an indication that it was time for me to do some releasing.

Sometimes we like to add the stress because it makes us feel more necessary. We want to sort things as it can feed a sense of dependence from those around us. But that day my daughter was helping me see, just because I could doesn't mean I should. She got the bus and I made my appointment and the world did not fall apart for my lesser involvement.

Sometimes we need to take a step back and make sure our help is actually helpful both for ourselves and others. Progress sometimes means doing less. And helping someone move forward sometimes looks like holding a little more back. Today, ask yourself in different scenarios, should I be doing this or is it time to let them know, they are perfectly capable of doing this for themselves.

THINK IT ━━━━━━━━━━━━━━━━ **282**

SPEAK IT ━━━━━━━━━━━━━━━━

BE IT ━━━━━━━━━━━━━━━

God addressed Samuel: "So, how long are you going to mope over Saul? You know I've rejected him as king over Israel. Fill your flask with anointing oil and get going. I'm sending you to Jesse of Bethlehem. I've spotted the very king I want among his sons." 1 Samuel 16:1 (MSG)

There are times in life when we think our good idea is a God idea but though they sound similar, the difference couldn't be any farther apart. We can think our choice is God's choice but sometimes we have to learn the hard way that what we are convinced of is not something God is automatically going to bless.

The people of Israel became convinced they needed a king and so they asked and asked for Saul to lead them. His appearance was impressive and the people impatient and impulsive. Though this was not God's choice, He gave them Saul, whose name means 'asked for', as king. Sometimes God will let you have what you ask for to teach you what you actually should have trusted Him for. Saul went from being what they thought they needed to everything they did not need. So God told Samuel, who had anointed Saul as king, to go and anoint another who was God's choice, not man's.

Samuel began to mourn the loss of Saul even though God was about to bring forth a far better replacement. In response to Samuel's grieving, God simply told him to get up and get on with it. There are times in all our lives when we have to leave what we think is best to attain God's best. We have to stop being attached to Saul if we want to find our David. This new direction for Samuel was hard to take but he did it anyway.

Sometimes God won't even enter conversations that you think matter because He knows it is not taking you forward but holding you back. God can seem like He doesn't care when He doesn't respond but the exact opposite is true, He is concerned for you to reach your future. He will propel you forward but sometimes in order to do that He may completely ignore what you can't seem to stop talking about. Maybe you're in a season where you need to change the conversation, stop talking about Saul and say, ok God, lead me to where David is. Stop being in fear of what could happen when Saul finds out and be more in a fear of missing the thing that God has already planned for your future. Samuel knew the anointing was attached to serving God's plan not man's agenda. If you want to meet David, where is it time to leave Saul? Let's continue with how we make this transition but for today, pray for the clarity to see what God wants over what you are asking for.

THINK IT ━━━━━━━━━━━━━ **284**

SPEAK IT ━━━━━━━━━━━━━━━

BE IT ━━━━━━━━━━━━━━━

"The Lord does not look at the things people look at. People look at the outward appearance, but the Lord looks at the heart." 1 Samuel 16:7 (NIV)

Samuel had to make several internal decisions before he could actually get to the place where he was ready to anoint David. He was disappointed that the one who he had anointed to lead the people had ended up only trying to please people. He was saddened over Saul's drift from serving God to making himself the god the people served.

Though Samuel was upset, he allowed his obedience to override his feelings. He did as God asked, he got up out of his place of despondency and disappointment and he set off. When we read the words 'he arrived' we are seeing the first step in obedience. Obey what God says, arrive where He tells you to arrive, let loose what he asks you to lose. If we just obey even though we may be upset or we may feel scared, we will arrive in the place where God is going to do the anointing. The first step towards your future is to do the thing you have been avoiding, to do what you know God has asked of you and stop fearing what people will say about you. If God is asking then you need to start responding.

When Samuel arrived, he then had to reprogramme how he viewed what God was going to do. He was greeted by Jesse's seven sons and immediately Eliab caught his eye; he was strong and towered above the others and immediately Samuel thought, this must be the one. He was keen to anoint what was next and yet God interrupted his train of thought and reminds Samuel that He doesn't look at the outward but the inward. If we are going to move forward, we can't use the past as our parameters for what God will do next, we need to be comfortable even when it's unusual. David would look nothing like Saul or Eliab, God's choice was not to do with man's criteria. Before David appeared, Samuel had to say no to seven of Jesse's sons, David wasn't even in the room that day, he was out tending sheep. Sometimes we are in such a rush to move things forward we can try and force what God has not endorsed.

In seasons when God is moving you on, you need to allow Him to lead and that may mean you have to have the faith and patience for seven nos before you get a yes. If God ever asks you to leave something that has become a Saul, then you too will also have to detach like Samuel. Detach your feelings, wrong thinking and also resist your need to rush. Remember it's worth the wait, don't settle for a poor substitute but keep going until you connect with God's yes.

THINK IT ━━━━━━━━━━━━━ 286

SPEAK IT ━━━━━━━━━━━━━━━━━━

BE IT ━━━━━━━━━━━━━━━━━━

"Sing, barren woman, you who never bore a child; burst into song, shout for joy, you who were never in labour; because more are the children of the desolate woman than of her who has a husband," says the Lord. Isaiah 54:1 (NIV)

My daughter loves music, she spends hours searching for great bands to listen to and puts together playlists all the time, she's our resident dj. I love hearing her sing along to her favourite songs, I love that as she hums, she is expressing how happy the music makes her.

We all have a song to sing, we all have a melody to get out. Your heart and soul were made to worship your Heavenly Father. The power of that melody can pull you forward and lift you up. Praise can propel you and worship can still the stress and usher in peace. That's why you need to protect the song within you. The enemy would love to steal that song, he would like to weigh down your heart with troubles so that you lose the ability to sing.

The verse today tells the barren woman to sing. It's more than bursting into song, it's teaching us that we shouldn't allow a barren or burdened season to steal our song. We need to commit to keep singing even if we can't see anything to sing about; we need to find the song that stirs up our soul. David's psalms were his source, the vehicle for his frustration to be drowned in faith anthems. Everyone of us has lyrics inside our life, melodies to write to our Saviour. We may never become the next great songwriter but we need to listen to our soul that wants to sing, it needs to sing. We need to write lyrics that take us straight to the truth of who God is and all He has done. We need to keep repeating songs for the valley and praises for the midst of the problems. The Bible tells us in Zephaniah 3:17 that the Lord sings over us; how much more do we need to find our song and sing.

If fear, hurt, pain or offense stop you singing, know that the enemy wants to steal your strength and he often starts with taking your song. Don't let him remove the melody your heart wants to sing to your Maker. Fight for the strength to sing out the song within your soul. Even if your voice is weak and the words are faltering, sing. Sing a song that lifts up praise in the valley, a song that soothes and a song that magnifies your God. Like the words of that old and beautiful hymn: Then sings my soul, my Saviour God to Thee, how great Thou art, how great Thou art. If you can't find your own song today, maybe start with this one and you will find that as you get singing, the gladness of God will flood in.

THINK IT ━━━━━━━━━━━━━ 288

SPEAK IT ━━━━━━━━━━━━━

BE IT ━━━━━━━━━━━━━

EXHALE

Later that night, the boat was in the middle of the lake, and He was alone on land. He saw the disciples straining at the oars, because the wind was against them. Shortly before dawn He went out to them, walking on the lake. Mark 6:47-48 (NIV)

Beginnings of projects or relationships are exciting, a little scary, a step into new possibilities, an opportunity to write something new, start something fresh. Beginnings require energy and gain momentum from all the activity you have invested. When you begin a new job or more to a new area, it presents the opportunity to discover new things about yourself and others.

Beginnings add excitement to our lives and in their own way endings also add a sense of joy when you finally finish a project or you achieve the last thing on that long list. We celebrate when we reach an endpoint in our education, a graduation marking all that has been achieved. Endings bring a sense of completion and closure. The ending is something we appreciate and often have worked hard to attain.

However, there is another stage we are less celebratory of, a space we don't look forward to and rather than have momentum it often just seems to be mundane and even painful. Yep that zone is called the middle. The middle is the place where many people quit, they feel it's too hard to carry on. They can't see the end and they long to go back to the start. Yet if we quit in the middle we do ourselves and others a huge disservice. The enemy wants in your middle moments for you to sink, swim back to shore, he is nervous you may realise what he already knows, that if you push past your middle point you will be closer to your next shore than you were before. When Jesus told the disciples to take the boat out, it says it was in the middle of the lake that a storm hit, not as they set off or as they approached the distant shore but in the middle. The enemy loves to send a storm in the middle because he doesn't want you to get past the halfway point. He would rather you go back and lose all the ground you just worked so hard to gain. What the disciples discovered is, the only place where you will see a water walking Jesus is in the middle. There is a miracle in the middle if you don't quit; the middle reveals what's in the middle of you.

What middle are you in right now? Where has the excitement left and endurance had to kick in? Maybe it's a middle season in your marriage, job, education. My advice is keep going, push on, you just need to take another step. The middle is a passing place not a final destination. God can do miracles in the middle so hold on.

SPEAK IT ━━━━━━━━━━━━━━━━━━━

BE IT ━━━━━━━━━━━━━━━━━━━━

May my meditation be pleasing to Him, as I rejoice in the Lord.
Psalm 104:34 (NIV)

What captivates you, communicates through you. Taking time to make sure your meditations are strong is not just a good idea, it's a life changing discipline. Where your thoughts are allowed to linger will either liberate or imprison your future. It is the difference between health and stress, striving and trusting. We may spend all day trying to fix what actually a shift in focus would change forever.

If you were to keep a track on how much time you spent thinking on different things, I wonder how that would read at the end of a day, a week, a year? I wonder if we had a thought tracker, would we be more careful about where we spent our thought life? If our thinking shapes our being and doing then we need to make sure it is regularly adjusted and challenged. Proverbs 23:7 says, as a man thinks so he is. Well what does that make you? What kind of person is your thought life creating? How many thoughts do we allow to have free reign in our lives? How many times do we allow others to pick what we think on? If our thinking really is shaping who we are becoming then we maybe need to get a little more intentional about what we daydream, ponder and meditate about.

Thoughts can be taught, they can be trained. Your thoughts don't have to be random. Have you ever watched someone break a horse in? They take that wild stallion and they corral it and eventually they get the horse from a place of wildness to a place of willingness. They take what before was unbridled and they introduce the horse to a saddle; they now can ride on its strength instead of being scared by it. Our thoughts need breaking in, they need to be captured so we can saddle up the right thoughts. They need to take us where we need to go. Where have you let too many thoughts run wild and in so doing they have led to confusion and contradiction?

Today, maybe do a thought check up. Ask yourself, what am I choosing to think on, is it helpful or harmful, is it making me into the kind of person I want to be? Put energy into your meditations and you will find renewed strength in your everyday decisions. See what matters most and you will be less concerned with what doesn't even really matter at all. Take a hold of your thoughts and make them work for you not against you.

THINK IT ━━━━━━━━━━ 292

SPEAK IT ━━━━━━━━━━━━

BE IT ━━━━━━━━━━━━

EXHALE

"A faithful man will abound with blessings."
Proverbs 28:20 (NIV)

Faithfulness leads where pride rarely follows. Faithfulness is a quality that speaks volumes about a person's life. Often we give attention to characteristics like charisma or gifting, skill sets or achievements but faithfulness is the quieter partner that holds everything together. Faithful people have a way about them that immediately adds stature and strength. They bring a depth to the conversation that is different and they see things with a much longer perspective than those who want short term results. Faithfulness is more relaxed and not forced. It doesn't fluster when things aren't all together because it's not committed to a certain outcome, it's committed to stay faithful to its post. Faithfulness doesn't overreact as it knows time and seasons will have their effect in each changing circumstance. Faithfulness is more mature and has a perspective that impatience never sees.

Where in your life do you need to work on faithfulness? Who in your life do you need to commit to be faithful to? Believing and praying for them in every season and staying faithful in your friendship or commitment even when others may not. There is a promise that comes with faithfulness, it has its own reward, for when we are faithful in the little we become entrusted with much. Often we want the much to start with and then we think we will show how faithful we can be but God works in the reverse order. It's the faithfulness in the small stuff, showing up on time for that coffee date, believing and standing with that young person, being faithful when you have not much to give instead of saying I will give when I have much. Today, let faithfulness be something you celebrate and elevate, be faithful in your little today.

When we let faithfulness lead, it will always avoid the shortcuts pride or ego would prefer to take. It will guide you past the place of self and into the path of serve. Faithfulness won't push or press, it will trust and stay steadfast. Pride rarely hangs out in the places that faithfulness finds, as it largely stays under the radar and avoids the spotlight. But where faithfulness leads, favour follows. So even if the road is longer, stick with it because eventually your faithfulness will lead you to the much God wants to trust you with.

THINK IT ━━━━━━━━━━━━━━ 294

SPEAK IT ━━━━━━━━━━━━━━

BE IT ━━━━━━━━━━━━━━

EXHALE

A nagging spouse is like the drip, drip, drip of a leaky faucet; you can't turn it off, and you can't get away from it. Proverbs 27:15 (NIV)

It's strange that almost all the verses in the Bible about nagging seem to be connected to a woman. The truth is, as much as we don't want to admit it, we can all be found guilty as charged. We can call it by another name, suggesting, hinting, helping but if you examine the evidence you can find that it's just nagging. Why do we nag? Well, it's usually because we see something needs doing or we feel we are not being taken seriously and so we start to send reminders that we are still waiting. The longer the delay between the demand and the supply, the more incessant the nagging becomes. Why do we think if we say something over and over again it will ensure it gets done when actually sometimes the folly of nagging is it has the exact opposite effect.

Nagging is not flattering, it doesn't bring out the best in anyone and it can mean you lose far more than you gain. I once asked my husband to fix something in our home, I must have asked every day and then my asking moved to accusing him of deliberately ignoring me just to annoy me. The nagging got more intense but his response got more distant. Eventually my nag was background noise, it was just like that dripping tap that Proverbs refers to. Then I quit nagging about it, I got distracted with another project and guess what, that's when it got fixed. Men don't like to be spoken to like naughty boys, they don't want to be nagged at, they just want to be asked and then given room to answer. Sometimes the job or demand may not get done in your timescale but as my husband would say, if it matters to you that much, then maybe you can do it yourself.

So where is your nagging creating a drag effect? What relationship is it sabotaging? It's not easy to admit it but if we don't deal with our nagging, it will suck the life and energy out of our homes and relationships. Nagging is not asking, they don't sound the same: an ask is clear and it's not got a whining attached to its request.

If nagging has become more of a norm than it should, ask yourself, am I getting anywhere with this approach, is this worth all the energy it requires? Is what you are nagging about that important anyway? If I stop nagging about it, what would happen? I have found encouragement gets a lot more things done than nagging ever will. Don't allow your voice to become that one no one listens to anymore because it never has anything new to say. Don't be a dripping tap when you can be a fountain of life.

THINK IT ━━━━━━━━━━━━━━ 296

SPEAK IT ━━━━━━━━━━━━━━

BE IT ━━━━━━━━━━━━━━

EXHALE

God's glory is on tour in the skies, God-craft on exhibit across the horizon. Madame Day holds classes every morning, Professor Night lectures each evening. Their words aren't heard, their voices aren't recorded, but their silence fills the earth: unspoken truth is spoken everywhere. Psalm 19:1-4 (MSG)

Have you ever been to an event at a child's school where you are invited in to look at their artwork or school books? The child you are visiting eagerly waits for you to show up at the schoolgate and takes you by the hand to go and see what they have been up to. My son would take me around each station pointing out his different pieces of written work and arts and crafts. He wanted to show me what he had made for me. Sometimes God wants to do just the same with us. He wants to take our hand and show His children just what He has made for us. He wants you to come and see the sunset He has painted and admire the flowers He has planted. He wants to point out the stars He has hung in the sky. He wants to show you just how much He loves you by showing you the creation He has made for you.

I remember at those same school open days seeing the children whose parents couldn't make it. They looked on as parent's celebrated their children's achievements, wishing the ones they loved could see what they had made. I would often adopt an extra child and visit their work, knowing on some occasions my child would be the one whose parents were unable to be there and hoping when that happened, someone would scoop up my son too. How often do we not show up for those moments with God? How many times do we miss taking His hand just to see the things He has done for us?

A few months back I was packing up to go to the airport somewhere in the USA. After a powerful night of ministry I was tired and drained and my sole focus was to find caffeine before the next flight. Then I felt God whisper, 'open the curtains I have something to show you'. I was greeted with a breathtaking sunrise. God wanted to take a minute to say, look what I did for you, I painted the sky so beautifully, take a minute to enjoy what I have created, let it bless you and remind you of how much I love you. As I took in God's majestic artwork, I was reminded again His mercy is new every morning, His grace and goodness is in fresh supply.

God wanted me to show up and see His artwork and I was so glad I did. You need to make an appointment to do the same. Go take God's hand and let Him show you what He made for you. I guarantee it will make you smile and remind you just how much He loves you.

THINK IT ━━━━━━━━━━━━ 298

SPEAK IT ━━━━━━━━━━━━━━━

BE IT ━━━━━━━━━━━━━━━

EXHALE

He climbed a mountain and invited those He wanted with Him. They climbed together. He settled on twelve, and designated them apostles. The plan was that they would be with Him, and He would send them out to proclaim the Word. Mark 3:13 (MSG)

When does the role of a leader begin? Is it found in a name tag, a title or a position? Is leadership a gift of the few and a goal unattainable for the many? Or have we over complicated this whole thing by overlooking the dormant seeds to lead within one another, starving the world around us from the leader that is within us? You don't need a platform or microphone to lead, leadership isn't performance, it's practice.

Every life that is willing to follow Him qualifies to lead people to Him. Leadership starts when you are willing to see past yourself and notice someone else. When you can hear before you need to be heard, and when you can embrace even if you haven't been embraced. Leadership isn't preaching a sermon, starting a church, getting a podcast. It's helping someone, leading them in forgiveness, faith, truth. Leading in integrity, kindness, patience. We can either be deliberate about the decision to lead or leave it to coincidence. Some are leading by default, others by design.

Someone right now is looking up to you, a child, sibling, friend, student, colleague. Someone is asking, can you see me? Someone's brokenness is saying, will you lead me to wholeness? The hopeless looking to be led to hope and the lonely looking to be led to family. You don't need to have all the answers, no one does! Just be present and be willing to follow Him. The disciples followed Jesus, that was the entire way they learnt to lead. They followed Him into difficulty and followed Him into triumph. They followed Him as He fed thousands and as He ministered to the individual; what the many heard in a message, the disciples saw lived out everyday.

I have had some incredible leadership tips from amazing leaders over the years and their input has helped me and opened my eyes to see things differently. But I have learnt far more from those who I have shared a journey with, those I have followed as they have raised a family, built a home, the character it takes to keep the ground you gain. I have learnt more from the unspoken lessons than the great speeches. I have watched them lead as they have followed. So maybe we all need to follow on purpose in areas where we want to become a better leader to others. Who are you following now so you can lead later? Where is someone now following your life that you need to be more mindful of? Let's all make the main followership of our lives Jesus, ensuring a better journey for any that are coming behind us.

THINK IT ━━━━━━━━━━ 300

SPEAK IT ━━━━━━━━━━

BE IT ━━━━━━━━━━

EXHALE

For this very reason, make every effort to add to your faith goodness; and to goodness, knowledge. 2 Peter 1:5 (NIV)

Have you ever been to a store that sells vitamins and been overwhelmed by the choices? They have vitamins for your skin, nails, hair, whatever you need covering they seem to have you covered. These are not a substitute for the daily diet you eat but they are a supplement that will enhance your health if you take as advised. The word of God is our daily diet, if we eat it we will add life to our years and health to our bones. 2 Peter tells us that God has given us everything we need for a godly life, then it goes on recommend some additives, supplements we would be advised to take.

So let's look at those additives and examine which we may be a little deficient in and what we need to be more deliberate about adding to our life on a regular basis. The list of additives starts with goodness, something we choose to take in. The more goodness we add the more goodness can flow through us. It then says to add to our goodness knowledge. How can we add knowledge? Choose to be a learner, start to study more, ask more and attain more. Then add to that self control; this is an additive that some need a lot more of than others. God has given you this gift of life but He needs you to add self control so that the life you have lasts long and is healthy and whole. To self control add perseverance, have you taken that supplement recently? Have you made a deliberate choice to persevere more and made it part of what you add to the life you lead?

To perseverance we are to add godliness and to that mutual affection, love. These are our responsibility and it goes even further and reminds us we need to add them not once and not in small doses but in increasing measure. So the more we serve God, the more we should be adding. The reason for these additives is spelled out for us in 2 Peter 1:8 when it says they will keep us from being ineffective and unproductive in our knowledge of God; who wants to be ineffective?

God wants your life and mine to thrive and so He recommends what we should add. If we can add worry then we can add self control, if we can add fear then we can add faith. Maybe the problem is not the ability to add but the content of what is being added, maybe it's time to change up your supplements so that you increase your effectiveness and decrease you ineffectiveness. So today, what spiritual additives do you need to make sure you take?

THINK IT ═══════════════════ 302

SPEAK IT ─────────────────────

BE IT ─────────────────────

"The Lord who rescued me from the paw of the lion and the paw of the bear will rescue me from the hand of this Philistine." Saul said to David, "Go, and the Lord be with you." 1 Samuel 17:34-37 (NIV)

Sometimes you just need to remember what you have come through so you can gain perspective of all God is able to do. David, a young man who had no previous giant slaying experience, faced a pretty daunting enemy in Goliath. However, he had a moment of memory recall; he was on the hillside when a lion and a bear both tried to take the flock he was entrusted to protect. David was unsure how to tackle the wild animals who had his sheep as their dinner choice and yet in his uncertainty he trusted in God's ability and he chased off a predator that could have also had him for dinner. David had never faced a Goliath before but instead of focus on what he didn't know, he recalled what he did know. He knew that God had helped him defeat wild animals and that gave him confidence in God's ability. If He could help him with a lion, why wouldn't He help him with this giant?

Sometimes when we face situations that seem far too big for us to navigate, we need to do what David did and replay a few of the highlight reels from what God has done for us. Just a glance at the path you have previously trodden will reveal not only how much you have overcome, but it will also show that you never took one step alone. Alongside your footprints you will find His. You will capture afresh just how steadfast His love has been. How in your weakness He was strength. In weariness He was water to your soul. You will see on the path travelled a trail of His provision and protection. You will catch a glimpse of where you walked with goodness and mercy as your companions.

What seems overwhelming in this moment will soon be overwhelmed by the power of how He has worked in all those other moments. So what right now do you think you can't do, what is daunting to you? Think how that list used to read, maybe back then your battle was with shame or your giant was insecurity but now you are free and stand confidently. Let that previous victory give courage for the present reality. If God can do that for you, why wouldn't He help you now? If you can overcome those giants why not these? The same God is with you and the same God is for you. Remember how far you have come and take courage for where you are about to go. So go ahead, take a glance, recall His goodness, lift up your thankfulness and remove the fear from your future. God is able my friend, so let's go!

THINK IT ━━━━━━━━━━━━━ 304

SPEAK IT ━━━━━━━━━━━━━━━━━

BE IT ━━━━━━━━━━━━━━━━━

He measured off another thousand, but now it was a river that I could not cross, because the water had risen and was deep enough to swim in - a river that no one could cross. He asked me, "Son of man, do you see this?" Then He led me back to the bank of the river. Ezekiel 47:5-6 (NIV)

Have you ever been to a swimming pool and seen a sign that says, shallow end? It's letting you know that the depth in this part of the pool prohibits your movement, you can't dive and you will find it harder to swim. The shallow end is for those who aren't able to swim well and usually it's filled with children who are just learning how to navigate the water.

In life we also need to know when we are in the shallow end and when it's time for us to leave. Here are a few things that will let you know if you are in the shallows in different areas of your life.

1. Shallows are where your feet are firmly on the ground. That means you are in control in a way that is maybe a little too safe, you can resist any waves. Shallows are not going to challenge your swimming ability, it's easy to find the bottom. Where in your life are your feet more fixed than they should be? Where has stubbornness become your shallow end? Where should you be diving but the shallow end means you are only standing?

2. Shallows mean you are never fully submerged. Sometimes we need total immersion for progress to happen. Where are you holding back from fully letting go? Are you fully immersed in faith or half in and half out in fear? Are you fully committed or undecided; shallows will hold back what total submergence will welcome.

3. Big fish can't survive in the shallows. A while ago, I was with a friend in South Africa and we had booked to go cage diving to see great white sharks, my friend convinced me this was what my life needed. However, the dive was cancelled because a whale had beached itself in the shallows, it couldn't survive there so the sharks were eating the whale carcass. Shallows won't allow big dreams or big ideas, they will be beached and die if you don't go beyond and into deeper water. So stop trying to birth in the shallows what can only live in the deep.

Where do you need to take your feet off the ground? Stop living half in and half out where it is time to jump in. Fear loves the shallows but faith wants you to go further and realise you were made for deeper. Write down some deep end decisions so that the shallows become less and less where you are living.

THINK IT ━━━━━━━━━━━━━━ 306

SPEAK IT ━━━━━━━━━━━━━━━

BE IT ━━━━━━━━━━━━━━━

**"The Lord gave, and the Lord has taken away; blessed be the name of the Lord."
Job 1:21(NKJV)**

I am sure you have played the game of snakes and ladders at some point in your life. One minute you are up and the next roll of the dice you are going down. The game is frustrating and can be a little like life; we can go from the high to the low, sometimes so suddenly you didn't see it coming. It's the redundancy you weren't expecting, the health issue that you discover out of the blue, it's the tragedy that happens. One minute things were good and now they are not good at all. No one is immune from the rise and fall of life. Success happens and so does failure so rather than being caught off guard, we need to build in a way that understands both of these are on the board of life and we need to know how to carry on playing either way.

In success we can forget to acknowledge God because things are so good we don't feel we need to pray as much. We can get so busy managing our success we can think we don't need to talk to God or seek His wisdom. The high can change us and even distance us from those around us. I have watched people with successful careers who lose perspective, those who say, I am doing it all for my family, but have lost their family. In the times when we are doing well, we need to also make sure spiritually we stay well. Every win should be enjoyed but remember, sometimes we have ladders and other times we have snakes, so don't let success blind you.

In failure we can tend to feel so disheartened and embarrassed we withdraw. We can quickly forget all our wins because we feel so overwhelmed by this loss. We have to keep perspective and know that rise and fall, ebb and flow are just a part of our story. Failure isn't final and therefore we should not make decisions in failure that turn what's temporary into something permanent. In failure we may pray more but we can also panic more and in panic we can make poor choices. So when the snake moments appear, we need to keep our head clear. Job knew this game all too well, from everything to nothing to everything again. Moses went from prince to fugitive to deliverer. The disciples would experience success and failure all the time with Jesus: one day they would be healing and helping people, other days Jesus was rebuking their unbelief and cleaning up their mess. One day they would be praying for the sick, another day they couldn't even stay awake to pray for their Saviour. Jesus wanted them to find a strategy to stay in play. So today, maybe it's snakes or maybe ladders, wherever you are, make a decision to stay in the game.

THINK IT ━━━━━━━━━━━━━━━ 308

SPEAK IT ━━━━━━━━━━━━━━━

BE IT ━━━━━━━━━━━━━━━

EXHALE

Jesus then took the loaves, gave thanks, and distributed to those who were seated as much as they wanted. John 6:11 (NIV)

There are times when we need to think on our feet, where the guests we didn't know were coming arrive and the people who were dropping by stayed all night. The moments where you need a plan and quick so that you can keep momentum. Jesus had these moments too. He had taught all day but the crowds weren't leaving and needed feeding; He wanted to take care of their needs and so He asked His team, what shall we do?

It's in these scenarios you soon find out about the way people respond to problems. The first reaction is a good indication whether they are someone who adds to problems, subtracts from problems or multiplies the possibilities. Jesus wanted His disciples to have a multiplication anointing; the ability to multiply answers and subtract problems. He wanted them to know how to reduce the need and not add to the stress. Scripture says Jesus already had in mind what He was going to do, but He wanted to know, what would they do?

Jesus first asked Philip, where shall we buy bread for all the people? The answer that came back was not one that helped reduce the problem, instead Philip added to it. He let Jesus know how expensive this shopping trip would be, yet Jesus didn't ask him how much money it would cost. Some people after hearing about the situation you are facing will begin to add more problems, they will introduce thoughts you hadn't even entertained that don't make the problem smaller but larger.

Then it was Andrew's turn, he was a subtractor in this scenario. He offered Jesus a way to take the problem down from 5000 hungry people to maybe 4995 as he came forward with the fives loaves and the two fish. He introduced an option; though it was nowhere near enough to feed everyone, it could help someone. He brought forward something to start to subtract the stress, not add to it. God loves our subtracting contributions, the suggestions that make the miracle possible, the ideas that may only help a few but in His hands can help the many.

Finally, Jesus showed what it looks like to not add problems or just subtract but to multiply the answer. He broke the bread and began to feed the crowd. His hands had a multiplication anointing, one answer led to another and then to another. I wonder what your first response is in a crisis? Do you add, subtract or multiply? What do the people in your world do when asked how to deal with the problem? We all need friends who subtract but we also need to believe for hands that learn how to multiply the miracle.

THINK IT ━━━━━━━━━━━━━ 310

SPEAK IT ━━━━━━━━━━━━━

BE IT ━━━━━━━━━━━━━

EXHALE

"Let me tell you why you are here. You're here to be salt-seasoning that brings out the God-flavours of this earth. If you lose your saltiness, how will people taste godliness? You've lost your usefulness and will end up in the garbage. Here's another way to put it: you're here to be light, bringing out the God-colors in the world. God is not a secret to be kept." Matthew 5.13-14 (MSG)

Just because you don't always understand something doesn't mean you can't appreciate it, even come to find a place for it in your world. I travel often and have got used to the many different pieces of documentation I require but over time things change and now instead of the paper ticket, it's all barcodes and downloads. I often feel that I need the security of my piece of paper, it's easier to see my name and my seat but that barcoded box has now replaced all the written information with a digital code. I have no idea how those lines inside the square tell the airline that my seat is on the flight pending, but they do. This little invention that took years of someone's life to discover, is now saving hours of my time and causing me to be more efficient when I travel.

Often we can throw away the ideas, wisdom, advice we don't understand, because we become nervous to try things we haven't initiated ourselves. We can be so organised and safe, we have left no room to be spontaneous. Or alternatively we can be so spontaneous and free, we have no time to listen to someone's order and strategy. The truth is we need both and both need each other. Don't be so quick to discard the ideas others have, don't throw out the things you don't understand. Give people time to get creative and allow new thinking to become part of what causes you to grow in curiosity, instead of going in the opposite direction and deepening in your predictability.

Embrace team in your world, the crazy, the creatives, the young and old, loud and silent types, traditional and comical. Give space for ideas to breathe and thinking to expand. I love when I get around my team or a group of leaders all full of amazing ideas and different ways of seeing and doing the same thing. Where do you need to find a willingness to hear what you may not even yet see, and see what you may not fully understand?

Colour in your future with new ideas and new shades, don't get stuck in the predictable. Don't be afraid of the changes just because you aren't in control of them. As long as we are all putting the ball in the same net, then how it gets there is irrelevant. Do what needs to be done and in doing so, have fun. Today, make some room for something new.

THINK IT ━━━━━━━━━━━━━━ 312

SPEAK IT ━━━━━━━━━━━━━━━━

BE IT ━━━━━━━━━━━━━━━━

EXHALE

For His anger lasts only a moment, but His favour lasts a lifetime.
Psalm 30:5 (NIV)

Everyone has a boiling point, some are quick to boil while others are slow burners. Some people never seem to be angry but don't let that fool you, we all express our boiling point differently. We all have certain things that flip our switch, maybe it's when you're disrespected, when you don't get your own way, when you feel taken for granted. The Bible says that His anger lasts a moment so even God gets angry but notice the anger has a short leash.

Raising our children we have always kept a very short account when it comes to those anger issues. We have had to teach our kids that boiling points need to be identified and neutralised. If you know what flips on the boil switch then you better know how to switch it off. Jesus had a moment of anger recorded in the Bible; His boiling point was the disrespect of His Father's house. He was angry at the way money lenders and traders were taking what was a holy place and using it for business. Jesus boiled over and cleared out that temple but then He regained His composure. The episode was short but its impact was felt. The anger was expressed but the damage was controlled. So how do you deal with anger? Here's a few things that I hope will help you as you seek to control this emotion.

1. Identify what flips that switch - what is it that always gets your temperature rising and your frustration overflowing? Once you know who and what has the ability to make you angry, you can then ask for help and wisdom in this area. You can start to take the power back and you can put strategies in place to avoid unnecessary fall out.

2. Fasten a leash - put things in place that restrict what your temper gets to do and say. When you're angry, don't get on the phone, don't start a conversation you will later regret, find an outlet. I used to tell my son to count to ten to slow down what's about to explode. Maybe your leash is not to say certain words like divorce or hate, words that cause huge damage way beyond the heated moment.

3. Don't go to sleep in anger - however you turn off that switch, do it before you close your eyes. Don't let anger fester, if you do it will take less and less to flip the switch. Say sorry, pray until it passes, do whatever it takes to switch off what rage wants to keep on.

Today, face what angers you and then find a way to not allow it to have control over you. Let's have anger management that will lead to a lot less damage in the long run.

THINK IT ━━━━━━━━━━━ 314

SPEAK IT ━━━━━━━━━━━━━

BE IT ━━━━━━━━━━━

EXHALE

"For who has despised the day of small things? For these seven rejoice to see the plumb line in the hand of Zerubbabel. They are the eyes of the Lord, Which scan to and fro throughout the whole earth." Zechariah 4:10 (NKJV)

Not all growth is equally visible. Sometimes the growth you are looking for is happening in the places you aren't looking. I know this is true in the natural because many times as a parent I have noticed my kids are growing out of their clothes and so I have bought new jeans or longer sleeved shirts but I have failed to check their feet. That's the growth that I couldn't see but it didn't mean there wasn't growth happening. It would only come to my attention when one of the children would say how uncomfortable their shoes were. I provided for what was obvious but neglected the growth that was not as visible.

Our spiritual growth can be just like that, we can get excited or disappointed by the growth or lack of it in the areas we see everyday but we forget about the growth that is happening that is more hidden away. I have often spoken to church leaders who feel like quitting because they don't think they are growing. All their focus is on who comes on Sunday and if that doesn't show increase, they determine that what they are doing has simply stopped working but if you start to ask a few more questions, it often turns out they are doing better than they think. They forgot to take into account the growth in their discipleship programme, they didn't add in the fact that the team had grown in wisdom and unity, they never saw the growth that happened in the kids ministry. So the truth was though in an area that was maybe more obvious there wasn't the growth expected, that didn't mean nothing had grown.

Maybe right now you are struggling with a sense of disappointment because the growth you wanted to see in a certain area hasn't happened but what about the other areas? Check the feet and you may find that growth has been happening all along. Maybe you didn't grow into the promotion you wanted but what about the new skills you learnt in the preparation process? Perhaps your finances didn't grow as quickly as you hoped but what about the growth in your budgeting and stewardship? Maybe your kids didn't grow in the area of responsibility you had hoped for but they grew in the area of understanding what needs to happen so they can move forward.

Growth spurts are great but so are those small and steady increases that happen over time. So today, celebrate the growth, not just in the big stuff but in the small stuff too.

THINK IT ━━━━━━━━━━ 316

SPEAK IT ━━━━━━━━━━━━━━

BE IT ━━━━━━━━━━━━━━

EXHALE

Pouring yourselves out for each other in acts of love, alert at noticing differences and quick at mending fences. Ephesians 4:1-3 (MSG)

A while ago we had a rabbit appear on our lawn, no big deal. It was a novelty, our kids thought it was cute and wanted to adopt it as a family pet. My husband was less keen; he knew that the bunny had somehow found a hole in the fence that surrounds our garden and is designed to keep out wildlife. The rabbit soon decided that he liked our lawn and brought his entire rabbit family over for a visit; they happily chewed on the plants and left a whole pile of droppings behind. Still, life is busy and we didn't take the time to find the hole in the fence that was letting our visitors in. This led to a much more sinister problem as the rabbit hole became the entrance point for a fox, who came through the fence and into our neighbour's garden, where he proceeded to eat all of their chickens. Suddenly the cute rabbit had led to a much more devastating set of events.

If we had been quicker to fix the place where the rabbit had got in, then all of this could have been avoided. How often has this very same scenario played out in our own lives, how many more times do we have to learn the hard way? This verse in Ephesians tells us we need to be quick to mend our fences if we want to build a life that has peace and a sense of unity. We can all have holes in our fences caused by bitterness, disappointment and failure. These moments put a hole in our confidence, faith and trust and if we are not quick to fix them, we will find the enemy wastes no time in sending devastation through them.

So how do we start to mend the hole? The first thing this verse says is, we need to be alert to noticing differences and quick at mending fences. Alert and quick: those two words are essential in the process of mending things that the enemy has a vested interest in destroying. We often ignore the thing we know needs to be dealt with, we put up with the dysfunction instead of addressing it. If you have a hole in your fence from something that happened a week, month, year ago, then the word quick is not applicable.

Where are there holes in the fence that need some attention, problems relationally that have been left for far too long? Maybe it's time to ask God to give you the strength to mend the fence. The great news is, if you are up for the work, God is able to make all things new. Let's carry this thought on over the next few days but right now, make your focus a renewed willingness to fix what has been left for far too long in disrepair.

SPEAK IT ═══════════════

BE IT ═══════════════

And I went out by night...and viewed the walls of Jerusalem which were broken down and its gates which were burned with fire. Nehemiah 2:13 (NKJV)

We are thinking about the verse in Ephesians that asks us to be alert at noticing differences and quick to mend fences. Let's take some lessons from Nehemiah, who literally rebuilt the broken down walls of Jerusalem. He had a burden to rebuild the city walls from the rubble they had become, so the people could come back together and worship, getting God back as their centre. Nehemiah applied principles to mending these physical walls that are so instructive for mending the fences in our own lives.

1. Examine the walls. Nehemiah took a trip under the cover of darkness, he went out with just a few helpers to find out just how bad the destruction of the walls was. He went to examine the places that were damaged so he could determine how much work was needed to rebuild. If we are going to fix the fence, we too have to take a journey of examining our walls. We need to be honest and open enough to walk around the places where things aren't right and identify where it went wrong. We need to not just say there is an issue but locate the place of the injury. Examining the walls may mean asking God to help you highlight where the problem lies. Today, can you identify where the hole is, can you take a walk around your relational, financial, personal life and examine the walls and then find the place that needs a little more attention?

2. Manage the mission. Nehemiah saw there was a lot of work to be done but instead of being overwhelmed, he made the mission manageable. He didn't call everyone together into some big building operation that was complex and hard to follow. He had a plan that was so simple but so effective. He gave everyone an instruction to fix what was in front of them. In Nehemiah 3, he told the priests that everyone was to work on what was outside their door, to fix what they could see was broken when they opened their curtains in the morning. How often do we point out all the things others need to fix but what if we all agreed to just fix what was in front of us? Practically, what does that look like? Well, if you have impatience in front of you, then that's your place of work; if the thing in front of you is your critical comments, then start there. Surely our gift to one another is to work on our own holes before we try and tell others what to do with theirs.

So today, start the journey and examine your walls, write down the place that needs attention and then make some decisions that are going to help you fix what's in front of you.

THINK IT ━━━━━━━━━━━━━ 320

SPEAK IT ━━━━━━━━━━━━━━

BE IT ━━━━━━━━━━━━━━

EXHALE

ACT
JUSTLY
LOVE
MERCY
WALK
HUMBLY

MICAH
6:8

But they were scheming to harm me; so I sent messengers to them with this reply: "I am carrying on a great project and cannot go down. Why should the work stop while I leave it and go down to you?" Nehemiah 6.2-3 (NIV)

So let's wrap up our train of thought from the past few days with some final wisdom from Nehemiah's commitment to rebuild. Let's see what he did after examining the walls and fixing what was in front of him. Nehemiah had everyone focused and progress was being made; people left the rubble and started seeing that restoration was possible. The enemy was getting increasingly uncomfortable and he's always the same - he doesn't want you to close those holes in the fence that he has for years used as his access point for all kinds of pain. We can't expect our new commitment to fix things to go without resistance. When Nehemiah was up the ladder, he had an adversary show up; the enemy came to invite him into a conversation. Yet Nehemiah knew this invitation was not to help but to hinder. We all need to become wise to the enemy's plans to try and get us off the reconstruction and back down into the rubble. The enemy wants to call you down from the progress and drag you back into the mess, he wants the conversation that kept the walls in ruins to flourish. However, Nehemiah knew this invite was to harm him and so he refused to leave the great work he was a part of.

We also, like Nehemiah, need to know how to stay on our ladder and avoid the chatter that wants to pull you back, the gossip that wants more company. The chatter that is about delaying and derailing the work you are restoring. Nehemiah reminded his enemy he was about a great project and he wouldn't be coming down today. Where do you need to do the same? What conversation do you need to exit so you can stay busy reconstructing? If you're being distracted by things from the past, voices in the rubble, stay focused on the great work in front of you and keep building. Stay on your ladder until the work is done. The enemy didn't just come once but four times. On the fifth he started to falsely accuse Nehemiah and yet his response was the same, to ignore what needed no more of his time.

The air is different on the ladder, it's cleaner and less toxic when you start getting out of the mess. If you're about the work of mending the fence you will also be asked to leave your ladder but like Nehemiah, remind your heart this is good work and remind your soul to stay strong. What you are rebuilding is to do with the generations who will follow on after you so don't stop now, stay on the ladder, you got this and God's got you.

THINK IT ━━━━━━━━━━━━━━━ 322

SPEAK IT ━━━━━━━━━━━━━━━

BE IT ━━━━━━━━━━━━━━━

EXHALE

"Does the clay say to the potter, 'What are you making?' Does your work say, 'The potter has no hands?'" Isaiah 45:9 (NIV)

Have you ever worked with clay before? Maybe you once made a pot at school or went to one of those pottery painting parties or maybe you have just played with kids and their playdough. The clay has to be pliable enough so that the potter can have free reign to create whatever masterpiece they choose, the clay doesn't get to tell the potter what to do, it's the clay's job to just work in the potter's hands.

The Bible describes our relationship with God like one of a potter and his clay. We are the clay and God is the Potter to our life and He is making our lives into the vessel of His choosing. I think sometimes we get these roles confused, we want to be the potter. We try and dictate what shape we will be, however I have learnt that I don't want to put my life in the kiln and set my shape before God has finished His work. How sad if the size and shape we decide we should be is far less than what the Potter had planned for you and I. Our role in this relationship requires trust and continual pliability. We have to stay on the Potter's wheel and allow Him to keep working and keep molding how He sees fit for our future.

We have to allow the shaping of God to be consistent so we don't become hardened in areas that He hasn't finished with yet. Heartache and hurts will all have a hardening effect on our clay, that's why we have to stay on the wheel. Just like a potter uses water in their hands as they shape the clay, God wants you and I to use His word as water to our soul to wash and lubricate what pain and disappointment wants to harden and suffocate. If we allow, even in the worst of times, God to mold us and to bring out the best in us, then our pliability will become a way in which we are to able to repurpose that pain. Imagine if Job had got off the wheel in his worst moment or if Samson had put his life in the kiln when he lost his strength. We have to stay on the wheel even when it hurts to avoid our lives taking the shape of pain, fixing around what happened to us rather than letting the Potter reshape with His wisdom and grace something more beautiful to work in and through us. If we stay like that clay on the wheel, then God can help fix the cracks and remold the things that have been destroyed.

Let these words of the old song by the beautiful Darlene Zschech resonate in your heart today: 'take me, mold me, lead me, guide me, I give my life to the Potter's hands'.

THINK IT ————————————— **324**

SPEAK IT ————————————

BE IT ————————————

Every good and perfect gift is from above, coming down from the Father of the heavenly lights, who does not change like shifting shadows. James 1:17 (NIV)

Sometimes the best gift to receive is a gift voucher. It may be less exciting to open but the older you get, the more you start to appreciate the possibilities that the voucher allows you to have. It may save you from having to awkwardly accept something that was chosen for you but is definitely not something that will be worn by you. The gift voucher presents options but it also presents a responsibility to activate its potential. How many times have you received a gift voucher and thought to yourself, I will go and redeem it later and then the later never happens? The voucher has the potential to purchase something for you but only if you remember to take it with you. It comes with a dreaded expiry date that may seem months away when you receive it but suddenly that huge amount of time you thought you had has disappeared.

In our spiritual lives I wonder where we have unspent gift vouchers, where are we sat with an ability to do something and we keep thinking, I will do it later. We have a talent that we could be using to make a difference but we say to ourselves, I am waiting for the perfect opportunity. As time goes by we become more and more selective about what opportunity we will take. Where could we take our gift of service and use it but instead we leave it on the shelf of our life? God has placed gifts inside you but you have to go and redeem them. You need to use them now and not leave them for some time that may never actually be the right time. Remember Esther when she told her uncle she couldn't help her people. He sent word back to her to remind her, if you don't speak up a nation will suffer. Esther was in a place where she needed to find her voice now, approach the king now. Without using her position, others would perish.

Often we hesitate on using the gift we have because we fear making a choice; what if something better comes along and I used this on something I don't like as much? This is faulty thinking: God doesn't give you everything all at once, He staggers those gifts, He keeps putting things in your hand to do, serve, give. Hoarding vouchers serves no one, especially you. We have a birthday every year, we don't need to hoard our gift vouchers as if another will never come. So what do you need to check the expiry date on and where do you need to stop deliberating and start investing? Today is a great day to take what you have to give with you and look for ways to start using that gift.

THINK IT ━━━━━━━━━━━━━━

SPEAK IT ━━━━━━━━━━━━━━

BE IT ━━━━━━━━━━━━━━

EXHALE

I have considered my ways and have turned my steps to Your statutes. I will hasten and not delay to obey Your commands. Psalm 119.59-60 (NIV)

Have you ever been sat in a lane of traffic and grown increasingly frustrated at the lack of movement? Recently I had left our church services to find myself stuck in a huge lane of traffic with no one moving anywhere. As time progressed and the traffic didn't, I began to get annoyed at what seemed to be a set of temporary traffic lights that were causing a permanent problem. As I sat complaining to myself there was a knock on my car window, one of our church members was in the same lane and had come to inform me that she thought the lights were broken, everyone was stuck at the other side of a red light that was not going to turn green any time soon.

Though I was several cars from the front, this lady assured me if I just went past the stop light, others would follow. So that's exactly what I did, I put my foot on the accelerator and pulled out of the lane of traffic so I could then go straight through at the stop light. Sure enough, the light was broken and the traffic did follow my lead. Suddenly, where we had been stuck for what seemed like hours now had movement because what we naturally assumed was working, we discovered was actually broken. What had been set up to help the flow of traffic keep moving had become the reason the traffic was at a standstill.

Too often we pray against or talk about the obstacles in our way whilst never examining the possibility that we may be getting in our own way. We can sit at the stop light complaining when we could start changing. When we make every problem external, we can overlook our own internal limitations that may be just as responsible for holding us up. We need at times to get out of our own way, remove our own smallness, cut back on our own negativity. We need to remove selfishness or insecurity as they are imprisoning our potential. Gideon had to get out of his own way, telling God he was the weakest of the weak. God's reply was simple, Gideon stop talking and go in the strength you have, stop putting the breaks on your own breakthrough.

Be diligent in leading yourself to a place of greater learning and deeper understanding. Choose to exit lanes you don't need to be sat in and avoid delays that can be of your own making. Move out of your doubt, move away from your lack. Speak to your soul, proclaim good things and stop saying, I can't, when you serve a God who has no limitation. Clear the way and stay diligent to keep the internal conversations propelling you past the external delays.

THINK IT ━━━━━━━━━━━━━━ 328

SPEAK IT ━━━━━━━━━━━━━━

BE IT ━━━━━━━━━━━━━━

EXHALE

"So now, go. I am sending you to Pharaoh to bring my people the Israelites out of Egypt." Exodus 3:10 (NIV)

"Sir, a woman preaching is like a dog walking on its hind legs. It is not done well but you are surprised to see it done at all." This quote jumped out at me when I heard it in a movie. I began to give thanks once again for those who have gone before us and fought so many can have a voice. Think of heroes past and present that have stood up in the face of prejudice, be it racism, sexism, ageism, those who have said to the dictators, the freedom takers, the narrow minded, we will not listen to your lies or give into your demands any more.

Sometimes we forget how far we have come and how many fights have been fought for freedom, whether it be in the church, workplace or life in general. We can take the liberty we have for granted, we can assume it's always been that way but everytime we forget the fight that was fought for us, we also forget to keep alive that fight within us. The enemy doesn't give up that easily, hatred and bigotry can affect every generation so we must not forget what was won so that it cannot be lost.

I hate how evil seeks to separate and confuse what God created to unite and compliment. I have been on the receiving end of sexism several times and it is not something we should be ok with. I love the family of God and how we are made to serve and build alongside each other. We are in this together. We need to do better, expect better and model better. Let's always see the best in one another, no matter the skin colour, social background, male or female, old or young. Insulting and making jokes about others isn't innocent, it is cowardly and ugly. When Peter received a vision about preaching to the Gentiles, he had to address a hidden prejudice. God was going to make Peter unite what he was happy to keep divided. Peter's struggle was acceptance of difference but Jesus' example was that without difference, we can never reflect God's greatness.

Let's be students of the ones who fought without thanks and let's pass on the lessons they taught us. God used people like Esther and Moses to fight injustice, to save entire peoples from slavery and genocide. God used everyday people to bring freedom to millions and that is still the way God works today. He looks for those who are willing to say, enough is enough and places within them the tenacity to say what needs to be said even when it is tough. So today, let's face our lack of tolerance, let's ask God to give us more understanding and let's pray with those who fight what many would ignore.

THINK IT ━━━━━━━━━━━━━━ **330**

SPEAK IT ━━━━━━━━━━━━━━━━━

BE IT ━━━━━━━━━━━━━━━━━

EXHALE

As they were walking along the road, a man said to Him, "I will follow you wherever you go." Jesus replied, "Foxes have dens and birds have nests, but the Son of Man has no place to lay His head." Luke 9:57-58 (NIV)

When people wanted to follow Jesus and become His disciples, sometimes His answers were rather shocking. In Luke 14 He says, "If anyone comes to me and does not hate father and mother, wife and children, brothers and sisters - yes, even their own life - such a person cannot be My disciple." He would tell people they wouldn't have a place to stay or that they would be persecuted. Jesus made the job one few brave applicants would apply for. What Jesus was checking was, do you have a point of no return? Is there a line you just won't cross? Is there an ask that would be one too many? He wants to know if things get tough, would you be able to tough it out? When it comes to following Jesus, there is no room for keeping your options open.

The Bible says there is one way and that way is narrow. Jesus is trying to help us by challenging us with this question, are you past the point of no return? Have your reached the point where you have nowhere else to go, you are lining up no more options, you're all in? Many who said they would follow Jesus did while it was working for them but disowned Him when the following looked like a cross and nails.

In Luke 9, Jesus challenges three types of people: the enthusiastic, the nostalgic and the apologetic. The enthusiast says he wants to follow Jesus anywhere, so Jesus says great but just so you know, that means staying anywhere, sleeping rough, no home comforts. He wanted to see if he had a point of no return and whether the discomfort and inconvenience would turn this follower into a sideline observer. For the nostalgic, Jesus challenged their commitment to move ahead when all their focus was on what they were leaving behind. For the apologetic, the one who needed to leave things tidy before he could follow, Jesus pointed out that it wasn't going to work without full commitment to the task in hand. I wonder which you would be or are you a little of all three?

Do you have a point of no return? If you're asked to give do you back out? If you're corrected do you disappear? We need to make sure if we really want to follow Jesus that we have removed any other options so that when we say, I will follow You, that's exactly what we do. We have no hidden clauses, and no small print in the contract. You don't need an escape plan when God's your life planner. So ditch the life boat and back up plan and go all in.

THINK IT ━━━━━━━━━━ 332

SPEAK IT ━━━━━━━━━━

BE IT ━━━━━━━━━━

EXHALE

Ants are creatures of little strength, yet they store up their food in the summer. Proverbs 30.35 (NIV)

In my cupboard at home you will find milk chocolate, you will find tea bags, you will find cookies, strong English mustard and coconut milk. You may think those items don't sound unusual and I agree but for them to be in my cupboard is unusual. I don't eat or use any of these things. I don't like milk chocolate and, sorry to shatter the British stereotype, but I don't drink English tea. I buy these things because I have people who regularly come to my house who love tea and a cookie, they like milk not dark chocolate. I am always mindful of who may pop over in the week and I want to make sure if they do come, they know I have already thought about them.

We all need to have something in our cupboards that is there simply to bless someone else. Living with a cupboard that had just enough for you to get by is not the abundant life you are called for. I remember in my student years I shared the house with three girls who would write their name on every tin they bought. If we are not careful, that mentality can carry over into our lives, we can say we are being wise in our management of our resources but we need to be careful that's not become an excuse for stingy living. We need to have a life that doesn't label the tins but has extra for others who may come over. We need not a little wisdom but a cupboard full of it, not just enough patience but more than enough to go around. We need to fill our cupboards with what others may need. Imagine Noah's shopping list for the ark; I'm sure he had to fill it with all kinds of grains, hay and plants, not for his consumption but because his house guests were about to arrive two by two. If Noah had empty cupboards then that ark would have become survival of the fittest. Selfishness never stocks the shelves for others and as a result, it receive less visitors who want to be a part of that life.

Let's restock our shelves now instead of having to do an emergency shop later. Store some knowledge for others that may need to learn from you. Put some extra joy on the shelf; if you've got enough for your day, put some in the cupboard for someone else's day. If you have some spare time, put it on the shelf to bless someone's life. I love when friends come and open my cupboard and say, those are my favourite and I say, I know, I got them just for you. I think that's how God is with His kids and so maybe He wants His kids to carry on that family tradition.

SPEAK IT ━━━━━━━━━━━━━━━

BE IT ━━━━━━━━━━━━━━━

"When two of you get together on anything at all on earth and make a prayer of it, My Father in heaven goes into action. And when two or three of you are together because of Me, you can be sure that I'll be there." Matthew 18:18-20 (MSG)

I confess I love the Star Wars movies. They bring back a lot of childhood memories, watching them over and over, and now I am rewatching them all with my own kids. The films are the classic fight between good and evil, a battle of the forces. Anyone who has ever watched the movies knows that the Jedi in training have to find and use the force that is within them, the invisible force that has tangible results, a force that sends out power and fights against their enemy. Maybe we all need a Jedi training moment, a reminder that we are also carrying a force within us, that we need to use that force and let it flow through us.

We have a force on the inside: His name is Jesus. His power and His presence reside within us and that force needs to be used more often and more deliberately. The Spirit of God that abides in the people of God is not to be contained but released and we need to use that force everyday to fight for what is ours and for one another. You may not feel like you have power today but that's not true, you do. Maybe you just need to activate that force with faith, to start to draw on what's within you and place a demand on the power that flows through your life.

One of the ways we need to activate our force is by joining it with others. The Bible tells us that where two or three are gathered in Jesus name, He is there too. Your force of faith, prayer, believing is meant to join with others. We activate things on a whole different level when we engage on purpose the power within us. We need more ways in which we use what we have to strengthen what maybe others lack. Today, who are you joining your force of faith with? Who on your prayer list is feeling your power in their situation? Where are you using your force of faith to uphold another who is faltering? Activate your force on a daily basis, engage on purpose for purpose, someone needs you to join forces with them today. Maybe you can start a prayer chain or intentionally let someone know you are going to add your faith to theirs by praying with them. The force of faith you have can strengthen someone, the force you are for good can bless someone. Today, where will you use the force? If we want to push back darkness then we need everyone to awaken the force within them; let's join forces and unleash the power that resides within us.

THINK IT ━━━━━━━━━━━━━━ 336

SPEAK IT ━━━━━━━━━━━━━━━━

BE IT ━━━━━━━━━━━━━━━━━

As water reflects the face, so one's life reflects the heart.
Proverbs 27:19 (NIV)

Have you ever asked someone if they are ok, they say they are great but their face tells you a different story? Our face tells a story all by itself, as we get older we can get better at faking it but usually it doesn't take much to spot the fake face from the real face. Kids have no concept of faking it, just watch them opening their presents on Christmas day and you can see the different expressions their faces make, the face that says I love this gift and the face that just can't hide they hate the gift.

Our faces are mirrors of what's going on inside us. The tears tell a story, the laughter lines express the joy, the tired eyes don't lie and the furrowed brow lets us know the concerns that run deep on the inside. So maybe we need to get better at facing what our face is saying, stop trying to tell a different story to the one our reflection is clearly shouting. If we don't like what we see in the mirror, then we need to go to the source of the reflection.

When I was growing up and I was feeling unhappy, upset or grumpy, I would often hear the expression, fix your face. What was meant was, we are not going out while you are giving off that vibe so fix what your face is saying. The truth is, what we should be saying is fix your heart, as the face won't change if the heart doesn't. So where does your face need a lift? Where does your downcast soul need to be told to praise God? Where does your moodiness need a dose of God's goodness? Maybe you're not even aware of the facial expressions you are making; you have become so used to your disposition you have accepted that's your look. You have resigned yourself as somber or morose but the truth is, you were made in the image of God and I somehow find it hard to imagine His face as being one that is hard to read.

We can actually fix our face if we choose to change our heart. Happiness won't last if it is based on what happens around or to us but a heart that reflects the goodness of God will always find a reason to smile; a heart that worships will always have a brighter countenance. So today, ask those around you, what is my face actually saying, what am I reflecting? Be willing to give yourself a face lift by meditating on something that will change your countenance, not on the loss but the gain, not on the work but the reward, not on what you have but on who He is. You never know, you may like your new look and decide to wear it more often.

THINK IT ━━━━━━━━━━━━ 338

SPEAK IT ━━━━━━━━━━━━

BE IT ━━━━━━━━━━━━

EXHALE

"As for me and my family, we'll worship God."
Joshua 24:15 (MSG)

You know the saying, 'you can choose your friends but you can't choose your family'. Well yes and no. We all have a family we are born into that we can't choose but we also all get the opportunity to have the family we decide to build and commit to. Our natural families come in all different shapes and sizes; some would say they have the best family, others would feel they had the worst start in life. Some families are close, others estranged. Some families are traditional, others less conventional. The family you were raised in may have shaped you but now it's your turn. We can't keep excusing what we are by what has gone before, we get to start choosing what we want to build. Just because your parents weren't loving doesn't mean you have to parent that way.

Steve and I both have great families but they are very different. We were raised in different nations and had all kinds of mixed up traditions. We had to decide how our family loves, laughs, shares, grows. The family we had in our hearts was something we would get to build with our own hands, our family could be unique, designer made, it could add in extra family members, it could be loud or quiet, it could be adventurous, courageous, it could play it safe or risk it all. Family was something we didn't just inherit but we actually got to invent.

As we began to build our family, we chose close friends that we knew would become like aunts and uncles to our children, extra voices of wisdom. Family would become our passion; as we grew in this understanding, we realised it was from that place of family we would also leave our legacy. The family of God means we have a lot of extra family members we get to connect and commit to. We have a new expression for family that is not geographical or cultural. How awesome is that?

So let me ask you a question: what family are you building? Maybe it's time to write down some family dreams; if you don't define them then it's hard for everyone to come into agreement about them. Our family has values we all uphold and things we defend. We have things that really matter and things that don't matter at all. Don't complain about what your family wasn't, instead use that energy to decide what your version of family will be. No family is perfect and so the aim is not to be something unachievable, the aim is to build something that you can love well. It's never too late to build what's in your heart and it's never too early to start praying and believing for what you see your future and family becoming, so why not start now?

THINK IT ━━━━━━━━━━━━━━━ **340**

SPEAK IT ━━━━━━━━━━━━━━━

BE IT ━━━━━━━━━━━━━━━

EXHALE

When you're given a box of candy, don't gulp it all down; eat too much chocolate and you'll make yourself sick. Proverbs 25:16 (MSG)

We can often be driven by an unreasonable need to figure everything out now. We want answers for all our unresolved questions by the morning, often causing more damage in haste than we would have ever incurred with more time and grace. It's kind of like eating cake...if you were given a whole cake to eat, though you may be hungry, common sense would tell you to eat the cake slowly. You would reason that just because the cake is given to you for eating, it doesn't mean it should all be eaten now. Eating the whole cake in one sitting turns what was supposed to be enjoyable and shared into something unpalatable and gluttonous. Cakes are to be eaten one slice at a time.

I have found that often the things we face in life, though they may all scream for attention at once, need just like that cake to be handled one slice at a time. We can cause spiritual heartburn and have emotional indigestion when we try and figure everything out instantly. You have heard the expression 'Rome wasn't built in a day', well it's true. I have been to Rome and it is breathtakingly beautiful; you sense as you take in the historical sights that they represent multiple lifetimes of dedicated commitment to keep building a little more everyday.

Our world wants instant but our reality is far different. Your marriage, friendships, ministry, home, did not appear overnight. Your problems can't all be solved in a day, it's going to happen one slice at a time. You and I don't have the capacity to eat the whole problem alone. We don't have the room to sort every unresolved issue out now. Stop forcing what needs more time and getting impatient when you need to allow for the process.

Maybe you have a lot to get through right now, but instead of giving yourself indigestion, why don't you choose your slice for today and start there. Maybe you have set some deadlines that are unrealistic, the intention was good but the application is untenable. Reset the deadline, create more room to breathe. There is often pressure from around us but sometimes the worst pressure is self inflicted. Take a step back and instead of trying to do everything, just do something. Instead of being there for everyone, just help someone. If you don't get everything done today, then give yourself a break and pick up where you left off tomorrow. Sometimes we are too hard on ourselves and we lose the enjoyment of what we have done because we are too overly obsessed by what is still to be done. Why not take a time out and enjoy a slice of life now, there will always be something to sink your teeth into later.

THINK IT ━━━━━━━━━━ 342

SPEAK IT ━━━━━━━━━━━━━━

BE IT ━━━━━━━━━━━━━━

EXHALE

Your kingdom is an everlasting kingdom, and Your dominion endures through all generations. The Lord is trustworthy in all He promises and faithful in all He does. Psalm 145:13 (NIV)

In the midst of what is temporal, let us stand on what is eternal. In a time where people are fighting for power, remember who holds the ultimate power. When many are making promises that may never be fulfilled, look to the One whose word never returns void. And in a season where much is being said in hate, pride and to degrade others, choose His way that speaks grace, honour and life. I am so very thankful that my world and my family's foundations are built on something far greater than policies or persuasive arguments. We are building on God's promises and kingdom purpose.

We serve a higher power, a King whose kingdom is being built on justice and truth, a King we can place our trust in. I, like you, don't have all the answers for the confusion in the world right now and I don't feel eloquent or smart enough to enter much of the debating and posturing politically and socially. We may feel out of our depth in offering practical solutions for such complex problems, yet that does not render us useless or sideline us as a spectator of where our hurting world finds herself. We have to wake up to the fact that we have a crucial part to play in our world, for we have knowledge and connection with the almighty God; therefore we can do something. Our response should not be to panic, or throw more anger or pain into the many problems that our world manifests. No, our best response is to understand our responsibility and capacity to change things through our willingness and earnestness to seek the face of God and to pray. Let us boldly approach His throne and pray with greater conviction and passion, let us serve our communities better and represent God's way to the many who have lost their way.

This is a time to draw closer to words that overwhelm everyone else's. This Psalm is a truth so powerful for us in our space and time in history. The words penned by those who have already fought the good fight are now words to strengthen our soul in our fight. These words are a safe harbour for those who may be trying to silence their fears today. Let your uncertainty and insecurity go to the feet of the one whose kingdom is unshakable and whose name is higher, the One who has kept His word for a thousand generations. The One who is the way the truth and the life, the One who has paved that way with love and grace for all. It is in God we trust, so like David, speak to your soul today, lift your head and let us all commit to panic less and pray more, 'thy kingdom come and thy will be done, here on earth as it is in Heaven'.

THINK IT ━━━━━━━━━ 344

SPEAK IT ━━━━━━━━━

BE IT ━━━━━━━━━

EXHALE

But in fact God has placed the parts in the body, every one of them, just as He wanted them to be. If they were all one part, where would the body be? As it is, there are many parts, but one body. 1 Corinthians 12:18-20 (NIV)

My daughter has an obsession with jigsaw puzzles; I think she got it from her nanny who likes to help feed her devotion. She can sit for hours and hours doing puzzles, she props up the box lid and then she gets the image in her mind of what she's building, then gets to work finding each piece. When I can see her getting frustrated at the seemingly ill fitting pieces, I also see her take another long look at the box lid, fixing the image again in her mind to inspire her to keep on searching for the pieces she is missing.

We have to choose in life whether we are looking at the pieces or the big picture. We need to know in the small that we are part of the big, and in the big we can achieve it by doing the small. If you lose the box lid, then the pieces soon lose their context and their purpose. Equally, without the pieces the box lid is just a picture that is painted but will never be constructed.

Sometimes if we over focus on pieces, we can become divided. We can think we have no need of one another but when we take a look at the box we can see we need unity because, if my piece isn't on the board, the picture can't be complete. As a family we all have our own piece we are working on but we need to not lose sight of the box lid that is the family we are adding our pieces into. In a church we need box lids everywhere so that the pieces are constantly reminded, you fit, so keep trying to find the exact place your piece was designed to be.

The box lid keeps you mindful of your bigger purpose. It says, you be you but at the same time, you belong with me. Have you ever picked up a piece from a puzzle and thought, this looks ridiculous, it's got weird colours and such an odd shape to it. When we isolate we can start to lose a sense of beauty, we can focus on what doesn't look right instead of realising, we are just right for the place God created us. If you weren't made that way, gifted that way, then when it came to the box lid you wouldn't be able to fit into the Master's design. Today, write down some aspects of the piece you represent. Consider ways you could fit and then ask, what is the box lid? Where have you lost sight of what this is all about? Let's get every piece on the board so we can complete each other not compare with one another.

THINK IT ━━━━━━━━━━━━━━━ 346

SPEAK IT ━━━━━━━━━━━━━━━

BE IT ━━━━━━━━━━━━━━━

EXHALE

Jesus loved Martha and her sister and Lazarus, but oddly, when He heard that Lazarus was sick, He stayed on where He was for two more days. John 11.5-7 (MSG)

A few years ago I was sat on an airplane desperate to get home to my family after a long time away speaking. I sat on the plane, seat belt fastened, when the captain made an announcement: ladies and gentlemen, we have to inform you that we have some major issues with the weather on our planned route, therefore we will face some big delays but the good news is, I will get you there, we just will have to go the long way around. Those words suddenly leapt into my spirit as I felt God say, that's how it is sometimes, I am the God of the suddenly but also the God of the slowly. There are times when the answer comes quickly and times when just like the pilot informed the passengers, for reasons we sometimes don't understand but have to trust, we will have to be willing to go the long way around.

I have experienced this in my walk with God on many occasions. I have sensed at times God preparing me for what will not come in an instant but could take months and has at times been years. When my husband and I were told we would probably never have children, I wanted God to move a mountain, preferably by the next afternoon. However, our infertility became a journey, we were going the long way around. For five years we believed, had treatment and nothing. Those five years were painful to navigate and very frustrating and challenging to my faith. I asked all the questions like, why me, what have I done to deserve this? I felt no answers but that reminder that we were going the long way around. Maybe that's where you are right now, your suddenly hasn't happened and you are sensing this is going to be a much longer journey.

Well, if that's you, my friend, let me encourage you today. God's got you and here's what I have discovered: when He takes you the long way around, He always gives you double for your trouble. Jesus didn't come suddenly to heal His close friend, Lazarus; He waited until healing was no longer an option because now he needed resurrection. Some may have thought Jesus was being unkind but He knew that Lazarus loved Him enough to trust He would come. That day Lazarus was raised, not only did he get a miracle but so did a whole crowd who watched and had their faith resurrected too. This miracle took double from the enemy with lives saved and God glorified. Today, maybe God knows you love Him enough to trust Him enough so stay strong, stay believing. If you are going the long way around, remember God will give you double for your trouble, so be encouraged.

THINK IT ━━━━━━━━━━━━━━━ 348

SPEAK IT ━━━━━━━━━━━━━━━

BE IT ━━━━━━━━━━━━━━━

EXHALE

Here is a trustworthy saying that deserves full acceptance: Christ Jesus came into the world to save sinners - of whom I am the worst. 1 Timothy 1:15 (NIV)

Sometimes we throw away what we deem imperfect and miss how beautiful the imperfections can really be. We have replaced uniqueness with usual and creativity with conformity. Yet when we learn to build with what's within, we start to trust that our creator God doesn't make mistakes. True beauty isn't being a copy of others but learning to see the purpose and joy in authenticity. I was recently in York, which is known for its historic buildings and ancient walkways. If you look down any of the town's main streets and alleyways, you will find no end of crooked buildings, some tall, some small, some leaning, others appear to be almost toppling over. The houses have stood for hundreds of years and despite their unusual building structure, they have withstood what many more conventional buildings could not.

On one particular street, The Shambles, these random and slightly awkward houses served a very unique purpose. Centuries ago, The Shambles became a place of great usefulness for the traders in this city. They discovered a benefit in the buildings' less than perfect structure, the leaning in of the walls meant they had shade in the street and so the houses provided a perfect place for local butchers to come and sell their meat. The closed in walls provided cover and cooled the temperatures; what could seem unusual became of great use.

Just like those misshapen buildings, we can all use the unique bumps and bends in our own walls to bless someone else's life. What we may think needs remodelling could very well be our unique gift to someone else's story. These buildings teach us to look for the beauty in everything and remember, what some walk right by as serving no purpose, to those who look with different eyes may become extremely useful. Remember Rahab, a woman who others would have said to stay away from, used by God to save the lives of His people. Or what about Saul, a murderer and persecutor of Christians who was then used to be the greatest evangelist. Or Moses, the stutterer who was called to be a deliverer. What about a widow who was penniless but became the host for a prophet to be fed. God loves taking what what no one thinks is worth using. God even used a donkey to redirect a stubborn man so don't you dare disqualify yourself because you don't look or sound like everybody else. The idea is not uniformity but unity and that means all our uniqueness can be used for His great purposes. So today, celebrate what others may have dismissed and know that in God, we all get to be used in the greatest call.

THINK IT ━━━━━━━━━━━ 350

SPEAK IT ━━━━━━━━━━━

BE IT ━━━━━━━━━━━

EXHALE

Finally, brothers and sisters, whatever is true, whatever is noble, whatever is right, whatever is pure, whatever is lovely, whatever is admirable - if anything is excellent or praiseworthy - think about such things. Philippians 4.8 (NIV)

Ok, let's be honest, we can all be guilty as charged. Overthinking everything leads often to doing nothing. It is a handbrake to your happiness and a stop signal to your sense of adventure. Yes, sure we need to be prayerful and thoughtful and there are things that need a lot of thinking. But that's not everything! You don't need to overthink every decision and conversation. Some people's overthinking leads to paranoia, they find conspiracy theories where they could be just getting on and enjoying the day.

Recently I was in a conversation and as I listened to one of the people in the room speak I suddenly interrupted. The thing they wanted me to think through wasn't a certainty or even a realistic possibility and even more astounding was that even if it did come about, it was eight years away. I had to stop the conversation as I decided I didn't need to overthink something that may never happen. Sometimes we need to check that our forward planning has not become a cover story for our overthinking. The Bible tells us not to even worry about tomorrow so I am certain worrying about something several years out is not good for your health.

So today, watch out for the overthinking syndrome. It can start subtly; I am a firm believer in making a plan but I also have learnt to not over plan. Overthinking leads to overplanning. It's like watching someone who doesn't travel much pack a suitcase; they can pack as if where they are going will need every type of clothing, shoe, food, medical supplies. They think so much about what might be needed they often pack for every emergency and forget to pack for the everyday necessities. Philipians 4 tells us some ways we should guide our thinking and not one thing on the list is to do with task or panic or stress. It's a list to build more life, peace and joy.

Where is your overthinking, over complicating, over indulging, over stressing, overwhelming your life? Let your mind have a break from mental gymnastics and just think on what is good, noble, true and enjoy what you have been missing due to overthinking. Stop imagining scenarios that steal the joy from your present because you have become over obsessed with the future. Worry will eat your time and you can't get back what it devours; do a little more living and a little less overthinking.

THINK IT ━━━━━━━━━━━ 352

SPEAK IT ━━━━━━━━━━━━

BE IT ━━━━━━━━━━━━

EXHALE

And He sent messengers on ahead, who went into a Samaritan village to get things ready for Him; but the people there did not welcome Him, because He was heading for Jerusalem. When the disciples James and John saw this, they asked, "Lord, do you want us to call fire down from heaven to destroy them?" But Jesus turned and rebuked them. Then He and His disciples went to another village. Luke 9:52-54 (NIV)

A while ago I went skiing with my family. I had never been before and for me this was going to be a huge challenge but a very persuasive family and some equally convincing friends meant I found myself on skis at the top of a mountain. My lessons had been going ok but I was definitely still cautious; my kids, who had also never skied before but were naturals, decided to ditch mum and join dad on some more testing slopes.

On my own and determined to catch up with the rest of my crew, I set off down the mountain. As I rounded the corner I skidded on the ice and my skis got crossed. Now gaining speed, I was out of control when I saw the ski school of five year olds who were criss-crossing the mountain in a group snow plough; I knew I was going to wipe them out. I had to decide how and where that wipe out would happen. To the left was a large cluster of kids and a snow bank, if I veered in that direction there would be some collateral damage but my pain would be less. To the right was a tiny opening in the ski school and if I tucked my head a little and gained even more speed, I could make it through with no one getting injured but me.

When we are out of control, when things are not going our way, when we know a collision is inevitable, we always have a choice between collateral damage and personal pain. So often we make the wrong choice, we blame others, involve people who didn't need to know, we take out others in our fall. That day I took the gap in the ski school and went off the edge of the slope. I hit my head, took a tumble and yes, it hurt, but no one else was injured.

We need to make more choices that save more lives, we need less collateral damage in leadership, ministry, homes and families. We need to learn how to trust God with our pain. Where right now are you facing a decision where one way will increase the mess and the other way won't make it hurt less but it will make less people hurt? Maturity reduces casualties, immaturity inflicts more injuries; which way will you go? Consider what that looks like in your life and then let's take a look at how we can save lives over the next devotional study.

THINK IT ━━━━━━━━━━━━━━━ 354

SPEAK IT ━━━━━━━━━━━━━━━

BE IT ━━━━━━━━━━━━━━━

EXHALE

Godly sorrow brings repentance that leads to salvation and leaves no regret, but worldly sorrow brings death. See what this godly sorrow has produced in you: what earnestness, what eagerness to clear yourselves, what indignation, what alarm, what longing, what concern, what readiness to see justice done. At every point you have proved yourselves to be innocent in this matter. 2 Corinthians 7:10-11 (NIV)

We've examined the moment that we can all face when we know something is going to go wrong and pain is going to happen. We have a choice which way to steer the situation, a proverbial wipe out taking others with us or taking the hit and dealing with our personal pain. Let's see how we can make better choices and reduce our casualties.

1. Blame vs ownership. When we start the blame game we spread what could have been contained. We move from this is a battle I am fighting to this is carnage I am sharing. Blaming can feel like the right response, why should you feel pain if they don't suffer too? But when we blame, we spread the pain, we involve more people in the argument and we increase the gossip. So when you feel you can either deal with it or blame others for it, know that's the junction of personal pain or collateral damage and choose wisely.

2. Self vs serve. When you are heading for a difficult collision, you have to decide, is my life about self preservation or serving? When we want to keep our ego intact, we will do everything we can to preserve our image or reputation instead of asking, how can I serve? Think of Jesus, if He had allowed self preservation to lead, we would not have eternity secured. At the cross His words were, not My will but Yours be done, and as a result His wounds became all our healing.

3. Private vs public. A social media post can parade as innocent but actually it has an agenda, it's someone using a public platform to express how they feel wronged. They Facebook scriptures that back up their upset and incite others to take sides. This is only going to lead to more collateral damage but in that moment they want public sympathy instead of private pain. Jesus never once asked for the sympathy of the people. When they said, crucify Him, even though He knew He had only healed and blessed them, He took the pain and won a victory. Today, stop asking for sympathy if it's just spreading more damage, be brave enough to take the hit and allow God to heal you.

Where can you make a decision that in the short term may be harder for you but in the long term will save those around you? Personal pain doesn't mean it won't hurt, it will, but God will heal if you allow Him to so don't hide the bruises from Him. He is well able to help you to a full recovery.

THINK IT ━━━━━━━━━━━━━ 356

SPEAK IT ━━━━━━━━━━━━━━

BE IT ━━━━━━━━━━━━━━━

EXHALE

**How beautiful on the mountains are the feet of those who bring good news.
Isaiah 52:7 (NIV)**

Have you ever had something amazing happen or been told some incredible news and you were bursting to share it with your friends? I remember when we finally found out we were pregnant, after 5 years of infertility. I was bursting to tell my parents. Good news is something everyone loves to hear; in a world dominated by horrific headlines the arrival of good news is like a ray of sunshine to the soul.

So if good news has the power to bring so much happiness, why do we often forget that we all have the greatest news to share? We have news that will not only help people but has the potential to change them forever, news that is the difference between everlasting life and death. News that offers freedom and forgiveness, love unlimited and new beginnings. The good news of the gospel of Jesus Christ is entrusted to all of our hands and hearts to share with all the lives we encounter. The enemy wants to make it difficult for this news to be heard, he wants to make you feel awkward and embarrassed but the gospel is not supposed to be a secret shared with a few, it's for everyone, always, everyday. God said, how beautiful are the feet of those who carry this message. The world needs more beautiful feet, more heaven sent messengers. If we identify the reasons for our reluctance then maybe we can overcome them and start to get more good news out.

1. We worry what people will think. What would you think if someone had the cure to cancer and kept it to themselves? We have the cure to loneliness, emptiness, hopelessness, we can't hold it back because we're not sure what someone may say. What matters most, our embarrassment level or people's eternity? Your job isn't to convince them but to share with them.

2. We think we have to know everything. This is not true, just say what you know, that's the most powerful thing. How has this good news saved you? People need to see transformation and your life is the good news in action. Tell your story, give your testimony, that's your personal good news that only you can share.

3. I'm shy. The spirit of God is in you and He will lead you. He wants to speak through you, don't let your nerves talk you out of something that if you will just commit to do, will become more and more natural to you.

We can all share good news because we all do it in our everyday lives. We share about our family, achievements, adventures. So let's make sure in all the news we share, this is at the top of the list.

THINK IT ━━━━━━━━━━━━━━ 358

SPEAK IT ━━━━━━━━━━━━━━

BE IT ━━━━━━━━━━━━━━

EXHALE

When Jesus landed and saw a large crowd, He had compassion on them, because they were like sheep without a shepherd. So He began teaching them many things. Mark 6:34 (NIV)

We all like to feel in control of our lives to differing degrees, some are very casual about the amount of control they need but others are, for want of a better term, control freaks. For them, the idea of being out of control strikes fear in their hearts as they imagine all the scenarios that could happen without their permission. Where are you on the scale? Having order and control are two different things. A life that is planned and has strategy is helpful but a life where those plans are set in concrete and the strategy is a military operation, that's a whole different story. Somewhere between the plan and the paranoia is a healthy balance for our lives.

The problem with being too controlling is that while you may have a plan for your day, home and life, you will want to ensure that those who interact with your life are controlled too. You need them to fall in line with the things you have deemed can never be out of line and that's where control gets out of control. I have learnt over seasons of life that some of the things I may feel I need to control most are the very things that I need to let go, and the things I paid less attention to are the things that needed me to express more control. Why do I need to control everyone's plans and not take control of my own tongue? Why am I so concerned to control the running of my home and ignore my own health and wellbeing?

Jesus was not a control freak but He also wasn't out of control. His ministry saw all kinds of crazy situations; to the demon possessed He took spiritual control over the evil. To the crowds who were disorderly and needed leadership, He put a plan in place to seat them and feed them. Jesus never controlled people, He gave them free will, He offered them a better way but never forced them to do things His way. He let the disciples make poor choices but He didn't try and control them. He loved and He guided, He spoke truth and He gave wisdom.

Where do you need to find some balance? Where has your control issue created problems? Maybe you are controlling in a relationship, dictating how everything must be done or maybe you're controlling in a work scenario, containing those who may handle things differently. The motivator for control is often fear so maybe the way to start to deal with the control freak is to ask, what am I frightened of? Perhaps the areas in your life that are the most tense are the ones where you are holding just a little too tight.

INHALE

THINK IT ━━━━━━━━━━━━ **360**

SPEAK IT ━━━━━━━━━━━━━━━

BE IT ━━━━━━━━━━━━━━━

EXHALE

SOMETHINGS YOU
WILL NEVER
KNOW

UNLESS YOU ARE STILL LONG ENOUGH

PSALMS 46:10

The stew was poured out for the men, but as they began to eat it, they cried out, "Man of God, there is death in the pot!" 2 Kings 4:40 (NIV)

This story about Elijah has been one I have learnt so much from over the years. Here is the prophet of God taking care of dinner when something is put in the stew that threatens to ruin the whole meal. A zealous young prophet has thrown a wild vine in the pot and what tasted good a moment ago is now full of poison.

In our lives this analogy runs true; often we have times when we have worked hard to make something and one person's contribution means potentially all we have done could be ruined. This can easily happen, we can all be working together and either through deliberate sabotage or a careless contribution, everything is upset. A bad comment can be spoken, a wrong assumption can be made, a rumour can be tossed in and suddenly what was tasting good can become toxic.

That's what the prophet had to deal with and here's a few things we can learn from him, so that instead of making drastic decisions in the face of these dilemmas, we use a little flour power to rescue what could have been wasted.

1. When you taste it, say it. One of the people eating the stew that day realised that this wild vine had poisoned the pot and as he tasted it, he said it. It was his shout that saved everyone eating the stew. How many times do we know something is toxic but we don't want to mention it? The longer it's left the more people are going to get sick, so say it if you taste it.

2. Everyone was ok with saying it's not ok. I love that as one person shouts, there's death in the pot, three other people don't start defending the pot. Everyone is ok with talking about the fact this is not ok. We need to build our lives relationally with those who are strong enough to hear the tough stuff as well as eat the good stuff.

3. Save the stew. How many times when something isn't right do we throw away what we have worked so hard to make? We throw out the relationship, we disband the group, we tear up the agreement. But Elijah didn't waste what could be saved. Instead he threw some flour in and saved the stew. We need more flour power, more people with a remedy in their pocket, ways to neutralise what was bad and keep what is still good.

So today, look for the areas where you can save the stew; you may need more flour in your pocket to restore what is currently spoilt but if the stew is worth saving, then save it, don't waste it.

THINK IT ━━━━━━━━━━━━━ 362

SPEAK IT ━━━━━━━━━━━━━

BE IT ━━━━━━━━━━━━━

EXHALE

He came to a broom bush, sat down under it and prayed that he might die. "I have had enough, Lord," he said. "Take my life." 1 Kings 19:4

Ok admit it, have you ever sulked about something and I don't mean when you were a toddler, I mean in your adult life. That look and expression we give to someone because we didn't get our own way or we feel things should have turned out differently. Sulking is often that silent mood we can get into and it's very hard to get out of.

Elijah went and lay down under the tree out of breath and exhausted as he was running away from Jezebel. He had one very big sulk, he was frustrated and tired and so told God to take his life. This was Elijah who had just called down fire and outrun chariots but today, because things were not going his way, he decided to quit. Elijah was throwing a tantrum and it was a big one. God sent an angel to Elijah to get him out of his mood and put him back onto his mission.

Maybe you, like Elijah, are having one of those bad days, weeks or years and you are about to lay down under the tree and quit. You are certainly sulking, things haven't gone your way. Well today, maybe learn from the lesson that God taught Elijah. The angel came and wanted him to see this was not the place that he belonged. Elijah was instructed to eat and rest. Sometimes when we find ourselves in these moments we need to do the exact same thing; you don't need to quit forever but you may need to take a break, have some sleep, recalibrate some thinking, gain some strength. Often our sulking comes when our energy is low and our soul is weary.

The angel then asked again, what are you doing here? Elijah again answered from his sulk and so he was told to stand in the cave as God was going to pass by. God wasn't in the wind or the fire, He was the still small voice. Maybe you also need to hear that still small voice. Maybe you need to stop looking for some big word to get you back on your feet but allow the whisper of God to restore you. Sometimes our redirection comes with a fanfare but sometimes it comes with a whisper. God recommissioned Elijah from his sulk back to his calling and gave him fresh energy for what the enemy tried to steal from him. Today, if you are in a sulk, maybe be honest with yourself and allow God to help you get back up because there are still things for you to do. Things may not have gone your way but that doesn't mean that God won't still do things His way. So shake off the mood and let's get back on with the mission because you're not finished yet.

THINK IT ▬▬▬▬▬▬▬▬▬▬ 364

SPEAK IT ▬▬▬▬▬▬▬▬▬▬▬

BE IT ▬▬▬▬▬▬▬▬▬▬▬

EXHALE

He led me back and forth among them, and I saw a great many bones on the floor of the valley, bones that were very dry. He asked me, "Son of man, can these bones live?" Ezekiel 37:2-3 (NIV)

So you have made it. You have reached the end of this journey of recalibrating, of taking some breaths. A journey of setting time aside to pause and think, taking the time to inhale God's truth and then making time to exhale His life. Making changes in your thinking, your speech and then adjusting some small and even larger things so that your actions and daily disciplines would line up with the words God has spoken over you.

As you began this devotional, my prayer was that where you felt short of breath, you would catch your breath once more. Where you had felt some things were a waste of your breath, you would make the much needed adjustments and save your breath for what mattered most. In and through it all, I prayed you would come to know more than ever before that life is not a sprint, it's not a catwalk we have to perfect, it's a journey that will require commitment and longevity and therefore being breathless is not an option. We all have to learn to find that rhythm, to keep breathing no matter the conditions we may be facing, for without breath there is only death.

So let's end where we began by looking at Ezekiel who was asked by God, when he saw all the dry bones around him, can these bones live? Ezekiel was faced in that moment with the reality that he was part of the very answer God was about to deliver. It was God's plan to use the breath in Ezekiel's lungs to breathe life. It was his words that were to speak life and his voice that was to command the dead to live.

Over the past year, the power of your confession and actions has been a recurring theme, not by default or coincidence but by design. Too often we think the answer is somewhere out there, when more than often the answer begins from within. So what new courage have you found that can help you conquer the things around you? What new confession are you harnessing so you can change the direction of your future? Where are you going to not suggest but speak what you know is the truth God has planted in your heart?

As this next season unfolds in your life friend, let me remind you again you are made to make a difference. We all face storms but we all have a voice, so just keep breathing. When life tries to make you breathless, breathe again and again. You can do it: take a deep breath and breathe in truth, exhale life.

Chad

Miracle In The Middle   **Turnaround God**   **Identity**

Be That Girl
Bible Study

We Are One
Bible Study

Outrageous Women
Bible Study

Teaching CDs   **DVDs**   **Apparel**

For a wider selection of Charlotte Gambill's resources, please visit:

WWW.CHARLOTTEGAMBILL.COM

Cherish Women's Conference UK

The Cherish women's conference unites women from all walks of life as one, to use their voice to glorify heaven and change earth. Cherish was founded more than a decade ago and now, every year thousands gather and lives are changed forever. We'd love you to join the party, just visit: *www.cherishconference.com*

Life Church UK

Life Church is a vibrant, growing and multi-cultural church. We believe that the Church is the hope of the world and a place where everyone can thrive. One church in four locations, Bradford (UK), Belfast (UK), Leeds (UK) and Warsaw (Poland). For more information, visit: *www.lifechurchhome.com*

Dare To Be Women's Ministry USA

When God put Charlotte's life together with her now best friend, Natalie Grant, they knew He was about to dare them to do something. Dare To Be was born out of simple obedience that has led to an incredible harvest. This annual event tours across America and invites women from all ages and stages of life to dare to be all God has purposed for them. To find out more about the Dare To Be tours, visit: *www.daretobe.com*

Further Information

For more information regarding Pastor Charlotte's ministry, itinerary, podcast, social media or any other enquiries, please visit: *www.charlottegambill.com*
Twitter: @Charlgambill
Instagram: @Charlgambill

CHARLOTTE GAMBILL

has an infectious love for life, a deep love for people and zealous love for God's House. Her passion is to build the local church across the earth, to see people reach their full potential and to develop and strengthen leadership. Charlotte is known for her practical, humorous and passionate application of God's word. Her messages of life and purpose are rallying a generation to embrace the broken and become ambassadors of hope.

Charlotte is an author, speaker, pastor and mother. She is founder and leader of Cherish conference and co-founder of Dare To Be, which reach thousands of women in the USA and Europe. She also leads Life Church alongside her husband Steve and together they have two children, Hope Cherish and Noah Brave.

Stay in touch with Charlotte on:

Twitter: @Charlgambill
Instagram: @Charlgambill